The Women of Faith Fiction Club presents

A Time to Dance

By Karen Kingsbury

WestBow
PRESS

A Division of Thomas Nelson Publishers
Since 1798

visit us at www.westbowpress.com

A Time to Dance
by Karen Kingsbury

Copyright ©2001 Karen Kingsbury

Published by WestBow Press, a division of Thomas Nelson Company,
P.O. Box 141000, Nashville, Tennessee 37214.

WestBow Press books may be purchased in bulk for educational, business,
fundraising, or sales promotional use. For information, please email
SpecialMarkets@ThomasNelson.com.

Published in association with the literary agency of Alive Communications, Inc.,
7680 Goddard Street, Suite 200, Colorado Springs, Colorado 80920.

ISBN 1-5955-4064-4 (repak)
ISBN 0-8499-4282-9 (sc)
ISBN 1-5955-4041-5 (tp)
ISBN 1-5955-4178-X (mass market)

Printed in the United States of America
06 07 08 09 10 QWB 9 8 7 6 5 4 3 2

Dedicated to

Donald, my lover and playmate and best friend of all. With you, all of life is a dance, and I can only pray the music continues for all time. Thank you for stating early on that the *d* word would not be part of our vocabulary. And thanks for modeling in Christ what it means to truly love.

Kelsey, my sweet girl, who stands on the brink of those tough and tender teenage years. Already you are old enough to understand love, to know that you're a one-in-a-million catch and to believe no one will ever love you like your daddy or your heavenly Father. You once said you wouldn't marry a boy unless he was like your daddy. Keep that, honey; believe me, your standard couldn't possibly be any higher than that.

Tyler, my dreamer and doer, who wants so much from life and whom God has chosen for great and mighty things. I will hear your voice singing to me on faraway nights when my hair is gray and our family days are but a memory. Thank you, buddy, for always making me smile.

Austin, my boy of boundless energy, better known as Michael Jordan. You defy man's wisdom each day by merely breathing. You grace our home with constant dribbling and shooting and slam-dunking, sounds that have almost made me forget those hospital machines in intensive care. Almost, but not quite. And each time your arms come around my neck, I thank God for the miracle of your life.

E.J. and Sean, our chosen sons, who have brought us all together in a common cause, a common love. Thank you for defining our family's eternal perspective and for giving us reason to celebrate God's plan. Remember, dear sons, although you did not grow under my heart, you most certainly grew in it. I look forward to all that God has planned for you.

And to God Almighty,
Who has, for now, blessed me with these.

Acknowledgments

The dream of writing a book that might show love—marital love—for the glorious thing that God has intended it to be, was inspired in my heart long ago and given wings here, by the grace of our Lord. Still, it would not have been possible to write this book without the help of many people. First and foremost I'd like to thank the Women of Faith organization: everyone from Steve Arterburn to Mary Graham and all the wonderful WOF friends I've had the privilege to meet in the process of pulling this project together. What a great idea—a line of fiction for all women everywhere . . . fiction that will entertain and change lives, encourage love and inspire hope. Bravo, for giving readers an option! Also to my fellow WOF fictionettes for being excited alongside me and for helping make this and the next three books in the WOF Fiction Club a reading experience like none other.

Professionally, a special thanks to Greg Johnson, who

is brimming with ideas and without a doubt the world's best agent. Greg, your enthusiasm and creativity, energy and devotion to God are a constant testimony to me. You inspire me to new heights, and I'm blessed and honored to be among those writers in your care.

Also to my editor, Karen Ball, who has been with me along the entire fiction journey and who makes my work sing. God has gifted you, friend, and I am grateful to benefit from the fact. Also to Ami McConnell, Mark Sweeney, and all the wonderful folks at Word Publishing. I'm honored to be writing for you now and in the future.

Thanks, too, go to Joan Westfall for doing a read-through of this book at the last minute. You are an amazing person, Joan—always encouraging others, looking for the good, and taking the time to catch even the smallest detail in this book so that it will be that much more professional. I treasure you more than you know.

And finally, on a personal note, a special thanks to Kristy and Jeff Blake for loving my precious Austin through the process of writing . . . and to Sorena Wagner for being the most amazing nanny anyone could have. You are wonderful, and I am blessed for knowing you. Also to my true friends and self-appointed publicity crew Christine Wessel, Heidi Cleary, Joan Westfall, Jan Adams, Michelle Stokes, and Debbie Kimsie . . . Thank you for being excited about the stories I tell and for bringing me such encouragement. God has used you more than you know.

A humble thanks also goes to my prayer warriors, Sylvia and Ann. The two of you are the most selfless, amazing servants—listening to Christ's call and lifting me and my work to His throne room daily. I don't deserve you, but I am grateful all the same. You won't know this side of heaven how much your constant intervention and love for me has affected the lives of our readers.

Always a special thanks goes to my family for their love and support and for understanding when dinner is macaroni and cheese three nights running. And to my parents, Ted and Anne Kingsbury, and siblings, Susan, Tricia, David, and Lynne, for your love and support. Also to Shannon Kane, one of my best and most faithful readers and certainly one of my favorite nieces. One day I'll be reading your work, honey!

Finally, a special thanks to the readers who have taken the time to write me over the years. I remember each of you and pray for you often. And to the Skyview basketball team for always giving me something to cheer about—even on deadline.

There is a time for everything, and a season for every activity under heaven: . . . a time to weep and a time to laugh, a time to mourn and a time to dance.

—ECCLESIASTES 3:1, 4

One

WITHOUT QUESTION, IT WAS THE MOMENT ABBY Reynolds had waited for all her life.

Beneath the Friday-night lights in the biggest college stadium in the state of Illinois, Abby's husband was on the brink of winning his second high-school football championship. Moreover, he was about to do so largely on the talents of their older son, the team's senior quarterback.

Abby pulled her blue-and-gray Marion Eagles jacket tighter to her body and wished she'd brought a thicker scarf. It was early December, after all, and though snow hadn't fallen for more than a week, the air was biting cold. "Football weather," John always said. Cold and dry, straight from heaven. She stared beyond the lights to the starry sky. *Even God is rooting for you tonight, John.*

Her gaze fell across the field, and she picked out her husband on the sidelines, headset angled just so, body bent over, hands on his knees as he waited for the play to unfold. She could remember a million afternoons when his eyes had sparkled with laughter, but here, now, they were hard and focused. His face was the picture of concentration, lined with the intensity of the moment as he barked commands in a dozen directions. Even from her place high up in the packed stands, Abby could feel the energy that emanated from John in the final minutes of this, his most prized football game.

No doubt about it, coaching was his gift.

And this was his finest hour.

If only everything else hadn't gotten so—

"Come on, Eagles. You can do it!" Abby's daughter, Nicole, clapped her hands and gritted her teeth, holding tighter to her boyfriend, Matt's, hand, every ounce of her energy focused on her younger brother.

Tears nipped at Abby's eyes, and she blinked them back. *If only I could freeze time, here and now . . .* She turned and squeezed her father's knee. "I can feel it, Dad. They're gonna win."

Her father, an old man who barely resembled the dad she'd grown up with, raised a shaky fist partway into the freezing night. "You can do it, Kade!" His hand dropped weakly back into his lap.

After tonight there were bound to be few moments of light for any of them.

"I kinda hate to see it end." Her father grinned at her through wet eyes. "All those years of football together. The boy's amazing. Plays just like his father."

Abby focused her gaze on her son, and the corners of her mouth lifted. "He always has."

"Mom, isn't it weird?" Nicole leaned her head on Abby's shoulder.

"What, honey?" Abby took her daughter's free hand and resisted the urge to close her eyes. It felt so good, sitting here in the thrill of the moment, surrounded by family . . .

"This is Kade's last high-school game." Nicole's voice was thick, filled with tender indignation, as though she'd only now realized a loss she hadn't prepared for. "Just like that, it's over. Next year he'll be at Iowa, and it won't be the same."

A stinging sensation made its way across Abby's eyes again, and she struggled to swallow. *If only you knew, sweetheart* . . . "It never is."

Nicole stared down at the field. "I mean, this is it. After tonight he'll never play for Dad again." She glanced at the scoreboard. "All those practices and games, and in a few minutes it'll be over. Just a box full of memories and old newspaper articles."

The lump grew thicker. *Not now, Nicole. Let me enjoy the moment.* Tears clouded Abby's vision. *Come on, get a grip. Life is full of endings.* She squeezed her daughter's hand and uttered a short laugh. "We're supposed to be cheering, remember? They haven't won yet."

Nicole stuck her chin out and shouted as loud as she could. "Go, Eagles, come on! You can do it!"

Abby's eyes moved toward the field where Kade was at the center of the huddle, relaying his father's plays to the team. Third down and eight, twenty-five yards to go for a touchdown. There was just over a minute to play, and Marion was up by three. This touchdown—and Abby could feel in her gut that there would be a touchdown—would seal the win.

"Let's go, Eagles!" Abby clapped her mittened hands together and stared intently at the field as the play unfolded. *Come on, Kade. Nice and easy. Like a hundred times before . . .*

Her strapping son took the snap and, with practiced grace, found his place in the pocket, searching downfield until he saw his target. Then, in the fluid motion that comes from being the talented son of a storied football coach, he fired the ball, threading it through two menacing defenders to land, almost like magic, in the hands of a Marion receiver.

The home crowd was on its feet.

Over the din of ten thousand screaming fans, the announcer explained the situation: the Eagles had a first and goal on the three-yard line with less than a minute to play.

The opposing team called a time-out, and Abby breathed in slowly. If she could savor this moment, bottle it up or capture it forever, she would. Hadn't they dreamed of this time and place since Kade was born, first joking about it and then realizing with each passing year the chance of it actually happening? Dozens of yesterdays fought for her attention. The first time she saw John in a football uniform . . . the way his eyes loved her as they spoke their wedding vows and toasted to forever . . . Nicole playing in the backyard . . . the gleam in four-year-old Kade's eyes when he got his first football . . . the thrill of Sean's birth seven years later . . . years of meeting on the pier at the end of the day . . . the music that they—

A whistle blew, and the players took their positions.

Abby swallowed hard. Her family had spent a lifetime getting here—two decades of memories, many of them centered around a white-lined, hundred-yard field of mud and grass.

The crowd remained on its feet, but despite the deafening noise there was a quiet place in Abby's heart where she could hear her children's long-ago laughter, see the way John and the kids tickled and tackled on the Marion High field every day when practice was over. For years John had known instinctively how to involve their children in his role as coach, how to put the game behind him at day's end. The image and voices changed, and the stadium noise was only a distant roar.

"Dance with me, Abby . . . dance with me."

There they were, on the pier. Dancing the dance of life, swaying to the sound of crickets and creaking boards long after the kids were asleep on nights when summer seemed like it might last forever.

A gust of wind sent a chill down her arms, and she blinked back the fading visions of yesterday. No matter how he'd betrayed her, no matter what happened next, there would never be a better father for her children than John Reynolds.

Another memory rang in her mind. She and John on the lake, adrift in an old fishing boat a year after Kade was born. *"One day, Abby, one day Kade'll play for me, and we'll go to state. All the way, honey. We'll have everything we ever dreamed of, and nothing will stop us. Nothing . . ."*

Now—in what seemed like the blink of an eye—they were here.

Kade took the snap and raised the ball.

Come on, Kade. It's yours, honey. "Go, Eagles!" she screamed.

The ball flew from Kade's hands like a bullet, spiraling through the winter night much the way Kade himself had flown through their lives, a blur of motion. *Come on, catch it . . .* Abby watched as Kade's best friend, T. J., the team's tight end, jumped for the ball. *Fitting*, she thought. Like the perfect ending to a perfect movie. And she realized that everything about Kade and John and their football days—even this final play—had somehow been destined from the beginning.

It all seemed to be happening in slow motion . . .

T. J. wrapped his fingers around the ball, pulled it to his chest, and landed squarely in the end zone.

"Touchdown!" Abby's heart soared and she leapt up and down, her fists high in the air. "I can't *believe* it! We did it! We *won!*" She pulled her father and Nicole into a hug and high-fived ten-year-old Sean three seats down the row. "State champs! Can you believe it?"

On the field the players kicked the extra point and then lined up for the kickoff. Fifteen seconds more and the Marion Eagles would be state champs. The Reynoldses' father-and-son team would forever be part of Illinois prep football lore.

John, you did it . . . you and Kade.

In honor of everything they'd ever been—of the beacon of light that had been their love, their family—Abby felt nothing but pure, unhindered joy for her husband.

Two tears spilled from the corners of her eyes and burned their way down her freezing cheeks.

Not now, Abby. Not when it's supposed to be a celebration. The crowd was shouting in unison: "Five . . . four . . . three . . . two . . ."

As the stands emptied onto the field, a swirling blue-and-gray mass of celebration, Abby's father hooted like he hadn't since he'd been relegated to a nursing home. Sean bounced along behind Nicole and Matt as they rushed down the stairs to join the others.

Abby sat frozen in place, soaking in the moment. She searched the crowd until she found John, watched as he ripped off his headset and ran like a madman to meet Kade. Their hug put Abby over the edge, and the tears came in quiet streams. John pulled their son into a solid embrace that shut out everyone else: teammates, coaches, members of the press. Everyone but each other. Kade gripped his helmet in one hand and his father's neck with the other.

Then it happened.

While Abby was still savoring the moment, Charlene Denton came up behind John and threw her arms around his shoulders. A rock took up residence in Abby's stomach and began to grow. *Not now . . . here in front of everyone we know.* John and Charlene were easily fifty yards from Abby, but it made no difference. She could see the way the scene played out as clearly as if she were standing beside them. Her husband pulled away from Kade and turned to hug Charlene briefly. There was something about the way John brought his head close to hers and kept his hand on her shoulder that conveyed his feelings for Charlene. Feelings he had long had for her. Charlene Denton, fellow teacher at Marion High, John's greatest stumbling block.

Abby blinked, and suddenly everything good and memorable and nostalgic about the night felt cheap and artificial, like something from a bad movie. Even the tenderest thoughts couldn't stand against the reality in front of her.

Abby's father saw them, too, and he cleared his throat. "I'll be fine here by myself, honey. You go be with John."

She shook her head, but her gaze never left her husband and Charlene. "No, I'll wait."

Her eyes were dry now, and anger pulsed through her, glazing her heart with hard, empty bitterness. *Get away from him, lady. This is* our *moment, not yours.* Abby stared at Charlene, hating her. John's voice echoed in her heart once more, but this time his words had nothing to do with dancing.

And everything to do with divorce.

This was the weekend they'd agreed to tell the kids. The weekend they would shatter their family's mistaken belief that Abby and John were perhaps the most happily married people in all the world. Abby sighed. No matter how it felt to see John with Charlene, the reality was he could talk to the teacher or any other woman for that matter. In a few months, John would be single, after all. As would Abby. She hugged herself tightly, trying to will away the nausea that swirled around inside her. *Why does it still hurt, Lord?*

No magic answers came to mind, and Abby wasn't sure if she wanted to disappear or bolt down onto the field and join them so that Charlene would feel too uncomfortable to stay.

I thought I was past this, God. We've already agreed to move on. What's happening to me? Abby tapped her foot against the concrete stadium floor and shifted positions, hating the way the other woman seemed unfettered, lovely and young and without the burdens of two decades of marriage. What was this feeling assaulting her? Jealousy?

No, it felt more like regret. Abby's pulse quickened. It couldn't be, could it? What was there to regret? Hadn't they *both* realized the place they were in, the place they were headed?

Or was this how it would always feel to see John with another woman?

Her vision clouded over, and again she heard John's voice from long ago. *"Dance with me, Abby . . . dance with me."*

The silent words faded from her mind, and she blinked back fresh tears. One thing was certain: if this was how being divorced was going to feel, she'd better get used to it.

No matter how much she hated it.

Two

THE STADIUM WAS EMPTY, STREWN WITH CRUSHED Gatorade cups and half-eaten hot dogs. Assorted remnants of blue and gray hung from the student section, proof that the Marion Eagles had indeed been there, that John and Kade had accomplished their lifelong dream and won a state championship together.

Abby wandered down the steps to the field and across the grass toward the locker room. John would still be inside, talking to the press, going over the game's great plays with the other coaches, picking up after his team.

Savoring the moment as long as possible.

There was a bench just outside the visitors' door and Abby sat down, gazing across the empty field. Kade, Nicole, Matt, and Sean were holding a table for them at Smokey's Pizza a block down the street from the stadium. Abby's father was waiting in the car. She studied the muddied lines and the way the goalposts stood proudly erect on either side of the field. Had it only been an hour ago that the place had been packed, an entire crowd holding its collective breath while Kade threw the final touchdown?

Abby shivered and buried her hands deep in her pockets. The temperature had fallen, but that had little to do with the terrifying cold that reigned in her heart.

A Marion assistant coach walked out and stopped when he saw her. "Hey, Abby." A smile took up most of his face. "How 'bout them Eagles?"

She chuckled softly. No matter what painful twists her life was about to take, she would remember their football days as absolutely wonderful. Every player, every coach, every season . . . all of it a mosaic of memories she would cherish forever. "Amazing. A dream come true."

The man huffed slightly and shook his head, gazing into the winter sky. He was the biggest coach on staff, a former lineman with a reputation for getting in kids' faces. But here in the quiet shadows of a stadium void of cheering fans and the guttural grunts of sixty teenagers in full warrior gear, Abby noticed his eyes glistening with unshed tears. He cleared his throat and caught her gaze.

"If I live a hundred years, I'll never forget the way John and Kade worked together tonight. They're magic, those two." He crossed his arms and stared up at the stadium lights, trying to compose himself. In a moment, he looked at her again. "What a ride, Abby, you know? I'm just glad I got to be part of it."

"Me, too, Coach." The corners of Abby's mouth lifted slightly as a layer of tears clouded her vision. She gestured toward the locker room. "Is he almost finished?"

"Yep, last reporters left a few minutes ago. He's just

getting his things." The coach smiled at her again as he set off. "Well . . . see ya next year."

Abby nodded, afraid her voice would betray her if she tried to speak. *There won't be a next year for us . . . for me.*

When the coach was gone, Abby thought about John, about their wedding more than twenty-one years earlier. What had happened to the people they were back then, the people who had walked through fire together and come out stronger on the other side?

Forget it, Abby. The coach was right. It was over now; she was just glad she'd been a part of it. Abby wished with everything in her she could go back in time, even an hour, back to the moments before the final touchdown when John's long-ago dreams all were coming true.

All but one.

Five minutes later, John came through the door and saw her there. Abby thought of Charlene, her arms around John after the game. *Do I hug him like she did? Do I nod politely?*

There was an uncomfortable silence while he held her gaze.

"Abby . . ." He spoke softly, but every word was coated in exhilaration. "We did it!" His eyes sparkled with an electricity that would take days, weeks to diffuse, and it beckoned her in a way she was powerless to resist. As sure as gravity, they came together, and Abby circled her arm around his neck, burying her head against his shoulder.

"I can't believe it! State champs!" She savored the comforting feel of his heart thudding inside his chest, and it occurred to her that months had passed since they'd hugged this way.

"I know." He pulled back, his eyes as full of life and hope and promise as they'd been two decades earlier.

There was a smudge of mud on his cheek, and she erased it gently with her thumb. "Best in the state, you and Kade. Amazing."

He drew her to him again, and they stayed that way, their bodies close, swaying slightly. His arms securely around her waist, hers holding on more tightly than usual.

Every moment was steeped in a desperate finality.

John pulled away first, and Abby hugged herself to ward off the sudden chill. "Could you believe that last touchdown?" He grabbed his gym bag from the bench and grinned at her. "Kade was something else . . ."

Abby smiled back. "Beautiful."

John stared out at the field as if he were watching a replay in his mind. "I've pictured this day ever since Kade first learned to throw."

They started walking toward the stadium steps, their feet keeping time in a familiar rhythm. John swung the bag up onto his shoulder. "Abby, about this weekend . . ."

The rock in her stomach grew. "What?"

He studied the ground. "I don't feel right about it . . . what I mean is, the kids . . ." His eyes found hers as they kept walking. "I don't care what the counselors say; we can't tell them now." His forehead was creased with concern. "Not after tonight. They'll be celebrating right through Christmas, Abby. They have a right to that."

Abby felt her shoulders tense as a burst of nervous tension spewed into her veins. "They have a right to know the truth."

His eyelids were heavy with sorrow. "We'll tell them soon enough." His steps slowed and he stared hard at her, begging her to understand. "Come on, Abby. This is the happiest day in Kade's life. And before you know it, Christmas'll be here. Can't it wait?"

She stopped walking and stared at her husband, one hand on her hip. "What are we supposed to do, John? Pretend forever?"

His jawline hardened, but he said nothing.

Stop, daughter. A kind word turns away anger.

Abby heard the still, small voice somewhere in the distant corners of her soul, but she shook her head. John had brought this on, after all. Why cover for him now?

"What good does waiting do?" She crossed her arms and huffed. "We should've told them last month." She hesitated. "You can't be the good guy forever, John." *Don't say it, Abby . . .* "Even if you are state champs."

"Here we go." John removed his Marion High baseball cap and dug his fingers through his damp, dark hair. "What do you want, Abby? A fight? Right here on the fifty-yard line?"

She thought of a dozen quick comebacks but held her tongue. "I'm just saying we should have told them by now. For goodness sake, John, we're filing in January. They won't know what hit them if we don't say something soon."

His face twisted, and she thought he might cry. He looked like a little boy who'd lost his best friend, and for a crazy instant she wanted to take him in her arms and beg him to stay, beg him to break it off with Charlene and love only her, Abby, for the rest of his life. Her heart softened. *We're both wrong, John. Isn't what we've built worth another try?* But before she could find the courage to voice the words, the feeling vanished. *I must be crazy. We're too far gone for second chances . . .*

Nothing is impossible with God, My child.

Abby closed her eyes. That time she was sure the silent voice in her heart belonged to the Lord. *We tried. You know we did . . . But even You would grant me an out in this situation . . . Your word says so, doesn't it?*

I hate divorce, daughter . . . Nothing is impossible with—

It's too late . . . Her eyes opened. "Listen, I just want to get through this."

He was still watching her, but his sadness had changed to determination. "We can file in February. We've waited this long. Let's get through Christmas."

The image of John and Charlene taunted her. "Ho ho ho," she whispered.

"What?" John's voice rose a notch.

She cocked her head. "Let's just say I'm not in the mood for the holidays."

John gritted his teeth. "I swear, Abby, all you ever think about is yourself. It's Christmas, remember? That used to mean something to you."

Don't do this to me, John. Don't pretend like it matters when it doesn't. Images came to mind of her and John wandering the hallways of their house in recent years . . . silent, tense, loveless. "Yeah, back when *I* used to mean something to *you.*"

They stood planted there, face to angry face, the chasm between them growing with each breath. Abby broke the silence first. "Don't make me the bad guy. I don't want to ruin their Christmas, either." She gestured at herself. "I'm just trying to be realistic."

"Selfish, you mean?" He was struggling to keep his voice down.

"No, *realistic!*" Her words were little more than a hiss. "I hate pretending!"

The muscles in John's jaw flinched. "You think I like it? I'm not talking about *us* here, Abby. I'm talking about the kids. We'll tell them after the holidays, and that settles it."

He started walking, and Abby wanted to scream. "Wait!"

John stopped, and after a beat, turned back to her. "What?"

She exhaled, struggling to control the emotions that rocked her heart. She couldn't imagine another moment trapped in a house with John while he was in love with another woman . . . and through Christmas?

Then it occurred to her that the holidays were apt to be busy anyway. Her shoulders slumped. Oh, what did it matter? Maybe John was right. Maybe it wouldn't hurt if the kids had less time to get used to the idea. Maybe she could survive waiting for their sake. As long as the divorce came quickly after that. "Okay . . . fine. After Christmas." She hesitated. "But keep your hands off Charlene in public, will you? At least until after we've told the kids."

John's eyes widened, and his anger became indignation. "What's that supposed to mean?"

"Come on . . ." Her mouth hung open. Why did he insist on lying to her? What was the point? "It means I have no intention of looking the other way while you run around with your *girlfriend* just so we can give the kids a happy Christmas."

John took a step toward her, his expression growing hard as flint. "You know, I'm sick of you blaming this on Charlene. Our decision to divorce is separate from my friendship with her. It's because you've changed . . . we've both changed." He sighed and stared into the moonlit sky, and she wondered if he were searching for answers—as she'd done so many times. She watched his jaw work and knew he was trying to control his temper. "We're not the same people we were, Abby."

She rolled her eyes. "Don't tell me it's not about Charlene. No matter how much we've changed we could've worked it out; we had an obligation to work it out. But when you took up with Charlene, it was time to get out." She uttered a short laugh. "I mean, come on, John. Don't tell me you aren't having an affair with her when I walked into your classroom and found her in your—"

"That was a hug!" John spat the words at her. "I told you she was upset about her . . ." His voice trailed off, and Abby felt her blood pressure rise a notch. How dare he deny it when she'd caught him in the act? When she'd been hearing about John's relationship with Charlene from a dozen different sources ever since then?

"A hug? Really?" Her voice dripped with sarcasm. "And what was she upset about tonight when she was hanging all over you in front of ten thousand people?"

John's body hunched forward, as though the fight had left him. "Forget it." He buried his hands deep in his pockets and resumed walking, his strides long and purposeful. "Believe what you want."

Abby was furious. He was lying, of course. Like he'd done a hundred times before. She jogged the few steps to catch up and fell in place beside him again. "I believe my friends, and they've seen the same thing I have."

He said nothing, his eyes straight ahead as he continued up the stadium steps toward the car.

Jerk. "Fine, don't talk to me. Just don't make a scene with her, okay? If we wait 'til after the holidays, at least give me that."

They were at the top of the stairs. John stopped and

glanced at his watch. "Whatever." His voice was void of any emotion. "I'll meet you back at the hotel in a few hours."

"What?" Abby's heartbeat doubled. *Don't do this to me, John, not tonight.* "You're coming with me. The kids are waiting for us."

Even before John answered, Abby knew she'd pushed him too far. Her husband was staring down the street, lost to her and their children and all that had given them reason to celebrate an hour earlier. "The coaches are meeting at the pub down the block. Tell the kids I'll see 'em later."

Then without making eye contact, without the slightest appearance of remorse or regret, without even a single look back, John walked off into the night. Abby stood stone still, watching him go.

Turn around, John. Come back and tell me you love me; tell me this is crazy and that somehow everything's going to be okay.

He kept walking. *Make him stop, Lord; the kids need him tonight.*

Silence.

She watched as John looked for traffic in both directions, jogged across the street, and headed further down the sidewalk. *Fine. Let him leave.* Turning, she blinked back tears and refused to entertain the ache in her heart. It was time she got used to seeing him walk away. This was all they had left now, all they would ever be: two people, two strangers, walking alone in separate directions into the cold, dark night of their future.

She knew it; John knew it.

And sometime after Christmas, the kids would know it, too.

Three

THE MOST WONDERFUL THING ABOUT GROWING up on a private lake, at least as far as Nicole Reynolds was concerned, was not the endless grassy hillside that spread from their back door toward the water or the old wooden pier where they gathered so often for diving contests and sing-alongs. Those things were wonderful and would always be a part of the fabric of her family's lives, of course. But the most amazing benefit was the trail that wound its way through shadowy thickets of trees and brush, then back out into the open along the water's edge. As children, Nicole and Kade would ride their bikes around the water pretending they were explorers in a foreign country or journeying across enemy territory to reach a safe place—usually the lakeside home of one of their friends.

At twenty, Nicole was too old for imaginary play and romps through the woods, but she still cherished the old trail. Nowadays it was the place where she and Matt

Conley could get away from the demands of college life and walk hand in hand, sharing ever more about themselves.

Years earlier, Nicole had liked the path best in summer when the ground was warm and the leaves in full display. But now, with Matt by her side, there was something magical about walking the three-mile trail even in the heart of winter.

That afternoon, a Wednesday nearly three weeks after Christmas, Nicole got home from classes early, started a fire, and fixed lunch. Matt would be there in less than an hour with something important to tell her. Something very important. She pulled the bread from the refrigerator and ripped two paper towels from the roll. His voice came back to her, urgent and certain, telling her that no matter what else happened that day, they must meet right after classes.

Her palms were sweaty, and she rubbed them on her jeans.

I'm not worried. She thought about that for a moment. What did she have to be worried about? She and Matt had been inseparable since meeting at the university's debate club two years earlier when he was a senior. Every day since then had been more wonderful than the last, and the relationship they'd started had been filled with romance and laughter. Their struggles were typical for people their age— people determined to serve God and put Him first. For that reason they'd set boundaries soon after their friendship turned to dating. But never—not once in two years—had Nicole feared Matt might break up with her.

It can't be that.

She reached for the mayonnaise, opened it, and grabbed

a knife. Matt was always so thoughtful, surprising her with her favorite smoked-turkey-and-swiss-cheese lunches, bringing her wildflowers, giving her space when she had to cram for an English exam.

She thought about the bond between her and Matt, and a deep ache formed in her chest. He didn't want to see someone else, did he? *No, it isn't possible.* They were too good for each other. Matt was twenty-four, in his final year at law school, an athlete with a brilliant mind and a way of making her feel taken care of. He was strong and determined and very much in love with her. Though Nicole knew he found her physically attractive, Matt seemed most drawn to the way she made him laugh. Nicole had been a cheerleader in high school and thrived on silliness and smiley moments. She was playful and affectionate and loved closing his textbooks, pulling him outside, and having an impromptu snowball fight or a walk along the frozen trail. He was her pillar of strength; she was his reminder that life was meant to be savored.

They were perfect together. Weren't they?

Is there something wrong with our relationship, something I can't see?

Be still and know that I am God, daughter.

Nicole drew a slow, deep breath. She loved the way God spoke to her, swiftly and with loving authority, in a quiet voice that echoed from someplace in the depths of her soul. For years she and the Lord had been this way, and the certainty of His presence, His voice, brought an intimacy to their relationship that was the very rock upon which Nicole was building her life. If God wanted her to be at peace over this meeting with Matt, then deep inside she knew she had nothing to fear.

Thank You, Lord. Just keep my heart from beating out of my chest, okay? The curiosity's killing me.

Throughout lunch, Matt's eyes danced, and he seemed about to burst with excitement. But he talked only about his classwork and current projects. At first Nicole played along, but when they finished their lunch she wiped her mouth and set her napkin down hard.

"Okay . . . stop."

He grinned at her. "What?

She could feel a smile playing at the corners of her lips, but she huffed anyway. "You had something *very important* to tell me, remember? That's why we're here."

He sat back in his seat and gazed out the window, his eyes twinkling as he drew a long breath. "Let's see, something important . . ." He murmured the words under his breath, as though trying to jog his memory. "What was it . . . ?"

Nicole's exasperated grunt filled the silence, and she grabbed his right arm with both hands, pulling on him like a petulant child. "Matt, this isn't funny. I'm serious, come on. I've been waiting all day."

He grinned at her but said nothing.

She huffed. "Okay fine, I'll guess. You're moving to Antarctica to take up ice fishing? Moving to Zimbabwe to be a missionary? Quitting law school and joining the circus?"

They both laughed and their foreheads came together. "You're funny—" he wiggled his nose against hers—"did you know that?"

"And you're a brat." Her voice was a whisper, their faces

still touching, and in an instant the mood changed. Matt cradled the back of her neck, adjusting her head so that their mouths met in a kiss that started out sweetly but filled with urgency in very little time.

Flee!

The Lord's voice was clear, as it always was in times like this. An empty house, a warm fire, snow falling gently outside with no one expected back for more than an hour.

They pulled away and studied each other, their faces inches apart.

"Let's take a walk . . ." Matt's voice was thick.

"Now? I thought you wanted to talk?" Nicole caught her breath and sat back in her chair.

He nodded, motioning toward the backyard. "Out there. On the path."

Nicole shrugged. "Okay." They moved in reverent silence into the backyard and onto the trail, each enjoying the presence of the other, remembering their kiss minutes earlier. Then, as though he'd planned it, Matt stopped and kicked the snow off a fallen log. He took his scarf from around his neck, laid it over the soggy wood, and looked deeply into Nicole's eyes.

"Sit." It was not a command, but part of some sort of mesmerizing ritual Nicole couldn't recognize and had never taken part in.

She dropped slowly to the log and stared at Matt. "Okay . . ."

Moving in what seemed like slow motion, Matt reached into his coat pocket and pulled out a tiny package wrapped in gold paper. It glittered in the shadows, and suddenly Nicole had trouble feeling her arms and legs, like she was floating somehow, living out a dream she'd carried with her since she was a little girl. Tears stung at her eyes, and she moved her gaze from the package to Matt's face. "Matt?" Her voice was barely audible, but full of love and questions and disbelief.

Without hesitating he bent down and planted one knee firmly in the snow as he held out the gift for her to take. Gingerly, her gloved hands shaking, Nicole took the box and stared at it. Could it be? Had he chosen today to ask her? *Dear God, help me open the ribbon . . .*

She worked her way through the paper, pulled out a blue velvet box, and opened the lid. The diamond ring inside captured the light and sprayed brilliance in a thousand directions as Nicole's breath caught in her throat. It was a wedding set, a single solitaire engagement ring and a matching wedding band with a trail of tiny diamonds across the top. *Oh, Lord, I can't believe it.* Tears clouded her vision and she blinked, sending a steamy trail down both cheeks. "Oh, Matt . . ." She pulled him to her and held on until he gently freed himself and caught her gaze with his eyes.

"Nicole Michelle Reynolds, I love you more than life itself." He gently brought his hand to her face and brushed away her tears with his gloved thumb. "I've loved you since our first day . . . and I love you more each time we're together."

He paused, and two more tears spilled onto her cheeks. So this was it . . . he was asking her the question.

Thank You, God. Thank You for this man.

She waited while he considered his words. "All my life I've been afraid of commitment, afraid that if I promised myself to a woman I'd wind up like my father one day . . . angry and alone and . . . well, pathetic, I guess." He smoothed a tendril of hair from her eyes. "Then I met you."

There were a hundred things Nicole wanted to say, but she was silent, memorizing the moment, soaking it in because she knew she'd never forget it as long as she lived.

"I see the way your parents have built their love for . . . what, twenty-one years now?"

Nicole nodded, a smile punctuating her tears.

"Twenty-one years." Matt shook his head. "Amazing." Tenderness shone in his eyes. "What they have together, Nicole, I want that for us, too. A family and a house where traditions and memories are built, where we can make a life together that will last until God calls one of us home."

Her happiness spilled over, and a gleeful laugh escaped her. "Oh, Matt . . . I love you so much!" She tried to hug him again but he put his hand up, stopping her from coming closer. Studying him, she saw that his eyes were wet. In all the days and months they'd spent together, she'd never seen him so serious.

"Nicole, I want you to be my wife." He framed her cheekbones with his fingertips, and she felt so safe in his powerful gaze. "I've asked your father, and he's given us his blessing." He paused for what seemed like an eternity. "Will you marry me?"

The tears came harder now, and she threw her arms around his neck, holding on as she would the rest of her life. How precious and perfect and beautiful were God's plans for His people. To think that her mother had prayed for her future husband hundreds of times over the years and now here he was. She was ready—pure and whole the way God intended—to cleave to Matt and become his wife. Just like her mother had prayed. She could hardly wait to tell her parents.

Oh, Lord, thank You . . . I'm overcome with gratefulness. We can tell my parents at the family meeting this week!

"Yes, Matt." She would remember this moment as long as she lived. "Yes. I would love to marry you . . ."

Four

IT WAS FRIDAY NIGHT, HOURS BEFORE THE FAMILY meeting, and Abby was exhausted beyond belief. Despite a series of joint sessions with their counselors, she and John had refused to come to any sort of last-minute agreement. Instead, they'd met at a restaurant outside of town and talked through the details, finally settling on a scenario that would work well enough for the future.

Abby would stay in the house; John would find a place of his own. The kids were old enough that custody wouldn't be an issue. Sean would stay with Abby during the week and with John on weekends or holidays—whenever he liked, really. Otherwise life would go on pretty much the same. Kade would move to a dorm at the University of Iowa sometime that summer, and Nicole would continue living at home while she took classes at Southern Illinois University.

Abby's tiredness was understandable. For years she and

John had been merely going through the motions, pretending to be happily married, but these last few weeks Abby had been repulsed by their charade. She'd found herself wanting to scream at John, the kids, anyone who would listen that she was sick of her life being little more than an act. The children had been caught up in their Christmas excitement, what with Sean's new skis and Kade's specially made class ring, complete with the insignia declaring him state football champion. Nicole was wrapped up in her life, working through the tougher classes that came along with being a junior and spending nearly all her free time with Matt.

As John had predicted, the excitement of a state title was still very much the buzz of family conversation. He continued to field weekly calls from reporters and other coaches wanting to congratulate him and compare plays, hoping perhaps that some of Coach Reynolds's success might rub off or spark an idea that would play out in their own lives. People seemed to think John had the answer for everything, everyone.

Everyone but her.

Abby exhaled slowly and pulled an old flannel nightie from her dresser drawer. She and John still shared a living space, but not a bed. Not for months now. She would dress in the bathroom, brush her teeth, and when she was sure the kids were asleep or too busy to notice, she'd sneak down the hall to the guest room. She'd always been the first one up in the morning, so none of them had ever caught on.

It was early, and John was at a league meeting that would last until after ten o'clock. *Just as well. I'll be asleep before he gets back.*

A bitter wind howled outside as she slipped out of her

clothes, donned the nightgown, and realized her feet were cold. *One of these days I'll have to buy my own socks.* But for now, this one last night anyway, she could use his. They were bigger and thicker and kept her feet warm even on the coldest nights.

After they told the kids about the divorce, John was going to talk to one of his coaching buddies about staying at his house for a while, until the whole thing was final and he could find a place of his own. Either way, he planned to be out of the house within a week. Abby slid the drawer open and dug her hands inside, looking for the thickest pair of socks she could find. Instead, her fingers felt a folded piece of paper. She pulled it out, staring at it. Hadn't she just cleaned the drawers a few weeks ago?

Her heart began pounding in her chest, shouting at her to drop the wrinkled note and avoid the message inside. She ignored the warning. Perching on the edge of her bed, Abby unfolded the piece of paper, which bore handwriting that—though not her own—clearly belonged to a woman. She began to read.

John, thanks for talking with me the other night. I don't know what I'd do without you. I mean it. You're the best friend a girl could ever have. Abby doesn't know what she's losing. Anyway, I'll meet you early Friday like usual. Can't wait to see you. Love, Charlene.

Abby stared at the note as angry feelings galloped about in her gut. Unable to stop herself, she read it a second time—then she ripped it in half and in half again, and again and again until she could no longer recognize any of the woman's words.

She couldn't decide whether to race for the bathroom or punch a hole in the wall. In the end she did neither, only stayed there on the edge of the bed, imprisoned by the hurt in her heart. *How could you, John? Can't you wait until after the divorce? Isn't what we shared worth at least that?*

Abby could hear her husband's voice, indignant and defensive whenever she'd brought up Charlene's name: *"She's just a friend . . . just a friend . . ."*

She huffed as her eyes scanned the shreds of paper. Just a friend . . . what a joke. Booster club members had reported to Abby several times that they'd seen John and Charlene together in his classroom. And at least once a person had walked in and found the two locked in an embrace. *"She was having a hard day . . . she's all alone . . . she's just a friend."* The excuses were endless.

Fine. John could be all the friend to Charlene he wanted after tomorrow. As long as he moved out and stopped the terrible lie he'd been living these past few months.

She scrunched the pieces up and moved into the bathroom, dropping them in the toilet and flushing them. On the way out she caught her reflection in the mirror. Was she not pretty enough? Had she gained weight in the past few years?

Abby studied herself and knew it wasn't a weight problem. She wore the same size-seven jeans she'd always worn, and at five-foot-eight she was thinner than most women half her age. She walked the treadmill early each morning and was careful about what she ate.

It has to be my age.

She scrutinized her skin and saw the visible pores and fine wrinkles that hadn't been there ten years ago. How old was Charlene, anyway? Thirty-two, thirty-three? Abby anchored her fingertips along her hairline and lifted up, watching as her face took on a look she was more familiar with, the look she'd had as a teenager and young woman.

Was that what their love had come to? After surviving so much, celebrating so much, after raising a family together . . . had it really come to this? To losing her husband because the skin on her face showed wear?

I gave you those years, John . . .

She took a step back and studied herself again. Her hair was a mass of short stylish layers that still turned men's heads. Old men, maybe, but men all the same. And with a little help from the salon, her hair was still blonde. Abby angled her face this way and that, trying to see herself the way John saw her. Okay, so she'd just turned forty-one, so what? Charlene would turn forty-one someday, too. That couldn't be the reason things hadn't worked between them.

Abby frowned. She was being ridiculous. Their breakup had nothing to do with looks. It was because their marriage had become an old sock years ago, threadbare in all the important places and too worn out and stained to bother saving.

She turned away from her reflection and padded through the bedroom door, down the hall to the guest room. Without turning on the light, she shut the door and climbed into bed.

She was fast asleep in a matter of minutes.

An autumn wind blew through the trees knocking leaves of every shade and color onto the walkway that surrounded an oversized stadium. Abby was inside yelling, *"Go, Blue! Come on, John, you can do it!"* He waved at her from the huddle, an impressive six-foot-four quarterback with dark hair and aqua blue eyes—by far the best-looking player on the field.

"Wait a minute, Abby . . . I have something to tell you . . . something to tell you." John drew his arm back and threw the football into the stands where it soared and dipped and finally landed in Abby's hands and became a bouquet of pink-and-white baby roses. A grin worked its way across John's face, and Abby noticed that the other players seemed frozen in time. Then, as though it were the most normal action in the world, John raced up the stadium steps toward her, his uniform clanking and jostling about as he came. He drew closer, and the crowd and bleachers and football team disappeared. In their place was a well-dressed congregation staring straight at them, smiling and motioning for her and John to move closer to each other.

"So, Abby, will you marry me . . . huh? Will you, Abby?"

She looked, and instead of his uniform, John was wearing a black tuxedo. She glanced nervously at her jeans, then shrugged and began reciting her vows.

"I, Abby Chapman, promise to love and cherish—"

But before she could finish, a doctor ran into the church waving his hands and shouting, *"It's a girl! It's a girl!"* Behind him came three nurses, the middle one carrying a tiny baby. The church crowd vanished, and they were in a hospital room. Abby was sobbing, crying as though her heart was being torn in two, and she took the baby from the nurse. But it wasn't the baby at all, because now Nicole was standing at her side, and John was holding their daughter's little-girl hand. The new baby, the one in Abby's arms, wasn't moving, wasn't breathing.

"I don't know what happened. She was taking her nap

just like every other day, and when I went to wake her up she was—"

"A boy, Abby. Can you believe it? We got ourselves a boy!"

She looked down. The dead baby was no longer there, and Nicole was older now, dancing in her ballet costume, doing toe-raises and spins and singing a song Abby couldn't understand. Without warning Nicole's spins became a whirlwind, and the whirlwind became a tornado, angry and menacing and building with each passing moment. In the distance Abby could see her mother, smiling, waving.

"Congratulations, Abby, you've got yourself a real beaut there. Congratulations, Abby . . . Congratulations . . ."

The tornado switched directions and headed for Abby's mother, shaking the ground and filling the air with the sound of a thousand blazing freight trains.

"Mom! Help yourself . . . run! Get out before it kills you!"

Suddenly the room was empty except for a hole in the ground. John crawled out of it holding the baby boy in his arms. Kade . . . it was Kade; Abby knew it. She ran a finger over the infant's forehead and then saw Nicole climb out of the hole as well.

"Nicole, you're okay!" She hugged her daughter, convulsing with tears and stroking her golden hair. Before Nicole could say anything, the baby in John's arms let out a loud sound, and Abby turned to him. Only now he was three years old, and he and John were having a burping contest in the middle of the living room. Abby looked at John, and they both laughed until tears were streaming down their faces. She glanced out the window and saw that their house was in the middle of the football field. Through the fifty-yard line ran a street where

Nicole was sitting, playing in the middle of the road, unaware of the car speeding straight for her . . .

"Nicole!" Abby's voice echoed into the night, and she was deathly afraid, utterly alone until she felt the arms around her. Warm, strong, reassuring arms. John's arms. *He's here . . . he's come.* She turned and hugged him close. *Oh, John, I love you . . . thank God you're here . . .*

Instantly they were bathed in Friday-night-football lights, standing in the end zone at Marion High. Slowly, a distance began to grow between them, leaving John on the field and her in the stands—in the back row—squinting to see what was happening. The crowd was frenzied, and the Eagles were down a touchdown in what Abby knew was the biggest game of the year. *Halftime . . . it must be halftime.*

Over the loudspeaker someone was reading a letter.

"Mr. Reynolds, I think you're the worst man who's ever coached football. Maybe our boys might win a game or two if they could get someone at the wheel who knew what he was doing . . . knew what he was doing . . . knew what he was doing . . ."

The words echoed across the field, and Abby ran down the stairs as fast as she could toward John. Only it took longer than usual, and she was forced to run for what seemed like hours until finally she closed the gap between them. Then, with everyone watching, she wrapped her arms around his neck. *"It's okay, honey . . . God has a plan in this. It'll be okay . . . you've got a gift, and one day the whole world will know it . . ."*

Suddenly she was in the school weightroom, heading for John's office, finding him at his desk. *"John . . ."*

There were tears in his eyes when he turned to her.

"Don't tell me, Abby. It's been hard enough already, please don't tell me . . . don't tell me . . . don't tell me . . ."

She came up behind him and placed her hands on his shoulders. "It's my job to do this, John . . . even if it's the worst news you'll ever hear. I have to tell you . . ."

Without warning there was the sound of a stadium exploding with the cheers of thousands of football fans. *"And now—"* the stadium announcer bellowed over the crowd— *"the state of Illinois would like to award to Coach John Reynolds and the Marion Eagles the honor of—"*

John stopped him before he could finish. *"What I really want,"* he said, *"is my dad. He's supposed to be here. Maybe if someone could find him . . . find him . . . find him."*

"Congratulations! Here he is . . ." Only the voice no longer belonged to the announcer, but to another doctor . . . one in a green coat and strange glasses. And Abby wasn't in the stands, she was on an operating table. *"It's a boy . . . a boy . . . a boy."*

Sean smiled at his parents and gave them the thumbs-up sign. But before Abby could hold him or savor the downy fuzz of his newborn cheek, they were all in the car, the old sedan they'd driven back when they were newly married. At the stoplight John pointed to a building up ahead. *"What's that, Abby? I've seen it before, but I can't remember . . . can't remember . . ."*

It took her a minute to recognize it. The building was their church, the place where they'd taught Sunday school together, where they'd taken their children when they were young. Only it looked different now, and John was wrinkling his brow. *"That's not what church looked like, Abby . . . Are you sure? . . . Are you sure?"*

They stopped the car and climbed out, and she held

Nicole's and Sean's hands while Kade stood with John, and suddenly a crack in the ground developed between them. It began to grow.

"John! Quick, jump!"

He stared strangely at her. *"You jump, Abby. I like it on this side."*

"But it's better over here! I like my side. Come on . . . jump!" Her voice was shrill, filled with panic as the distance between them continued to grow at an alarming rate. Eventually she couldn't make out what he was saying, just that he was trying to talk.

"Come on, John. Don't you care about me? Jump! Jump, John! Before it's too late!"

Nicole started to cry, and Sean closed his eyes. *"I'm scared, Mommy. Make him come back. Make Daddy come back . . ."*

Then John grabbed a long piece of rope, and though the space between them was widening more with each passing second, he heaved it with all his might, and it spanned what was now a canyon. In a blink, the rope became a sturdy footbridge.

"I've changed my mind, Abby. I'm coming . . . I'm coming!"

Without waiting another moment, John and Kade ran as fast as they could across the bridge. They were almost there, almost to the safe place where Abby and Sean and Nicole waited, when the bridge began to give way. Kade caught his father's arm, and the two jumped the remaining feet, barely landing on solid ground.

"Oh, John, you could have been killed . . ." Abby ran to them and hugged first Kade, then John. *"You should have stayed over there where it was safe."*

He caught her eyes with his and drew her close, kissing

her the way he had when they had first fallen in love. *"I had to be with you, Abby. I love you! I'll always love you . . . always love you . . . always love you . . ."*

His words repeated, over and over again—*". . . always love you . . . always love you . . ."*—but his voice changed, and Abby pulled back, studying him.

No! It can't be . . .

Abby untangled herself, frantic. Instead of John holding her, it was a dummy made up to look like him. *". . . always love you . . . always love you . . ."* There was a recording playing from inside the life-sized doll, and as Abby moved backward, her heart racing, the dummy fell to the ground, eyes open. *". . . always love you . . . always love you . . ."*

Abby's scream pierced the night, and she shot straight up in bed, gasping for breath, her heart racing faster than ever before. What had happened? What had she just lived through? A dream?

No, a nightmare. A terrible, terrible nightmare.

She shook her head, trying to clear the strange words and images that had consumed her night. Everything about the dream—the voices and feelings, the way her body had felt wrapped up in John's arms—all of it had been so real. She struggled to catch her breath.

In the still of the night, she glanced at the clock on the bedside table. Four-fifteen. Bits and pieces from the pictures in her head still played in her mind, and she sank back down onto the pillow. Had any other two people been through as much as she and John and then decided to throw it all away?

Abby didn't think so.

And in the quiet hours before she and John would sit down with their children in the home where they'd been raised and tell them about the divorce, Abby grieved for all they'd been, all they'd done, all they'd never be again after today.

The grieving turned to quiet weeping. She sobbed in a way she hadn't done in years until she heard the early morning stirrings of John in the kitchen making pancakes and the kids taking showers down the hall. Feeling as though she'd aged decades overnight, Abby dragged herself from bed, wiped her tears, and drew a deep breath.

There was no point dwelling on the past. It was time to face the future.

five

ABBY PULLED ON A TURTLENECK AND MATCHING
sweatshirt and slipped into a pair of jeans. Might as well
be comfortable since they were bound to spend most of
the day in deep conversation, wiping their children's tears
and making shallow promises that somehow everything
was going to be all right.

The house was colder than Abby liked, and after she
made her way downstairs, she rounded the corner and
flipped on the heater. *At least our home will be warm, even
if we can't be that way toward each other.*

John glanced up from the skillet and spotted her.
"Pancakes are ready."

Abby stared at him and blinked. Didn't this day matter
at all? Had it been so easy for him to come home late, sleep
through the night, and pop out of bed to make pancakes
like everything was fine? "I'm not hungry."

She turned her back to him and wandered into the

living room where the meeting would take place in less than an hour. Everything was neat and tidy, but in the morning light she could see a layer of dust on the old photos that sat on the bookshelves—framed pictures from when they were young and just starting out. Abby thought about getting a rag and dusting them, then shook her head. *It's fitting that they're covered in dust. Just like our lives.*

She closed her eyes for a minute and considered the enormity of the announcement they were about to make. *So this is it, huh, God? Dusty photographs, dusty lives. How did we make such a mess of things?*

Seek first My kingdom and all these things—

Abby's comeback was quick and rude. *We did seek You, and look what happened.* Immediately she was seized with remorse. *I'm sorry. It's not Your fault.* She squinted and stared across the room, out the window at the front lawn she and John had landscaped themselves. It seemed like an eternity ago that they'd been able to laugh together, to love each other the way they'd once hoped to spend a lifetime loving. And now . . .

Now their lives were an unmanageable ball of knots too tangled to understand, let alone make right again.

Abby sensed someone else had entered the room and turned around.

"I think we should talk." The corners of John's eyes were lined; maybe he was more concerned than she had thought.

"About what? Haven't we been through it a hundred times with the counselors?" She crossed her arms and chided herself for finding him attractive. After all he'd put her through, all the lies he'd told . . . even now, an hour before their big announcement, she could not force herself to be unmoved by the sight of him.

John sighed and dropped into the nearest chair, anchoring his elbows on his knees as he lowered his head. After several beats he looked up and caught her gaze so powerfully she couldn't have blinked if she wanted to. *Do your eyes have to be so blue all the time?*

"Look, Abby . . . what I'm saying is . . . are you sure? Are you sure this is what we should do? Are you sure it's the right thing?"

Abby shifted her weight and released a short laugh. "I'm absolutely sure it isn't the right thing. The Bible tells us that much."

John sat perfectly still, his gaze still locked on hers. "Then why, Abby . . . why let it happen?"

She'd always hated the way her eyes stung with the initial onset of tears. This time was no different. "*I* didn't let anything happen, John, and you know it. *We* let it happen. And right now—to be perfectly honest—*you're* letting it happen. You and Miss Meet-You-Friday-Morning-Same-Time-As-Usual."

"What?"

"Don't look surprised, John. You're the one who saves her notes in your sock drawer. Did you forget I'm the one who does your laun—"

"Be quiet." He stopped her midsentence, the connection between them broken as he stared at his feet, shoulders stooped. "The kids are getting ready, and Matt'll be here any minute."

What? Abby felt like she'd been slapped in the face. "Matt? Why's he coming?" This was outrageous! The most difficult announcement they'd ever had to make, and now they had to do it in front of a stranger? John must be crazy to have allowed Nicole to—

"Oh, get off your high horse, Abby. Nicole wanted him here for the first part of the meeting. I guess he's got something to ask us. Talk to *her* if you're so frustrated."

"Stop blaming me for everything." She took a chair opposite him and lowered her voice. Even in this they couldn't get along. "You make it sound like I'm crazy to want just our family here when we tell the kids we're getting a divorce. I mean, seriously, John, why not invite the whole neighborhood? We could sell tickets, pass out popcorn. I don't know, I guess I thought it was kind of a private moment."

"It will be." His voice was a tightly controlled hiss. "We can take a break after Matt talks to us, and he'll be on his way. Nicole said he has a hundred things to do today."

"Then why come to our meeting?"

John forced the air from his lungs and shook his head, chuckling in a way that was completely void of humor. "Don't you ever let up?"

"I know, I'm the bad guy, the relentless one, pushy and demanding. Fine. So be it. But why does he have to come to the meeting?"

"Forget it!" John stood up and glared at her. Gone was the intensity in his eyes, the searching and questioning heart that had moved him to wonder aloud if this decision to dissolve their marriage was really one they should be making. In place of all that was a man with whom Abby was more familiar these days, a man who seemed neither to love her nor care for her feelings. "Ask Nicole."

He turned to leave, and Abby was instantly on her feet. *Not that quick, John. You started this conversation.* "Wait!"

He spun around, his expression cold as wet cement. "What?"

Don't say it, daughter . . . A kind word turns away anger . . .

Abby narrowed her eyes. "You asked me a question earlier."

John waited, silent.

"You asked me if I was sure if this was the right decision." Fresh tears stung at her eyes, and she blinked them back. There was a tightening in her chest, and she recognized what it was: the walls of her heart were growing higher, harder.

"And . . . ?" John's look had gone from cold to impatient, and she wanted to kick him in the shin. Maybe then he'd share some of the pain she was feeling.

"It's the right thing to do, John." Her voice was measured, barely more than a whisper as she fought for control over her tears. "As long as you're sleeping around behind my back, it's the only thing we *can* do."

Fire exploded in his eyes, and he clenched his teeth. "I am not sleeping with her, Abby. She's a friend."

"How can you stand there and lie to me?" She gave a shake of her head and glared hard at him. "I mean, you're absolutely amazing. Your sock drawer has a love letter from the woman, and you're trying to tell me she's only a friend? Be real, John. And when the kids ask why, make sure you mention your weakness for sad, lonely women, will you?"

A dozen emotions flashed in John's eyes, and his jaw muscles flexed. But he said nothing, only turned around again and disappeared into the kitchen.

Abby stood there, watching him go, and a strange, sad feeling came over her. In that instant, her hardened, walled-up heart felt like an unbearable burden deep within her.

"She's a friend . . . she's a friend . . . she's a friend." John's words beat at her relentlessly until she shut her eyes to make them stop.

He *was* sleeping with Charlene, wasn't he? He had to be.

Let he who is without guilt cast the first stone . . .

There it was again—that same voice. A piercing pang entered her consciousness, and Abby thought of her e-mail friend, a man she'd been talking with almost daily for the past two years. *That's not the same.*

Let he who is without guilt cast the first—

No! She shouted silently at the words assaulting her heart. *I've never even met the man.* Why would God want her to feel guilty now? She needed that friendship. Especially with John devoting all his attention to Charlene.

Daughter, hear Me. Let he who is without—

Abby closed her eyes and forced the words from her mind. *Okay, fine. We're both guilty. But it's John's fault, Lord. He's the one who broke faith first.*

Abby considered the number of times she'd found out from other sources that John and Charlene were together, and suddenly her mind was filled with the image of the two of them on the football field after the state game. It was amazing the kids hadn't gotten wind of their father's affair.

Like the old saying went, where there was smoke there was fire. And where Charlene and John were concerned, there had been enough smoke to indicate an outright inferno.

Lean not on your own understanding, but in all your ways acknowledge Me and I—

Why was this persistent voice rattling around in her heart lately? Ever since the football game. Certainly it had

to be habit, familiarity with Scripture, and not the presence of God trying to communicate with her. After all, it
had been years since they'd attended church regularly, and
at least that long since she'd prayed or read her Bible with
any consistency. *What would the Lord want with me now?
Now that John and I have gone against everything He ever
wanted for our lives?*

There was no answer, and she allowed her eyes to find
the dusty photographs once more. Every time there'd been
a chance to make things right, somehow she and John
wound up in a fight. *Just once, Abby, couldn't you have shut
your mouth? Couldn't you have walked straight up to him and
allowed him to hold you like old times?* She thought about
that for a moment and realized the answer was no. Fighting
words were all they had left.

Apparently today would be no sentimental exception.

They had no choice now but to move ahead with the
divorce and pray that somehow God—if He still cared
enough to listen—would forgive them and help them
make new lives without each other.

Sean and Kade were already downstairs in the living room,
but Nicole was reading her Bible on her bed, feeling as
though she might actually float if she tried to stand up.
She glanced across the room at her mirror and realized
that she had never felt more beautiful. Really and truly, she
was a daughter of the King, and He alone had set her apart
for this moment in time. It was overwhelming.

She scanned the pages of Jeremiah 29 until she found
the verse she wanted, the one she'd lived under and
believed since she was a little girl: *"For I know the plans I*

*have for you, . . . plans to prosper you and not to harm you,
plans to give you hope and a future."* Nicole let her eyes read
over the words several times. Never had her future looked
brighter than at that moment, and it had everything to do
with the nature and faithfulness of God Almighty.

Leaving the Bible open to that page, she found the velvet box that had been hiding in her jewelry cupboard. With
ease she placed the ring on the appropriate finger and
stared at it. *Oh, Lord, I'm the happiest girl alive.* Folding up
the fingers of her left hand so the ring wouldn't be obvious,
she danced down the stairs and peeked into the living room
where Matt, Kade, and Sean were watching an NFL pre-
game show. "Where's Mom and Dad?" It was already after
nine, and Nicole knew she couldn't wait much longer. If
they didn't start the meeting soon she might just have to
jump up on the kitchen table and announce her news for
all the neighborhood to hear.

Kade shrugged, his eyes fixed on the television set.
"Upstairs, maybe."

Nicole caught Matt's gaze and held it, grinning at him
as he spoke a hundred silent words with his eyes. He stood
and crossed the room, kissing her lightly on the cheek.
"You look pretty."

Sean grabbed a pillow from the sofa and threw it at
Matt. "Aw, quit it, guys. No ooey-gooey stuff before noon
on Saturday, okay?"

Nicole giggled as Matt linked his fingers through hers
and led her into the room. He patted Sean on the top of
his head. "One day you'll understand, little brother."

Everyone smiled, and Nicole's love for the man beside
her swelled. Already he thought of Kade and Sean as his
brothers. Her parents were going to be thrilled at—

"Okay, TV off." Mom and Dad entered the room together, and for a brief moment, Nicole felt a frown crease her forehead. Were Mom and Dad mad at each other? She had the oddest sense that there was something foreign—a tension or a wall or a wedge—something between them. Something big.

Nicole caught herself. She blinked away the image and looked at her parents again. There. Now they looked right. They were smiling and taking their seats next to each other. *Must be my imagination. Too much on my mind.*

The room was comfortably quiet. She and Matt sat on one sofa, Sean and Kade on the other, and Mom and Dad in chairs beside each other. Dad spoke first.

"Let's get started. You all know how busy football season is around here—especially this last one. And now that things have settled down there are a few things we need to discuss as a family. First, I'd like to—"

"Aren't we going to open in prayer?" Nicole looked from her father to her mother and back again. "We always start our family meetings with prayer, right?"

Nicole watched her mother cast a knowing look at her father, and a twinge of apprehension hit her again. He looked nervous . . . convicted, even. A feeling of fear came over her. *I can't believe he actually forgot, Lord . . . Wow, what's going on with them?* She shook the worry away. Everything was fine. Her parents were solid. Rock solid. Why imagine a problem where there wasn't one?

"You're right, Nicki." Dad looked at her, and the uneasiness of a moment earlier disappeared. She loved it when her father called her that. He was the only one who did. "Why don't you pray, honey?"

She shrugged and glanced at the faces around her.

"Sure." She bowed her head and focused hard on the Lord, on His goodness and kindness, on the plans He was bringing to fruition in her life. "Father, we come before You as one, one unit, one family, determined that our ways and plans and decisions will be only those that You have planned for us. Bless this time of communication, and let it bring us closer as a family, closer to You, and to each other. Thank You, Lord. In Jesus' name, amen."

There was a pause, and Nicole couldn't fight off the sense of something fearful and foreboding in the air. *Come on, Dad, say something funny like you usually do. This is getting weird here.*

Her father cleared his throat and looked in her direction. "Matt, we'll start with you. That way you can get on with your day and leave us here to finish up."

Matt nodded and squeezed Nicole's hand, the one with the engagement ring on it.

"Well—" he looked at her, and she knew she would never forget the way his eyes sparkled—"actually, Nicole and I both have something to tell you."

Nicole took in her mother's reaction, noting how her eyes changed from cool tension to wide-eyed disbelief. Her father still looked clueless, but that was typical.

Nicole drew a deep breath and looked expectantly at Matt. "Do you want to tell them?"

"Come on, guys . . . the suspense is killing us." Dad crossed one leg over his knee and settled back against his chair, his smile forced and stiff. *Why does he look nervous? Or does he?* Nicole couldn't get around her pesky suspicion that something wasn't right. *I'll find out later. Right now there's something more important to discuss.*

Matt grinned and then faced her family. "Okay, this is

it—" he gently lifted Nicole's hand so that everyone could see her ring—"I've asked Nicole to marry me."

Nicole wrapped her other hand around Matt's neck and gave him a quick hug. Without turning toward her family she spoke, her eyes locked onto Matt's. "And I told him yes."

She whipped around and saw that her parents were stunned, their mouths hanging open, their eyes wide.

"Mom, Dad . . . did you hear us? We're *engaged!*" Nicole hooted out loud, and then in a blur of motion her parents were on their feet, pulling her into a three-way hug. Mom squealed as Dad stepped back and shook Matt's hand.

"Talk about a shocker . . ." He pumped Matt's hand until he realized that the moment called for something greater than a handshake. "Come here." He grabbed Matt and pulled him into a hug.

At the same time, Mom braced her hands on Nicole's shoulders and kissed her on the cheek. "Nicole! I can't believe it. When did this happen?"

All feelings of impending doom had vanished like morning fog on the lake; Nicole was overcome with joy. "Since Wednesday. Matt took me out on the trail and proposed to me with his knee in the snow."

The group shifted so that Mom could embrace Matt and congratulate him, as well. Kade moved into the circle, gently grabbing the necks of both Nicole and her fiancé, pulling them close. "You crazy guys, keeping a secret like that." He punched Matt's arm lightly. "Hey, way to go, Matt. Welcome to the family."

Gradually the hugs ceased, and they returned to their seats. Nicole beamed at her father, who was tapping his fingers in a nervous rhythm on the arms of the chair. "Now, Dad, don't tell me you're shocked. Matt said he asked you about this a long time ago, and you gave him your blessing."

Her parents exchanged an uneasy look. "Really?" Mom raised one eyebrow and cast Dad a strangely partial smile. The uneasy feeling hit Nicole again. *What's Mom's problem? Why're they acting like this?* "I didn't hear about it."

A nervous laugh came from her father's throat, and he glanced from Mom to Nicole and back. "Matt said it could be . . . years. I thought . . . well, I had no idea that's what he wanted to tell us today."

Matt reached for Nicole's hand again, and she slid up next to him. Everything was going to work out just as she'd always dreamed. She nestled her shoulder against his much larger arm and studied him. He was something else, really. The complete package. Exactly what she and her mother had prayed for.

Sitting up a bit straighter, Matt faced her parents. "Actually, I had no idea I'd be ready this soon." He glanced down and gave Nicole a smile that echoed in the core of her being. *He loves me! Thank You, God, he loves me!* Matt turned back to her parents. "The change came sometime last summer, or maybe in the fall. I started thinking that I'd be finished with law school this June, so why not get married this summer? Nicole can keep taking classes. In fact, we both think it's a good idea for her to get her education so she can teach if she wants to."

Nicole loved the way he worded that. *If she wants to . . .* The truth was, married to Matt she would have a choice. The thoughts were almost too wonderful to bear.

Mom nodded and looked from Nicole to Matt. "That's

wonderful. I'm so happy for you." She hesitated, and Nicole studied her eyes. They were flat, and the happiness in her voice seemed artificial. *Why aren't you glowing, Mom? This is my finest hour here.* She wanted to mention the fact that everything about this day, this news, was an answer to the prayer her mother had prayed so often when Nicole was a young girl, but somehow the timing didn't seem right.

"Have you thought of a date?" Dad looked at them curiously, and his eyes, too, seemed strangely untouched by the joy of their news.

Nicole and Matt looked at each other and grinned as they turned back to Mom. "We figured it out last night. July fourteenth. Your anniversary, Mom and Dad! Isn't that great!"

Matt slipped his arm around Nicole and looked intently at her parents. "The truth is, Nicole and I want the kind of marriage you two have." He looked at Nicole again. "The kind that grows better every year."

Mom stood up, and her smile was strange . . . awkward. "How nice." She looked at Dad, and Nicole thought she conveyed some unspoken message. "I'm going to put the kettle on for tea. Nicole? Matt? Can I get you some?"

Kade raised his hand. "Actually, get some for me, too, Mom." He worked his face into an ultraformal expression. "English tea with a dash of sweet cream would be simply smashing."

Sean burst into little-boy laughter and tackled his brother until the two landed on the floor. Nicole smiled at her mother. "Sure. Thanks, Mom."

Without another word, without crossing the room for

a hug or asking Nicole to join her, Mom hurried from the room and headed for the kitchen.

Dad stood. "I'll help." He hesitated, looking at them strangely. "We'll be right back."

Kade and Sean were still wrestling on the floor, and when her parents were out of earshot, Nicole turned to Matt. "Are my parents acting weird, or is it just me?"

Matt shrugged. "I think they're happy." A concerned look crossed his face. "They are, aren't they?"

"Yeah, they seem like it." Nicole thought about her mother's reaction and worked her mouth into a smile as she snuggled closer to Matt. Of course they were happy. *It's only my imagination.* "Mom's probably just in shock. I mean, she turns forty-one last week and now I'm getting married. That's a lot to handle."

Matt laughed. "If I know your mother, once it sinks in she'll be bouncing off the walls."

"Yeah," Nicole ran her finger along Matt's face. "You're the answer to both our prayers."

Six

THE NOISE OF SEAN AND KADE WRESTLING IN THE next room was enough to hide Abby's convulsing whimpers as she braced herself against the kitchen sink and stared through her window at the frozen lake. Beside her, his back to the view, John stood silently, arms crossed, eyes cast downward.

Her heart was so heavy she could barely stand up under the weight. *Help me, God. I've never felt so alone in my life. What are we supposed to do now?*

What God has joined together let no one separate, My child.

Oh, quit! Abby was bone-tired of pat answers. That scripture couldn't possibly be from the Lord. Not when He knew what was happening with John and Charlene. *I need real answers, God. Please!*

Silence.

Her tears came harder, and she buried her face in her

hands. Nicole was going to get married in six months—on their wedding anniversary, no less—during the exact same time as the divorce proceedings were scheduled to take place. It was like something from a terrible nightmare. Was the pain of living in a loveless marriage fated to go on indefinitely?

For two minutes neither of them said anything. Abby glanced at John and felt the hatred rise within her. *Look at him, standing there speechless. Say something! Hug me or tell me we'll find a way to break the news to the kids despite Nicole's plans. Something. I mean, come on, John. We should be celebrating out there with them, not in here where there are no answers, no ways out.*

John shifted his weight and turned his head in her direction. "You gotta get a grip here, Abby. The kids could come in any second."

She stared at him, mouth open. Didn't he get it? Didn't he understand that Nicole and Matt's announcement changed everything? She yanked a paper towel from the roller, wiped hard at her eyes and blew her nose, reaching down to slam the wrinkled ball into the trash beneath the sink. When she looked up she caught his eyes and searched them, trying to understand.

"Get a grip? You want me to get a grip when our kids are out there celebrating Nicole's engagement?" She uttered a brief laugh and shook her head. "I mean, didn't you *hear* them? They want a marriage like ours, John. They're getting married on our anniversary, for goodness sake. You think we can go out there now and tell them we're getting a divorce?"

John clenched his teeth and stared at the ground, rubbing the back of his neck with his right hand.

Stand up and look me in the eye! Abby folded her arms

and glared at him. He was always rubbing his neck about one thing or another. It was too late for that now.

"Can't you say something?"

John brought his head up slowly, and Abby was not prepared for the transparency of his eyes or the sadness she saw there. "I'm so sorry, Abby. I feel . . . I don't know, I guess I feel like I failed you, failed God. Failed everyone."

She had expected him to snap back at her, but this . . . this broken man before her was someone she hadn't seen in nearly a decade.

Don't forget about Charlene.

The taunting voice flung darts at her compassion, bursting it like a cheap balloon. *Good point. We're too far gone to feel sorry for each other. Not with—*

Don't say it, daughter. The tongue is full of evil.

"Save your confessions for Charlene."

As soon as the words were out she wished she could snatch them from the air and shove them back inside, where she could sort through and filter them. She remembered something her father had told her once after he'd given his life to the Lord. *Trying to take back unkind words is like trying to put the toothpaste back in the tube. You can't do it, and you'll only make a mess of things trying.*

Abby uncrossed her arms and tapped her fingers softly on the kitchen counter. "I'm sorry. That wasn't very nice."

John cocked his head and studied her. "No, it wasn't, but then we haven't exactly been very nice to each other for a while now."

Abby felt fresh tears in her eyes as she turned to fill the kettle and light the fire beneath it. "So what're we supposed to do?"

"We pull it together, go back in there, and act excited for our daughter, that's what." John's voice was quiet and measured, the way it sounded when there was no arguing with him.

"What about *our* announcement?" Panic rose in Abby's chest; she desperately needed fresh air. They couldn't pretend another six months, could they? In the shadows of planning a wedding for Nicole and Matt? *Help me, God, I—*

She caught herself. What point was there in asking the Lord for help when He wasn't handing out answers anyway? At least not any she could use.

"We can tell the kids after the wedding. Really, Abby." John worked his face into an incredulous frown. "You think we can go back in there, ask Matt to leave, and then tell them we're finished? Nicole would probably pack her bags and elope. She deserves more than that from us."

"Well, that's why I don't have a grip here, all right?" Pain and sarcasm oozed from every word, and Abby fought to keep from spitting at him. "You're dating another woman right under my nose, and now I get to pretend everything's fine for another six months." He rolled his eyes and she continued, her anger building with each whispered word. "Not only that, but I have to act like our marriage is this shining *beacon* of an example for our daughter and her fiancé while we shop for wedding dresses and flower arrangements. It's enough to put me over the edge, John."

"For crying out loud, Abby, I'm not dating her!" It was the loudest John had gotten during the discussion, and Abby glanced toward the kitchen entrance then back at him.

"Keep it down. Please. And quit lying." If the kids

came in now, she had no idea what they'd say to explain why they were fighting in the kitchen.

John continued as if he hadn't heard her. "Okay, you want to know the truth? I kissed her. There, are you happy?"

Her world shifted wildly as she stared at him. He was finally admitting it; she had been right after all. John was having an affair. That could only mean one thing: he was in love with Charlene. Abby reeled backward until she came up against the place where the counter formed an L-shape. She had accused him often, yes, but somewhere in the recesses of her mind she had always hoped it wasn't so, that John's constant declarations of innocence were maybe, at least in part, the truth.

"You *kissed* her?" Abby's words were weak and hoarse, like the sounds that come from a dying old woman. A whistling began to build from the kettle, and without looking Abby reached over and flicked off the burner. Forget tea. Her head was spinning too hard to even think about putting something in her stomach.

John took a step closer, determination etched in his face. "Yes. You were right; are you happy? Isn't that what you wanted to hear? I did it; I kissed Charlene one night after practice because I was stupid and weak and not thinking straight." Another step in her direction. "But, Abby, I have not slept with that woman, and I'm not having an affair with her."

Abby's eyes fell to the floor, to the place where their feet now faced each other as they'd done so many times before. He was lying—she could feel it in her bones. She began shaking her head in short, jerky motions. "I don't believe you . . ." A surge of renewed anger filled her, and she found the strength to look him in the eyes again. "You kissed her? Why don't you just tell me the whole truth, John? That you're having an affair and you're in love with her."

His lips formed a straight, angry line, and all trace of sadness and compassion vanished from his face. He brought the palm of his hand down hard on the countertop.

There was a beat. "Hey . . . did something break in there?" Nicole yelled her concern from the next room.

Abby forced her voice to sound cheerful, normal. "No, dear. Your father dropped a cup. Everything's fine."

She shot an accusatory look at John and he narrowed his eyes.

"Believe what you want, Abby. I've told you the truth. I don't care how you want to handle this, but we need to make a plan." He paused and the tension left his face. "Our decision to divorce isn't about Charlene any more than it is your e-mail buddy, Stan. Things have been falling apart between us for years." Some of the warmth returned to his eyes. "Let's not go out fighting like this, hating each other."

New tears filled her eyes, and she crossed her arms tightly, gazing once more at the floor. He was right, and she hated him for it. Stan was her editor and friend, nothing more. But her marriage to John had been dead long before Charlene entered the picture. How in the world had they managed to keep everyone fooled for so long? Even the kids? Habit, Abby guessed. A lifetime of loving for all the right reasons had become a pattern of going through the motions. Nights of laughter and deep conversation had given way to silent isolation, hours of meaningless television, and using old magazines to pass the time and fill the emptiness.

And now they were left with this.

She nodded, wiping at a tear before it could slide down her face.

John sighed. "I'll stay away from Charlene as much as possible. I mean, I work with her, and nothing can change that fact. But I'll do my best." John reached out and gently lifted Abby's chin, and she felt even the small muscles along her spine go tense. He never touched her that way anymore. Now that they'd agreed it was over, she preferred his angry indifference to this . . . this reminder of all they'd once been.

"Can you do it, Abby? For six months?"

She held her breath, searching for another way and knowing there was none. This was Nicole's season, her time of becoming. Abby would do nothing to mar it, even if the pretending killed her. She turned her head slightly and John took the hint, allowing his hand to drop to his side. But she maintained eye contact. "We'll be busy, I guess. With wedding plans and all."

John nodded slightly. "Right. The weeks'll fly by and then later on—when they're back from their honeymoon— we can go on with our plans."

Abby considered the notion and knew it was the only way. Her thoughts landed on Charlene, and her heart skipped a beat in response. "Don't make a mockery of me, John." For the first time that morning, there was fear and vulnerability in her voice.

Again John brought his hand to her face and brushed a lock of hair back from her eyes. "I respect you, Abby. You have my word."

She wanted to push away his fingers, his kindness, shout at him that it was too late for that, but right then she needed his touch more than she understood. She shifted slightly, and he removed his hand once more. "So it'll be our secret, right? We tell no one?"

"Right."

She raised her eyes and studied the silk plants that lined the top of her cupboards. "I guess it won't matter, anyway. The next six months won't be about us; they'll be about Nicole and Matt."

"That's right." His hesitation drew her eyes back to his. "Besides . . . we're already basically divorced. We go our separate ways, spend time with different groups of friends, and sleep in separate rooms. The only thing we'll be waiting on is telling the kids."

Abby blinked. John's description of their lives sounded as appealing as cold oatmeal, and she willed away the wetness that returned to her eyes. It was true, wasn't it? They were separate people living separate lives. "Let's try to get through it without a lot of fighting, okay?"

"I'm all for that . . ." John chuckled lightly, and immediately Abby's ire ignited. What did he think? She caused all the fights? Before she could come back with a biting response, she stopped herself. *Deep breath, Abby.* If they weren't going to fight, then it had to start now. With her.

Abby thought of something. If he was conceding that things were separate, that meant he couldn't comment on the fact that they weren't sleeping together, weren't physically intimate. Of course, they hadn't been for six months—ever since the first time she'd caught Charlene in his classroom late one night—but that hadn't stopped John from making an occasional dig at her. Especially after sessions with their counselors. She leveled her gaze at him thoughtfully. "So for the next six months we'll be cordial roommates, nothing more. Agreed?"

John lowered his eyebrows, clearly confused by her statement. "Agreed."

"And none of this, 'Fine wife you are, sleeping down the hall' stuff, either. Right?"

A darkness fell over John's eyes, and the intimacy that had been there a moment earlier faded. "Don't worry, Abby, I don't want anything from you."

His statement left a pit in her stomach. With his words sounding again and again in her heart, she excused herself and went to the bathroom where she splashed her eyes with cold water. *"Don't worry, Abby, I don't want anything from you . . . I don't want anything from you . . ."* Wasn't that the problem? That neither of them wanted the other anymore? Abby waited until her eyes had cleared and some of the redness in her face had faded. *"I don't want anything from you . . . from you . . . from you . . ."*

Abby held back any further tears and stared hard at the mirror. John's words might hurt, but they were more than appropriate.

Because at this point, she had nothing left to give.

She drew a steadying breath and went to join John in the living room with the kids. None of them seemed to notice anything different, and Abby settled back into her chair, fixing her attention on Nicole and casting her an unspoken invitation.

Nicole immediately picked up on the message and joined Abby, taking a spot on the floor at her right side. "Everything okay?"

Oh, honey, if only you knew. "The steam from the kettle melted my makeup. It got in my eyes. I'm fine now."

Relief washed over Nicole's face. "That's good. I was beginning to think you weren't happy about it. You know, excited for us."

The boys had quit wrestling and flipped on the television again for the first of two NFL play-off games. In the din of activity and football noise, no one was listening to their conversation, and Abby was thankful. She needed time alone with Nicole, needed to let her daughter know from the beginning how excited she was about her impending wedding.

She stroked Nicole's dark blonde hair. "Honey, I'm so happy for you. Matt's a wonderful young man. Really."

Nicole smiled at her. "He is wonderful, isn't he?"

Abby felt another wave of tears, and she did nothing to stop them. Tears for Nicole's happiness were appropriate; tears about the death of her own marriage and the tombstone they would be keeping in the closet for the next six months would be absolutely forbidden. At least in public. "I can't believe you're all grown up." A single tear spilled over onto Abby's cheek. "My little girl, ready to make a home of her own and get married."

Nicole's eyes were suddenly brimming with tears, too, and she reached up and clasped Abby's hand. "You know what I read today?"

Abby smiled through wet eyes. "What?"

"Jeremiah 29:11 . . . 'I know the plans I have for you . . . plans to give you hope and a future' . . . Remember that one?"

The words hit Abby like falling bricks. Remember? Their pastor had recited those very words at their own wedding more than twenty-one years earlier. She swallowed hard. *How do I handle this, God? What do I tell her?*

The truth will set you free, daughter . . .

Abby wasn't sure the response had come from God, but she acted on it anyway. What would it hurt? "I remember it well. We read it at our wedding, honey. Did you know that?"

Nicole's eyes lit up. "No way . . . really? I thought it was *my* special verse. That's amazing." She thought for a moment. "Maybe we should use it, too." She started to rise as if she might approach Matt and ask him about the scripture right in the middle of the football game, then she paused and sat down again. "I'll tell him later. Hey, Mom, I almost forgot. I bought a *Christian Bride* magazine. Wanna look at it later, after Matt leaves?"

"Sure."

Pangs of nostalgia stung at Abby's heart. She remembered going over the details of her wedding with her own mother, planning the reception, searching for the perfect dress . . .

Would she feel this way every day for the next six months? Aching and grieving every time she drifted back through yesterday and revisited the days before she and John had taken this very step? She sighed inwardly. If she could get her perspective right, it wouldn't be so bad to walk through that time in her life. Sort of like recalling a friend who had died too young. Yes, that's exactly what their marriage was like. No amount of recall could bring it back, but certainly there would be nothing wrong with remembering the good times.

Sean interrupted her thoughts by muting the sound on the television and staring expectantly first at John, then Abby. "When do we finish the meeting?"

John glanced around the room. Abby wasn't sure

what to say, so she shot him a look that said, *Think fast; it isn't going to get any easier.*

There was a momentary deep-seated fear in John's eyes as he cleared his throat and sat up straighter in his chair. Shrugging lightly, he forced a smile. "Summer plans." He looked at Abby once more. "Right, honey?"

Abby felt like a character in a poorly written play. "Yep. Summer plans."

John clapped his hands in a show of closure. "And since Nicole and Matt have given us their news, I guess the summer has enough plans already."

Sean looked satisfied, and a quick glance around the room told Abby the others believed John, too. "Then can I go to Ben's? Please?" Sean was on his feet, already heading for the coat closet. "He got the new Play Station for Christmas. You should see the NFL game, Dad."

Abby couldn't stop herself from laughing. "Okay, go. But be back before dinner."

"Right . . . and make sure you're the quarterback," John yelled after him, winking at Kade who was now stretched out on the sofa grinning. "Reynolds men are always quarterbacks."

"You got it, Dad!" Sean was gone in a blur of flying scarf ends and a half-fastened coat.

Matt stood up, and after another round of congratulations, set off to take care of errands and pressing schoolwork. Abby watched him go, and someplace deep inside her she trembled at the charade she and John were living out, the way the kids were believing them and had been for months. *Just like everything's fine.* The whole family was plummeting toward a major disaster, and not one of their children had even the slightest idea what was coming.

What would the kids think when they found out? Would they feel deceived? Lied to? She forced the thought from her mind. Whatever price she and John would pay, they wouldn't have to face it until after the wedding.

John and Kade were lost in the football game as soon as the door closed. Nicole studied them and then giggled at Abby. "Never changes, does it?"

"Nope." Abby's mind flashed back to a long-ago celebration—a moment in John's career for which they had waited years—a time when she and John were madly in love in every way that mattered. John's arms had been around her, and everything had seemed perfectly right with their world. She could hear him, even now: "I couldn't have done it without you, Abby . . . couldn't have done it without you . . ."

Stop! The silent, harsh command forced the memory to disappear. It was one thing to remember how she and John had met, how they'd fallen in love and decided to marry. It was another to be hit by more recent memories, glimpses of their happy days together, back when they were halfway to forever.

Nicole squeezed her hand. "Did you hear me?"

Abby sat up. "Sorry, honey. I was drifting."

"I said, let's go check out my magazine."

Nicole led the way, and Abby looked to see if John would notice their departure. She should have known better. His eyes were fixed on the screen and the play about to unfold.

Up in her room, Nicole tossed the magazine on her bed, and Abby sprawled out next to her.

"I think I know what I want in a dress, but I'm not sure about the neckline, you know?"

Abby smoothed her forefinger over the images of fresh young brides in their assorted wedding gowns. "Lots to choose from."

Nicole sat up and crossed her legs, her eyes full of wonder. "Isn't it amazing, Mom? How faithful God is? Bringing Matt like this as an answer to all those years of prayers."

Abby pulled herself up and brought her knees close to her chin. Where was Nicole going with this? There was only one right response, of course. "He's always faithful."

Indeed, God had answered Abby's prayer for Nicole to find a godly husband.

But for the life of her, as she and Nicole poured over pictures of wedding gowns, there was something Abby couldn't understand. If God could answer her prayers for Nicole, why hadn't He answered her prayers for herself?

Seven

JOHN HAD NO IDEA HOW HE WAS GOING TO PULL OFF
pretending for the next six months that he and Abby were
happily married, but he did know one thing: if the problem continued to consume him, he would be useless in
the classroom.

He planted his elbows on the cluttered surface of his
desk in the back of the weightroom and closed his eyes. He
had to handle four health classes and two sessions of weight
training, do grades and tests for 152 students, and get ready
for spring league coming up in ten weeks. All while trying
to avoid Charlene Denton. Someone dropped a weight in
the next room, and John looked up. As he did his eyes fell
on his family's Christmas photo from . . . hmm . . . what
year? He looked at it more closely. Sean was two, so it had
to be eight years ago.

Lord, how did it all get so crazy?

It had been so long since he'd talked to God that the

silent question felt foreign, and he was struck by a pang of guilt. Maybe it was his fault. He was supposed to be the spiritual leader, after all. Maybe things would be different if only he'd—

There was a knock at the door and John turned. Charlene stood there.

Ah, Charlene . . . What am I going to do with you? He kept the question to himself and smiled big as he reached for the door and opened it. "Hey, what's up?"

She swept into the room and took a seat opposite him. John studied her for a moment, enjoying the easy way they had with each other. It wasn't so much that she was beautiful, really . . . There was just something about her—a Sandra Bullock look maybe—that made him want to spend time with her, to protect her from the dangers in her life.

"Wanna get coffee?" Her eyes twinkled, and John wondered, as he had a hundred times before, whether down the road a year or two things might work out for the two of them. She was willing; she'd told him as much. But he wasn't sure. He'd already made a mess of one marriage.

He resisted the urge to take her hand in his. "Not today." How was he going to say this? "Listen, Char, I have something to tell you."

Her expression changed, and John could see fear in her eyes not far from the surface. "Okay."

"It's about Abby and me."

Charlene shifted in the chair. "I'm listening."

"We're postponing the divorce." John watched as she sat straighter in her seat, more formal, further back from him, as though the words had sent a knife straight through her heart. When she didn't say anything, he continued. "It wasn't anything we planned. Nicole and Matt announced their engagement Saturday. Right before we were going to tell them."

Charlene moved her head up and down in a subtle motion, and John knew she was trying to be strong. "Okay, so for a few weeks or what?"

A few weeks? Didn't she know how hard this was going to be on his kids, his family? He uttered a disbelieving laugh. "No, until the wedding is behind us. Six months at least."

She held tightly to the arms of the chair. "And you want me to wait around six months?"

Her voice wasn't angry, but it was close. John closed his eyes and wished himself a thousand miles away—there had to be a place where life was quiet and uncomplicated . . . maybe a football field, where the main thing that mattered was the way his boys played the game. When he opened his eyes, she was waiting. "What you do is your choice. I haven't promised you anything."

"I matter more to you than she does. I know I do." Charlene sounded like a petulant child, and John felt a ripple of doubt. This was a side of her John had never seen before. "Ever since Rod left last year, you've always been there for me." Her voice showed she was back in control. "You know how I feel about you, John."

Yes, he did. She was in love with him. If he hadn't been sure before, her reaction now removed any doubt. "I only wanted your friendship, Charlene. I'm sorry if I've made you think there was more between us."

This time she was the one who laughed. "Who are you kidding? That was *you* I kissed that night after practice, right? Don't tell me all you wanted was friendship then."

There it was again. As though someone else had entered the room wearing Charlene's skin. He released a troubled breath. "I don't know *what* I want anymore, but I know this. I can't face a future with you—or with anyone—until my past is behind me."

The scowl on her face faded, as though the fact that he'd admitted a possible future with her somehow calmed her concerns. "You're right. We both need time to think about things." She grinned at him and tapped his foot playfully with hers. "Besides, it's not like we won't be together."

John felt his neck muscles relax. This was the Charlene he was familiar with, the one who was his buddy, his fun friend. The one who reminded him of the way Abby used to be. John leaned forward, resting his forearms on his thighs. He hoped Charlene would still be smiling when she heard what he had to say.

"Actually . . . I promised Abby I'd stay away from you as much as possible."

Charlene's eyebrows raised. "She knows about us?" The corners of her mouth lifted slightly, and the look in her eyes grew confident as though she'd notched some kind of victory. John wasn't sure why, but her reaction bothered him.

"How could she not know, Charlene? We're together all the time. People talk." He thought a moment.

What remained of Charlene's frustration and fear faded even further, and he could see in her eyes again the carefree, youthful exuberance he so deeply appreciated about her. "So I have to stay away, huh?"

Seeing her there, dark hair falling over her shoulders, green eyes glistening even in the fluorescent lights of his cramped office, made him long to take her in his arms and . . . His mind filled with the memory of their kiss, and he gritted his teeth. *Show a little control, Reynolds.* "We *both* have to stay away. I promised Abby."

Charlene's mouth curved into a full smile and she stood to leave. "Okay, if that's the way it has to be." She quickly kissed her two fingers and then touched them to his lips. "Whatever happens, I'll be here for you. If you need to talk, anything. I live alone, remember? I can make sure no one ever finds out. That way you can keep your promise to Abby."

With that she turned and walked away, weaving her lithe body between the machines and free weights and leaving without ever looking back.

The air in John's lungs leaked out slowly as he ripped the baseball cap from his head and tossed it on his desk. Charlene's words rang in his mind: *"I can make sure no one ever finds out . . . that way you can keep your promise to Abby."*

If that's how she felt, Charlene didn't know the first thing about keeping a promise. Doubts began to nibble at the ankles of John's conscience. What sort of future did he hope to have with a woman who could lie so easily? Who could justify an affair without a second thought? He had no answers for himself.

A sudden image flooded his mind—him kissing Charlene in the moonlight of the empty Marion High football field—and he hung his head. He had no room to judge her. He didn't know the first thing about keeping a promise, either. *At least she's gone. Maybe she'll stay away until fall, and then . . .*

Then maybe he and Charlene would find a way to make it work; maybe theirs would be a better relationship because of what he'd learned the first time around with Abby.

He turned his attention back to the stack of "Nutritional Supplements" tests that lay on top of the pile of player profiles and camp applications and advertisements for football equipment. Normally it took him less than an hour to correct tests like this—multiple choice answers and single-word fill-ins. But today he'd already been working on it for two hours and he wasn't even halfway done.

Focusing on the task at hand, he narrowed his eyes and made himself concentrate, but all he could think about was Charlene—how she'd looked and smelled and so easily presumed he'd take her up on her offer of being available and secretive.

"I can make sure no one ever finds out . . . no one ever finds out . . . no one ever finds out."

Who would have ever dreamed things would get this complicated with Charlene Denton? As if in response, he heard Abby's voice from years ago: *"I don't like the way she looks at you, like she doesn't care a bit that both of you are married."*

He set down his pencil and leaned back in his chair, lacing his hands together behind his head and closing his eyes. Forget the tests. The only way to figure out how things had gotten so complicated was to go back to the fall of 1993, the year Charlene was hired to teach at Marion High. The same year things between Abby and him went from fun-loving and unforgettable to busy and stressful.

Nicole had turned thirteen that year, and every hour the girl spent at the junior high seemed to require another two hours of Abby's time to sort through Nicole's problems and help her understand the pains of growing up. And of course there were the sports activities. That year Kade was ten and building a name for himself in youth football leagues around Southern Illinois. When there wasn't football there was baseball or basketball.

Abby always seemed to be driving Kade one place or another, and Nicole was just as busy. She needed to get to youth group and swimming lessons and piano recitals and soccer games. On top of everything else, there was Abby's father. The man lived alone, but he'd lost much of his independence since being diagnosed with Parkinson's disease. He'd sold the old house in Wisconsin in 1993, along with much of his furniture, then packed up his few belongings and moved to a retirement home ten minutes from John and Abby's house. So in addition to the kids' schedules, Abby took time to stop in and see her dad several times a week. Where once he and Abby had spent Sunday afternoons watching fall football, that year she spent those hours with her father.

Most of the time Abby was so busy she'd drive three-year-old Sean over to the weightroom at Marion High and leave him with John so she could attempt the insurmountable schedule of the day.

It was so different from those early years, back when the children were young and the only thing on Abby's agenda each afternoon had been getting the kids down to the high school so they could run around the grassy hills and watch the Marion Eagles' football practice. By the fall of '93, not only was Abby too busy to watch his team practice, she was no longer interested: *"It's the same thing, year after year . . . Besides, it's too cold out there on the hillside."*

He could hear her excuses, and even now, years later, they still hurt. In the early days she couldn't wait to hear who went out for the team and who made it. She'd pepper him with questions about players and strategies and upcoming games until long after practice was over.

Those were the days.

John opened his eyes and reached for his water bottle, taking three long swigs before setting it back down and staring hard again at the family photo. Why had she changed? Did football lose its appeal somehow? Or was it him she'd grown tired of? Either way by the time Charlene started teaching at Marion, life at the Reynolds house was little more than a functional blur. At least four out of five nights, John and Abby would see each other only when they met back at the house long after dark to grab a quick meal before putting the kids in bed.

Late evenings—a time Abby and John once had reserved for each other—became the only opportunity to clean dishes or fold laundry or for Abby to edit a magazine piece due the next day. Each season they told themselves things would get slower, they were *bound* to get slower.

But they only got busier. And the busier they got, the more lonely life felt.

John remembered the in-service training three days before school started in 1993, when Charlene came up and introduced herself to him. She had been twenty-five then, young and fresh and bound to catch the attention of hundreds of high-school boys. John had heard about her from one of the other coaches, but even their praise hadn't prepared him for the impact she made in person.

"Hi, I'm Charlene Denton. You must be Coach Reynolds." She held out her hand and he took it, taken aback by her directness.

"I guess I just look like a Coach Reynolds . . ." He grinned at her, and she laughed in a way that Abby had long since stopped doing.

"State title, 1989; quarterfinals, 1990. I'm a big Eagles football fan, Coach. Everyone knows who you are."

John pondered her statement now. Maybe that was why he'd felt so attracted to Charlene. She was a football fan, *his* fan. The way Abby had been before the hillside grew too cold and practices became too routine.

He remembered how he'd felt lost in her wide-eyed gaze that afternoon. "Well then, it's a privilege to meet you, Ms. Denton. We can always use an extra fan around Marion High."

That should have been the end of it, but Charlene was persistent—and he was weak. Surprisingly so. She stayed by his side, clearly enjoying his company and pumping him for dozens of details about the team and its chances that season.

"My husband's a fan, too." She casually tossed the comment his way, and he remembered feeling himself relax, relieved to discover she was married. There would be no threats for either of them that way.

Before the training session was over, he had found a way to invite her and her husband over for dinner that weekend. "Just to make you feel welcome," he'd told her.

Abby had been puzzled when John brought it up later that evening.

"We don't even know them, honey. I mean, it's the busiest time of the year. I have an article due Monday and school shopping for the kids. I wasn't exactly planning to entertain this weekend."

John had shrugged like it was no big deal. "She's new on

staff, that's all. Besides, I don't think she and her husband are Christians. It'd be a good witness."

Abby thought about that and smiled that weary smile she'd picked up by then. "Oh, all right. We'll barbecue. And maybe if you help me with the cleanup . . ."

The night had been a disaster from the beginning.

Charlene and Rod arrived, and it was obvious from the way they avoided each other and spoke around each other that they were fighting. Introductions were simple, and though Charlene was polite to Abby, she stayed by John's side throughout the night, pulling football stories out of him and laughing hysterically at anything he said that was even remotely funny.

Why didn't I see it back then? Maybe none of this would have happened . . .

John's question wasn't really directed at anyone, and there was no magical answer in response. He let his thoughts drift back again. The evening had been enjoyable enough for him, but Abby had seemed tense almost from the beginning. When Charlene and her husband left, Abby shook her head and headed for the kitchen. John remembered following her and asking—innocently—whether something was wrong.

Abby slammed the dishrag on the counter, splattering soapy water across the floor. "Come on, John. Don't tell me you didn't notice."

John had been baffled. Was she jealous? Just because a beautiful young woman enjoyed his company? "Notice what?"

Abby huffed. "Charlene."

A laugh escaped before John could stop it. "I don't believe it. You're jealous of her. Come on, Abby, be realistic."

Abby seemed to struggle with whether to scream or break down and cry. Instead, she pushed her hands in a controlled manner, palms down, until her arms were straight. Then she cocked her head, a gesture that meant she was forcing herself to be calm. "In case you weren't watching, the woman got all drippy around you and hung on everything you said."

"Come on, honey. She's married." John had approached Abby, but she took a step backward.

"You're married, too, and that didn't stop you from playing right into her little plan."

At the time, John honestly hadn't known what Abby meant, and her accusation roused his own anger. "Wait a minute, don't go blaming me about her actions. I can't help it if—"

"If what?" Abby's voice was louder than before. "If that woman has a crush on you? Well, for the record, John, I don't appreciate you inviting her here to parade around *my* house flirting with *my* husband eating *my* food at *my* table. Are you reading me?"

John had stormed out of the house then, refusing even to acknowledge Abby's tirade. Back then it had seemed ridiculous. Like maybe it was that time of the month or possibly Abby was frustrated about her hair or something. Looking back . . . well, he knew that she'd been more right than he could have imagined. From his current vantage point, it seemed Charlene had used the dinner to make her attraction to him known.

John leaned forward again and sifted through the papers on his desk. He'd asked Charlene about the dinner since then, and each time she'd denied having an agenda. "How could I have known things would get like this between us?"

How did *they get like this, anyway?* John had asked himself the question a hundred times if he'd asked it once. It wasn't really Charlene, was it? It was Abby. Too busy with the kids and their schedules and her father to even ask about his day let alone attend Friday night games. Basically, she had forgotten about him. Left him to live his own life while she managed the lives of everyone else around her, always complaining about something. Ever since life had gotten busier, she was constantly blaming him, accusing him of not helping enough around the house, not being involved enough with the kids' lives. He was doing everything he knew how to do, but it was never enough. She'd turned into a mean-spirited shrew.

All things considered, any man would have been weak in those circumstances.

At first it had been lunch with Charlene in his classroom, and then an occasional phone call after work. Still, it wasn't until four years later that Charlene began having serious trouble with Rod.

"I have no one to talk to," she'd tell him. "Meet me here before school. I just need someone who understands."

And so—without telling Abby or the kids—he began getting up earlier and arriving at Marion High half an hour before classes. John remembered that not once that year did Abby even ask why. It wasn't every day, of course, but in time he and Charlene began meeting in the weight-room and working out together before classes began. Occasionally there'd be teasing and rib-poking between them and a rare tickling match or two. But he'd been up-front with her about his situation.

"I don't believe in affairs, Charlene."

Once when he said that, she came up behind him and

started rubbing both sides of the base of his neck, seemingly concerned only about the tension in his back. "Who's having an affair?"

She was so innocent, so sweet and fun to be with. He'd convinced himself she was harmless, and there was nothing wrong with a backrub now and then after working out. He remembered laughing lightly and lowering his head, enjoying the way her fingers worked themselves into his muscles. "Okay, so it's not an affair. I just want you to know where I stand."

She ran her fingers lightly down the sides of his arms and whispered. "Don't worry, Coach. I'm not trying to seduce you."

John had done a quick check of his emotions and realized she didn't have to try. Just being near her . . . He'd reached up and caught her hands, firmly taking them from his arms as he turned around. "Look, Charlene. I care a lot about you, but I could never do anything to jeopardize my marriage. I mean it."

Charlene grinned at him then and shoved him roughly on the shoulder. "Yes *sir*, Coach. I'll just be your buddy, then. That's all I want from you, anyway."

John had risen to his feet and noticed that he towered almost a foot above her. "Let's keep it that way then, okay?" But even as he said the right thing, an intense desire began to take hold of him. He wanted to kiss her, could feel himself drawn to do so. It wasn't yet seven in the morning, after all, and the kids wouldn't come around for another half-hour.

Hypocrite! The accusation rang in his mind, as though his desire was mocking him. *Hypocrite!*

He'd nearly given in, but finally he'd stepped back and

released a breath, striving to alleviate the sinful feelings assaulting him.

Before he could leave that morning, Charlene gently took hold of his arm, her green eyes piercing his, begging him to understand. "Things are so bad at home, John. Just understand one thing. You're the best friend I have. I won't do anything to lose that."

That year and the next they kept their obvious attraction for each other at bay. Sometimes, when it seemed their feelings were getting too tense, he'd take a few days off and avoid her. But they always found each other again, whether in the weightroom or at lunch or after school out on the football field. She was, in many ways, his constant companion. And though he still felt deeply committed to Abby, Charlene was quickly replacing his wife as his best friend.

It wasn't until the fall of 1999 that Charlene and Rod's divorce became final. After that, things heated up considerably. The early morning times John spent in the weightroom with Charlene were charged with sexual tension. If she was within ten feet of him, John found himself almost unable to work out. The times their bare, sweaty arms brushed against each other in passing or their fingers met in the exchange of a dumbbell, John fought against scintillating feelings he was sure would anger a righteous God.

God.

The thought snapped John back to the present. Where did God fit into the mess that his life had become?

He pushed the papers around on his desk until they formed a neat stack. He still loved God, still believed the Scriptures and God's promises. It was just that sometime back in the early 1990s, when life got more hectic and Abby was busy with the kids and her father, it seemed easier to skip Sunday service and Wednesday men's meetings. The coaches who ran the kids' football and soccer games were not respecters of the Sabbath. Why should he be?

No offense to the Lord or anything. After all, by that time John had been a believer for so long it seemed he'd heard every sermon imaginable. He knew thousands of stories and analogies and illustrations, all designed to keep him on the straight and narrow. In fact, when John turned 35 in the fall of 1991, he calculated the Sundays and Wednesdays he'd spent in church and figured them to be 3,640 days total and counting. 3,640 days! He considered his schedule and decided he needed less time at church with a bunch of people he barely knew and more with his family or alone getting renewed for another busy week. After all, there was no law saying he had to go to church. Not when he could read his Bible each day and carry on a perfectly devout relationship with the Father from the comfort of his Sunday morning easy chair. That afternoon, in the hours before his birthday dinner, he made God a promise, something he remembered to this day.

Okay, God, this is it. I've got Your message memorized. You know my attendance record better than I do. Give me my Sundays and Wednesdays back, and I promise I'll be a godly man all the days of my life.

John considered his promise now, in the light of all that had happened in the years since then. *I still love You, Lord. I still believe . . .*

Remember the height from which you have fallen . . . repent and turn back to Me.

John sat back hard in his chair. Where had *that* come from? It had been years since the Lord had spoken to him by bringing verses to mind. Maybe it wasn't God. Maybe it was just his guilty conscience.

It was true, his plan hadn't worked exactly like he'd hoped. He'd started off with early devotions each day, but when Charlene made arrangements for them to meet in the mornings, something had to go. After a year of meeting with her, he no longer even knew where his Bible was.

And prayer, well, he still prayed at family dinners and meetings and—

He pictured Nicole's startled face from a couple days ago asking how come they weren't going to open the family meeting in prayer. John sighed and rubbed the back of his neck. So maybe they didn't say family prayers as often as before. Still . . . he was definitely a praying man, even if he hadn't prayed much for the past few weeks. Months. Years . . .

Repent and turn back to—

The thought rattled around in his mind as though his conscience had no place to file it.

What about the football games? Hadn't he led a prayer before each contest as long as he'd coached at Marion High? Hadn't he stood up to the powers of political correctness and decided that his team would pray even if no others did? Hadn't he been a pillar of example for countless boys who had gone through his program?

The image of Charlene standing beside him near the locker room on the Marion High field late that one night, of her in his arms as he kissed her, came to mind.

So I'm not perfect. At least it was just once. It's not like I haven't had my chances.

He remembered the time Charlene asked him to stop

by on a Saturday morning the previous summer so they could share teaching plans for the fall. Abby had been out of town with Nicole for a soccer match, and Sean and Kade were doing chores at home. Charlene and Rod had no children, and by then Rod had moved up to Michigan and taken a high-tech job with an engineering firm. So John had known Charlene would be alone.

He had knocked on the door that morning and found that it opened with little effort. "John, is that you?" Charlene's voice came from somewhere down the hall. *Her bedroom, no doubt.* John had swallowed hard and forced himself to take a seat in her living room.

"It's me. I'll wait for you out here."

Her answer was quick and lighthearted. "Come on back. My stuff's spread out on my desk."

Alert to the danger of the moment, John headed down the hallway toward the distant bedroom with mixed feelings. He and Charlene were already so close, such good friends, he knew he could trust her not to make a move. It was himself he was worried about.

He reached the doorway and poked his head inside. "Hey."

At the sound of his voice, she appeared from a closet area, her hair wrapped in a damp towel, her body bare but for a loosely tied bathrobe. She gestured toward a small desk covered with several sheets of papers. "Come sit down."

Had the warnings he felt been audible, the room would have been bursting with the clamor of bells and whistles. But since they were silent, he ignored them and moved closer, avoiding contact with her as he took the chair. As though she were unaware of the effect she had on him, she placed an arm casually around his shoulders and bent over the back of him, pointing out the plans she wanted to discuss.

The smell of her shampoo and the occasional drop of water on his arm made him unable to understand even a little of what she was saying. After ten torturous seconds, he pushed his chair back. "I can't do this." He looked deep into her eyes and saw that no matter what she said next, she knew exactly what he was talking about.

"The kitchen table then?" She smiled warmly, a smile that said she would not push him, would not force him to cross a line that made him uncomfortable.

He nodded. Without another word he walked through the house to her kitchen table, where she joined him fifteen minutes later. The rest of the morning he was overwhelmed with an aching desire that had nothing to do with Charlene Denton.

It had to do with his wife.

And why he was spending Saturday morning here, in this stranger's house, instead of side by side with the one woman he still loved more than life itself.

Enough remembering. John stood up and scooped the papers from his desk into his hands. It was time to go home and find a way to get his work done there. At least then he wouldn't be in Abby's way. His presence only seemed to make her tense these days.

Maybe I should go home and pray.

Do it now, son, before another moment goes by.

There it was again, that voice. Was it the same one that had spoken so regularly to him back when he was logging in his 3,640 church days? John dismissed the thought. He'd wasted enough time for one day without sitting alone in his office trying to sort it out before God. What was the point?

He and Abby had made the decision to end their marriage. A decision they were not going to back down from.

No, this time they were choosing to go it alone, without the help of Almighty God. He pushed his chair in, and before he left, he caught sight of the Christmas photo one last time. Abby was such a beautiful woman. So full of life and love. At least she had been. *Abby, girl, what happened to us? Did we just get busy and quit trying? Is that the legacy we'll leave our kids, our daughter as she starts a life of her own?*

There was only the buzz of the overhead lights in response, and John let his gaze linger a moment longer on the image of his wife. Without thinking, he brought his finger to her face and traced it tenderly. *I miss you, Abby.* For the first time in years, he was tempted to go home, sweep her into his arms, and tell her so, face-to-face.

Crazy. He shook his head and the notion vanished. *We don't even like each other anymore. How can I be missing her? Answer me that, God, how?*

More silence.

Figures. First Abby, now God. Next thing I know, the kids will turn their backs on me. He stood still, feet planted, and ached for the happy family in the photo. *What did I ever do to turn you against me, Abby?* He gazed up trying to see through the fiberboard ceiling. *Or You, for that matter.* He flipped the light switch and headed into the cold, wintry night, sure of only one very sad thing—whatever decisions he made about his future in the coming months, they would not involve the two people who once upon a time had mattered more than any other.

Abby and God.

John had no idea how he and Abby had arrived at the decision to divorce, a decision that would virtually eliminate both Abby and God from his life. He only knew that they had. He thought about them—Abby, for whom he once would have laid down his life; God, who had willingly died to give him that very life in the first place. Abby, to whom he'd promised forever; God, who had promised forever to him.

I was young and foolish.

You were happy, My son . . . holy . . . set apart . . . Repent and turn back to—

The bitter wind hit him square in the face, and he pushed on toward his car, ignoring the silent whispers in his heart.

No, regardless of guilt feelings, he would not change his mind about the divorce. Abby was angry and hard and distant; she'd been that way for years. Even if they wanted to they couldn't find their way back to the people they had once been, the lives they'd once lived. It was too late; they were too far gone. And if that meant losing God in the process, then so be it.

He pulled the hood of his state championship jacket more tightly around his head and fidgeted with his keys. Besides, God probably had checked out on Coach Reynolds a long time ago. The thought took root as John climbed into his car and began driving, the entire time resisting an urge that was stronger than ever before: the urge to forget about everything waiting for him at home, to turn the wheel of his car and drive straight to Charlene Denton's house instead.

Eight

THE WOMAN WAS DRIVING ABBY CRAZY, THREATENING
to ruin the whole outing.

Whose idea had it been to bring her, anyway? The afternoon was supposed to be a special time between Nicole
and her, hours of gazing at wedding gowns, searching for
the perfect dress.

Instead, she and Nicole barely had a spare moment to
exchange glances, let alone attempt breaking into the
conversation. *Be patient, Abby. Don't make a scene.* The
woman—Jo Harter, a divorced, single mother and a non-
believer—was Nicole's future mother-in-law, after all.
Maybe she was one of those women who talked a lot when
she was around people she didn't know well.

"So, anyway, like I was telling Margaret at the office
the other day, a girl's got to wear white." She was punishing her gum as though it were guilty of a crime. "I
mean it doesn't matter so much whether she's already

got the goods, if you know what I mean, but still it has to be white." A quick breath. "I mean, look at Nicole's complexion. The girl would be lost in something ivory or off-color. It has to be white; I absolutely insist." She smacked her lips, rubbing in an excessive coat of lipstick, and sorted hastily through a rack of gowns.

Nicole shot Abby a look. "Actually, I like white, but I'm looking for a—"

"I found it!" The woman's bright red hair stood out in stark contrast to the white dresses hanging on the rack. Her freckled face flushed an uncomfortable pink as she jerked a dress free. It had a high neckline, but the hem stopped short just below the knee, where the dress cut away and curved into three lacy trains that dangled from the back.

It's hideous; it looks half done.

Abby resisted the urge to say so but cast a knowing look at Nicole. *Oh, honey, I hope things'll get easier for you two. There's nothing more wonderful than sharing a friendship with your mother-in-law.* Abby remembered Hattie Reynolds and wondered how the woman was doing. She was in the throes of Alzheimer's disease and had been relegated to an assisted living home. It'd been months since they'd talked or even—

"Well—" Nicole interrupted Abby's thoughts and looked at the dress thoughtfully—"it's not really what I had in mind, honestly."

Jo's face fell. "It's the absolute newest style, Nicole. Haven't you been reading the magazines?"

Abby was proud of the way her daughter handled the woman—patient, polite, but firmly determined to go with her own tastes. Nicole took the dress gently and placed it back on the rack. "Actually, I'm looking for a more traditional dress. White, yes. But also elegant, unforgettable, that sort of thing."

Jo nodded, slightly dejected, then turned her attention on Abby. "By the way, I've been meaning to tell you . . ." She paused and Abby mentally braced herself. Jo was from North Carolina, and many times that day only a lack of oxygen had stopped the woman from going on for hours on every topic they'd hit on.

Jo adjusted her head so that her eyes were level with Abby's, her eyebrows raised dramatically. "That's one fine man you've got there in that John of yours. Yes sir. Big U of M football star." She waved a hand in the air. "I remember how it was. Me and Denny'd be wasting a day, nothing to do on the weekend, and we'd tune in to college ball. And that man of yours . . . mmhhhm." She carried the sound out as long as she could and then grabbed a quick mouthful of air. "Best-looking quarterback I've seen before or since."

The ache in Abby's gut took her by surprise. So what if John was handsome? That didn't hold a marriage together any more than paint held together walls. "Yes, he's always been good looking."

Jo gave Abby a quick once-over and grinned. "'Course, you're not bad looking yourself. Must be nice, that's all I can say."

Nicole—capitalizing on the fact that she was no longer Jo's target—moved on down the rack, lost in private thought as she carefully checked out each gown in the section. Again Abby felt her frustration rise. This was supposed to be *her* time with—

"How long you say you were married?"

Abby blinked. *Here we go.* "Twenty-one years last July."

"Twenty-one years, eeeewwwhheeeee!" Jo sounded like a farm woman calling the pigs in at the end of the day. Her last, loud note lingered in the afternoon air, and Abby glanced about in hopes that they weren't attracting an audience. Jo set her hands firmly on her hips. "You know what I think? I think twenty-one years is a miracle anymore." She poked Abby roughly in the shoulder.

Abby took the slightest step back and wished desperately that the woman would leave her alone. *Don't talk to me about miracles, lady. Those kind of miracles don't happen to people like me.*

Abby worked to hide her discomfort, not that it mattered. Jo was too busy enjoying the sound of her own voice to notice much of anything else. She examined her fingernails, admiring the way the ends were perfectly rounded and painted burnt orange to match her blouse. "You know, I might even step foot in a church one of these days if I thought it'd get me my Denny back. Yes, sir, I believe I just might." Her hands fell to her side, and she looked straight at Abby. "You're churchgoing folk, right? That's what Matt tells me. Ever since he went and got himself saved, that's the first thing he talks about. 'They're Christians, Mama.' 'She's a believer, Mama.' Seems like people making more and more a big deal out of spending time in a church building, but you know what I say?"

Abby opened her mouth but didn't have time to answer.

"I say more power to 'em. And you know what else? If I thought it'd get me my Denny back, I'd probably take it up, too." She refueled instantly. "Matt didn't tell me what you folks are exactly, anyway. You those Pentecostals or Presbyterians or Baptists or door-knockers or TV-watchers or what? 'Cause I don't have nothin' 'gainst any of it;

I want you to know you heard it from me first. Right here. Out of the horse's mouth. Don't want no arguing about religion when it comes to the kids' wedding." She hesitated, actually giving Abby a chance to speak, but Abby wasn't sure what to say. "Well, what is it? Which one are you? 'Course you don't look like a door-knocker, and I mean that as a compliment."

"We belong to a Calvary Chapel, actually." *The woman's a lunatic.*

Be prepared in season and out.

Abby was inwardly shocked at the words that filtered through her mind. *I can't even make my marriage work, God. You can forget me being prepared with this woman, especially if she's going to keep on—*

"Calvary Chapel . . ." Jo gazed at the store ceiling for a moment. "Sounds like a Christmas shop." She gasped. "Wait a minute! I think I know the kind. They the ones that get all wild and start laughin' and runnin' around in circles?"

Despite her frustration, Abby had to resist the urge to laugh out loud. That'd be great, to make her think it was true. "No, nothing like that."

Jo shifted her weight to one foot. "So what's the deal with the Calvary Chapel folks? What'd y'all believe? All that hellfire and brimstone stuff everyone's always talkin' about?" She caught herself quickly. "Not that I care, really. Never bothered me all that 'Gotta-get-your-ducks-in-a-row-Lord-might-be-comin'-back-tomorrow' stuff." Despite Jo's words, concern flashed in her eyes. "I mean it's okay for you and all, but I'm a very busy person. Sundays are my cleaning days, really."

Tell her the truth, Abby.

The voice was so strong and clear Abby wondered if Jo had heard it too. Out of habit more than anything else, she looked tenderly at Jo. "Our church is like a lot of churches. We believe in Jesus Christ and that the Bible is the only infallible Word of God."

Jo seemed intrigued, and she was silent nearly two full seconds, something of a record for the afternoon. "You really think so, huh? Smart woman like you?"

Abby nodded. She did, didn't she? She might not have been living like she believed it, but somewhere deep in her heart she knew His Word was truth.

Everything on earth will pass away, but My word will remain forever.

Longer than Abby or John or the fact that they'd chosen to divorce. God's Word was eternal. "Yes, I believe it."

Jo's jaw dropped. "Huh. Well, you and me'll have to have ourselves some down-home, old-fashioned, long, drawn-out conversations on that one. Especially between now and the big weddin' day. Denny and his new wife are split up now, and don't I know he was the best thing ever happened to me. I'm gonna lose ten pounds and dye my hair between now and then just to get his attention. And he'll come all right, know why?"

Abby studied the woman's hair and realized the red wasn't natural after all. "Why?"

"'Cause ever since Matt's been into this God stuff, Denny's been into it too. I think he's actually startin' to believe it. Nothing wild, mind you, but Matt says it's almost like there's something different in his tone. Something that wasn't there before." Jo smiled broadly, and Abby noted that the woman must have had her teeth bleached. They were whiter than the wedding dresses.

If she weren't so obnoxious, Jo would almost be a pretty woman—but if she had talked like this during the years she was married, Abby could only congratulate Denny for having had the good sense to leave.

What God has joined together let no man separate, My daughter.

Fear washed over Abby, and she felt the holy admonishment as strongly as if God had appeared and spoken it to her face. What was wrong with her? When had she begun feeling so jaded and cavalier toward marriage? The situation between John and her was one thing, but to agree so easily with divorce? Just because a person talked too much?

I'm sorry, God, I don't even recognize myself anymore.

Nicole was fifteen feet away, and she held up a dress. "Mom, what do you think?"

Abby cocked her head and studied it. High lace collar, fitted bodice, narrow waist, and a traditional skirt that glistened with sequins and lace. She pictured Nicole in it and smiled. "I like it."

Nicole glanced at her watch. "We still need to eat, and I have to meet Matt in a few hours. Maybe I'll ask them to hold it for me."

"Good idea."

When the dress was safely put away, the threesome headed for a salad restaurant a block away. Jo was talking about Denny again, and Abby reminded herself continually that the outing was nearly over.

"I told you the story about me and Denny, right? How we decided it was too much work and threw in the towel?" Jo was walking between them. "Worst decision I ever made."

"Uh . . ." Abby caught a glimpse of Nicole's grin and

she smiled at her daughter in return. *Oh, fine, little girl. Let me deal with her.* "I don't think you mentioned it." Abby kept a straight face and waited for the next chapter.

"Thing of it was, with me and Denny, we really loved each other. I mean really. Started off that way and seemed that way right on through about the seventh year or so. Then something happened, and good golly if I'm just stumped to tell ya what it was."

That last part caught Abby's attention. *She could be telling my story too . . .*

"One day we was flyin' high as a kite, spendin' time together, laughin' and lovin' and making babies and fishin'. The next—" Jo made a ripping sound with her teeth and lower lip—"the next we weren't hardly talkin' to each other. Before you could say cat-got-caught-in-the-washing-machine, we was livin' separate lives. I mean, completely separate. Him stayin' out in the trailer, and me not carin' if he did. And that wasn't the way it started out at all. Fact, if you have a minute I'll tell you about how we got started. Nothing short of a love story, tell you the truth."

Abby had the feeling there was no way around hearing it. They entered the restaurant, and Jo paused long enough to get the attention of the hostess. "Ma'am, we need a booth for three, and not too busy either." Jo smiled big at Abby and then Nicole. "We got us a lot of talking to do." She pointed a finger at the reservation sheet. "And not too close to the smoky section, if you don't mind."

"Smoking section?" The hostess was a brunette not more than sixteen years old, and she seemed genuinely confused by Jo's comment. Again Abby and Nicole exchanged a look that made them both bite their lips to keep from laughing.

Jo leaned closer to the girl. "The smoky section. That's what I call it, okay? The place where the air's so thick with smoke a girl could lose her voice in fifteen minutes. We don't want the smoky section 'cause like I said, we got a lot to talk about."

The girl stared blankly at Jo for a moment. "Sure. Okay."

Jo remained unmoved, obviously waiting for more information. "Well, how long a wait are we talking? 'Cause there's a Micky D's around the corner if this isn't going to work. Nothin' personal, mind you, but we ladies need a quiet place to talk."

And we'd get that at McDonald's? Abby kept her comments to herself and watched the hostess sympathetically as she checked her seating chart.

"Should be about five minutes." The girl sounded uncertain, as though she'd spiraled into confusion the moment Jo walked into the building and hadn't quite recovered yet.

"All right, five minutes it is." Jo grinned conspiratorially at the girl. "I'll be timin' you, startin' now."

With quick, nervous steps, the girl headed for the dining room, and Jo used her departure as a signal to resume her monologue.

"So anyway, like I was sayin', there's never been a love story like me and Denny, and I'm tellin' the God's honest truth about it . . ."

She rambled throughout their five-minute wait, pausing only long enough to follow the hostess to the table and fill her plate at the salad bar. By the time they were back at the table, Jo had talked about her love story with Denny for almost half an hour, and still Abby wasn't quite sure how the two of them had met.

Nicole seemed lost in her own thoughts, content to let Jo ramble. *She's thinking about Matt and the dress and the rest of her life.* Abby pretended to be listening, but inside she was smiling at Nicole. *You're so beautiful, honey. I couldn't be happier for you.*

How would Nicole remember this, her love story with Matt, when one day her own daughter was getting married? In some ways she was thankful for the distraction Jo provided. Otherwise she was sure Nicole would have been peppering her with questions about her and John's love story.

Someday . . . Maybe someday I'll be able to talk about it without feeling angry and hurt and frustrated, without wanting to punch my fist through a wall at the way John ruined everything. The way he let me take over the efforts of raising the kids and got so busy with football he couldn't so much as pick up after himself.

Abby tuned in for a moment.

"But after that day at the county fishing derby, there was no turnin' back, no sir. Denny had himself the shiniest, most man-size fish you or anyone in all of Marion, Illinois, ever saw before or since. I mean to tell you, it was a big fish. Truth be told—and I'm a truth-teller from way back—fish don't get any bigger than the way that one looked when . . ."

Abby's mind drifted again. Jo and Denny didn't have anything on her and John. Theirs was a love destined from childhood, like an amazing rainbow laid across the sky for everyone to marvel over. She swallowed hard and set down her fork, staring at the wilting lettuce on her plate. Of course, like all rainbows, their light had faded, and now all that remained were stormy grays and lackluster hues of beige. Very soon everyone would know tha[t] no matter how great a story it had started out to be, no matter how long it had lasted, it had long been doomed to an awful ending. The kind that made people leave movie theaters wanting their money back.

Oh . . . but once upon a time their story had been truly brilliant.

Back in their first decade of marriage, she had told the story often, referring to John as her Prince Charming and secretly savoring the way other couples tried to model what the two of them had together. Lately the tale of how they'd met as kids and eventually married seemed to belong to another time, another woman. As though maybe it had never happened at all.

Jo's voice interrupted her thoughts. "So there we were, all these belly-opened fish spread out on the kitchen counter at his mama's house, when what did we see but something shiny lying in the guts of one of the little fellers . . ."

Jo didn't need an audience. If Abby and Nicole leaned their heads back and fell fast asleep, the woman would continue talking. The story would go on as long as the two of them were breathing—maybe even if they weren't. She noticed Nicole picking her fork through a scoop of tuna fish on her plate. Fish guts. Great lunch conversation.

No, Abby was fairly certain there wasn't anyone whose love story topped hers and John's. She thought back, and at first the pictures seemed hazy. But after several seconds of trying, the images came more easily, and Abby realized something. It wasn't that she'd forgotten their past or convinced herself that maybe it never happened. She simply had stopped giving herself permission to go back.

But here, with Jo Harter going on about a story that seemed to have no real plot and yet was bound to last the rest of the afternoon, Abby allowed herself to remember as she hadn't done in years.

There, in the privacy of her own mind, she journeyed to a time and place when she was just a young girl, ten years old, and living in a wonderful old house on the back side of Lake Geneva.

"Abby, come in and get cleaned up . . ." It was her mother's voice, crisp and vivid as though she were still alive, still looking at Abby from the back porch and beckoning her to come in from the water—

"You're listening to me, right, Abby?" Jo's gravelly voice cut into the memory, stopping it cold.

Abby drew a settling breath. This was not the place. But maybe it wasn't such a bad idea, after all. Nicole's wedding plans were bound to bring up much of Abby's memories of the past anyway . . .

She took out a ten-dollar bill and set it on the table. "It's a fascinating story, Jo, but I'll have to hear the rest later."

Nicole practically lurched from her seat and joined Abby near the edge of the table, grabbing money from her purse and handing it to Jo. "Me too. Sorry . . . Matt's waiting for me."

Jo looked disappointed, but she collected the money and began calculating. "Well, now, don't you know something I never even counted on? It's been the best afternoon I can remember in a long time, spending it with you girls. I say next week we do it again, huh? Lots of shopping to do, and if there's one thing I love it's—"

"Not next weekend, Jo." Abby looked at Nicole and smiled. "I promised Nicole we'd take a couple of date days, just her and me." She shifted her gaze back to Jo. "We've done that ever since she was a little girl."

Jo's eyes lit up. "Well, then, I know. Thursday night, week from this. How 'bout say we go scrapping together?"

Get me out of here . . . "Scrapping?"

A laugh bubbled up from deep in Jo's throat. "Oh, I forgot . . . you 'Northern' types call it scrapbookin'. You know, getting together at the craft store and puttin' pictures down on paper. I'm makin' a book for Matthew for the wedding." She glanced quickly at Nicole and held a finger up to her lips. "Shhh, now, don't go tellin' him. It's a surprise. Just like when I used to bring homemade peanut-butter fudge to school after he got a good report card." She grinned proudly at Nicole. "And you, sweetie girl, are the best thing he's gotten since who knows when, and like I always say, the celebration has to fit the thing you're celebratin'."

Abby watched Nicole's eyes dance with possibilities as they turned to her, half expectantly, half apologetically. "Mom, I know you're busy with your writing." She batted her eyelashes in a gesture she'd used since she was a little girl. "Do you think you could? Find time to make me a scrapbook, I mean?" Nicole looked at Jo once more. "I think it's a great idea."

At that point, Abby was willing to do whatever she could to end the afternoon and get as far away from Jo Harter as she could. Besides, the idea wasn't bad. She'd started a scrapbook for Nicole back when her daughter was in grade school, but it was missing pages. Sometime after Nicole's tenth year, Abby had gotten too busy to work on it. If she was ever going to finish it, there was no time like the present. "A week from Thursday, then. What time?"

Jo grinned. "Six o'clock. Meet at the Crafter's Bin on Main and Sixth."

When the three of them were out in the parking lot, Nicole and Abby bid good-bye to Jo and watched her leave. Then Abby turned to her daughter and the two nearly collapsed in laughter. "I thought I was going to lose it for sure." Nicole could barely breathe she was laughing so hard.

"All I know is if I heard one more detail about fish guts and shiny objects slithering about I was going to lose my lunch." Abby caught her breath and held her sides. "I'm sorry. That wasn't very nice."

Nicole looped her arm around her mother's waist and walked alongside her to the car. "I understand, Mom. It's not like you're condemning the woman. And it could be worse. Marli's mother-in-law acts like Marli isn't even alive. At least Jo likes me."

"That's for sure." They were at the car, and Abby turned to her daughter. "You go on home. It's not too cold this afternoon. I think I'll walk."

Nicole frowned. "Mother, that's two miles. You don't want to walk two miles on frozen sidewalks. You'll break your neck."

Abby tousled Nicole's bangs. "Now you sound like me." She grinned. "No, really. Don't worry. I'll take the scenic route along Willow Way. That's a gravel path. No danger of ice."

"Are you sure?" There was concern in Nicole's eyes, and Abby worked as hard as she could to appear casual about her decision.

"Yep. I need the fresh air. Tell Dad I'll be home in an hour if he asks, okay?"

Nicole smiled and pulled her mother into a close hug.

"Okay. I guess I can understand wanting a little silence in light of the afternoon."

Abby laughed again and kissed her daughter on the cheek. "Drive safe."

"Walk safe." They smiled at each other again, and Nicole climbed into the car. "See you at home."

When her car was out of sight, Abby released the deep breath that had been building since they'd met up with Jo Harter. Especially over the past twenty minutes, while memories of another day, another time, beckoned her back to the hallways of yesterday. Abby could hardly think of anything else.

"Abby, come in and get cleaned up . . . The Reynoldses will be here in half an hour."

She could see the cotton sheets blowing on the line, hear the rustling of leaves in the oaks that lined the sides of their property. The smell of the lake, the feel of the sun on her tanned little girl arms . . . all of it was right there, so close she could touch it.

And now, with a two-mile walk of solitude and a future of loneliness lying just ahead of her, she was ready to go back and live the past again.

Nine

ABBY AND JOHN WOULDN'T HAVE MET AT ALL if it hadn't been for their fathers. Abby considered that as she set out toward home and remembered once more the stories her father had told. Stories of the glory days, back when Joe Chapman and Allen Reynolds had been football heroes for the University of Michigan Wolverines. Her father had been a receiver, John's father, the quarterback. Abby stared at the cloudy sky above and held her jacket a bit closer.

I wish I could have seen you play, Dad.

Instead she'd heard a hundred tales of game-winning touchdown tosses and crazy anecdotes in one of the most famed locker rooms in all of college football. Long after their playing days were over, her father and John's remained friends, the kind who sent Christmas cards and surprised each other with a phone call once or twice during the football season, just to be sure the other was watching a good Michigan game. The one against Ohio State, usually.

The Chapmans settled in Lake Geneva, Wisconsin, in a hundred-year-old cottage given to them by Abby's grandparents. The house bordered the lake on the far end, away from the area where tourists flocked each summer. With football rich in his blood, Abby's father taught and coached at the local high school. So completely absorbed were the Chapmans in football, that even now Abby remembered finding her father on the sidelines at half-time one cool Friday night and tugging on his jacket.

"Yes, honey . . ." Her father had always been patient, enjoying the way his family stayed involved in his passion.

"Daddy, when I grow up I'm going to play football for you, okay?"

Something about the night, the crimson and gold of the trees surrounding the stadium, the smell of burning leaves faint in the wind, caused the memory to stand out sharply in Abby's mind.

Football.

When she'd been old enough to realize that girls simply didn't play the game, she figured there was only one other option. She'd marry a football player. The realization had come when she was ten years old. The same year she first met John Reynolds.

For reasons Abby never fully understood, the summer of her tenth year her family's friendship with the Reynolds stopped being a Christmas-only correspondence and turned into something rich and personal, something the two families would continue the rest of their days. Back then Abby hadn't cared about any of that, only that Daddy's friends were coming for a visit and bringing along their kids.

Of course, she'd been bitterly disappointed when her mother explained that they had no little girls her age. Still, there was an air of excitement knowing they were coming. And that afternoon, when her mother called her in from the lake, Abby remembered running into the house, her child-blonde hair wispy in the wind, cheeks golden from the early summer days on the lake.

Abby hadn't wanted to be downstairs when they arrived, so she scurried to her room and held private watch from a bench just beneath her grand window. Maybe her mother was wrong. Maybe they did have a child her age, or at least near it. As she tried to imagine what the coming week would be like, a blue station wagon pulled up, and a family climbed out.

Even now, with Abby's and John's divorce a certain thing, with the bitter cold stinging her cheeks and summer forever away, Abby could remember how her face grew hot that afternoon the moment she first laid eyes on John Reynolds.

He was tall and muscled, with hair as dark as the mane on her old mare out in the barn. Abby recalled her little girl sigh, long and hard. Still, he was just a yucky boy. How much fun could they have together? Especially when he was so much older.

The reality had been surprisingly different. With no one else for him to play with, thirteen-year-old John had taken a liking to her that week. Together they rode horses on hidden trails and built sandcastles on the beach around the lake. There was a public pier a hundred yards down the shore, and they spent hours there, tossing rocks into the lake and telling silly jokes. She taught him how to somersault off the end of the pier, and he taught her how to throw a spiral pass.

Abby realized he wasn't attracted to her. He was three and a half years older, and she was only ten, after all. But as he held the football and ran his fingers over the leather laces, taking her hand in his and positioning it just so, she was overwhelmed with a feeling she had never been more sure of in all her young life.

One day, she was going to marry John Reynolds. And if he didn't know it now, that was okay. Because she wasn't going to stay a little girl forever, and when the years allowed, she had no doubt that he would feel about her the way she already felt about him.

Abby grinned as she walked, remembering the pixie she'd been and how hard she'd fallen for John that summer. She kicked a loose rock and let her eyes gaze up into the winter sky. *There was never any other boy for me, was there, Lord?*

Silence.

Abby didn't think too hard on the fact that there were no holy whispers in response to her daydreaming. *Maybe God's giving me space. After all the conversation today, I probably need it.*

She dug her hands deep into her coat pockets and kept walking. It hadn't taken long for John to come around. Not really.

Four years later, the summer she was fourteen, John and his family came back to Lake Geneva and this time spent two weeks. He remembered her, of course, and though he was going into his senior year in high school and she was only a freshman, they again found common ground. By then she could throw and catch a football better than most boys her age, and they spent hours barefoot on the beach tossing the ball back and forth.

"You're not so bad for a girl," John had teased her.

She remembered holding her head a bit higher. Older boys didn't intimidate her. After all, her father coached sixty of them every year at the high school, and oftentimes they hung out at the house, playing on the lake or eating barbecued chicken with her family. She cocked her head and stared at John, her heart dancing close to the surface. "And you're not so bad for a *boy.*"

John had laughed hard that afternoon, hard enough that eventually he took off after her, tickling her and pretending she could outrun him. The truth was, he had become a great quarterback in his own right by then and was being pursued by a dozen major universities, including their fathers' alma mater—Michigan.

How strange you were back then, John . . . seventeen, star football player, yet somehow content to spend two weeks running around with a little girl.

One night the two families brought blankets down to the sandy shoreline and her father built a bonfire. There they did something Abby couldn't remember ever having done before: they sang songs about God. Not the usual silly campfire songs about chickens or trains comin' round the mountain, but sweet songs about peace and joy and love and a God who cared deeply for all of them. When the songs ended and the adults were lost in their own conversation, John moved next to her and poked her with his elbow.

"You got a boyfriend, little Miss Abby Chapman?" He grinned, and Abby still remembered the way his blue eyes shimmered with the reflection of the moon on the water.

She had been sorely thankful it was dark, because her cheeks were hot from his question. Again, years of being teased by older boys paid off, and she kept her cool. "I don't need a boyfriend." She nudged his bare foot with her own.

He nudged her back. "That so?" A grin spread across his face, and Abby hadn't been quite sure how to take him.

"Yes." Her head raised another notch, and she leveled her gaze straight at him. "Boys can be very immature." She studied him for a moment. "Let me guess . . . you've got a different girlfriend every week, right? That's how it is with Dad's quarterbacks."

John's head fell back for a moment, and he laughed out loud before he looked at her again. "I guess I'm different."

Abby's eyes grew wide in mock amazement. "What? John Reynolds has no girlfriend?"

He reached for the football then—it had never been more than an arm's length away that entire summer—and tossed it lightly in the air a few times. *"This* is my girlfriend."

Abby nodded playfully. "She'll make a great prom date, I'm sure."

He pushed her foot again and lowered his eyes in mock indignation. "Shhh. You'll offend her." He chuckled, then his smile faded. "Truth is I don't have time for girls. I wanna play football at Michigan, like my dad and your dad. Either I work out every day and get better all the time, or someone else'll beat me to it. Girls can wait." He reached over and tousled her hair, and at the contact, something changed in his eyes. "Hey, you be careful next year, okay, Abby? Big high-school girl and all."

His comment seemed to come out of nowhere. *Be careful?* Butterflies fluttered wildly in her stomach. "Of what?" She thought she understood what he meant, but still . . .

He shrugged, his brown shoulders lifting in a way that showed the muscled lines in his arms. "Of guys." There was another elbow in her ribs, and she had the impression he was trying to say something serious without letting the mood become too heavy. "Know what I mean?"

"Guys?" Abby nudged his foot again and grinned at him. "Oh, you mean like you?"

"Come on, Abby . . ." John turned so he was sitting directly across from her. "You've looked in the mirror lately, right?"

"The mirror?" The butterflies were swarming now, and everything in her wanted to believe that John Reynolds was thinking what she thought he might be. *He thinks I'm pretty . . .*

John whistled in response and casually shook his head. "You're gonna be a knockout, Abby. And the boys'll line up from here to your front door. Especially your dad's players." His smile faded and his eyes connected with hers again. "Just be careful."

It was as if someone had opened a trapdoor to her heart and released the butterflies all at once. In their place was a feeling deeper than anything she'd felt before. More than a crush, more than what she'd feel for a summer friendship on the beach. Instead, in that instant there was something deep and intimate—like a best friendship—that took up residence in her heart and set down roots.

Abby sighed, drawn back to the gravelly pathway of the present and the light snow that had begun to fall.

Roots that held firmly to this very day.

What happened to us, John? How could anything have come between us?

Abby felt tears in her eyes, and she blinked them back. If she was going to remember how she and John had been, she might as well not stop now. Not with the best part, the sweetest days of all, just footsteps ahead.

John had gone back home with his family a few days later, and before Christmas he signed a letter of intent to play football at Michigan—just like his father and hers decades earlier. Three years passed, and instead of summer visits John's family sent newspaper clippings. He was easily one of the most talked about quarterbacks in the country and often the topic of conversations in the Chapman household. Once a year Abby's parents drove to Ann Arbor and took in a game, but Abby stayed home, busy with high-school life and certain that John Reynolds had forgotten about her.

Then one September afternoon in 1977, the phone rang in the Chapman house.

"Hello?" Abby was out of breath, seventeen, and busy cheering for her father's high-school team.

"Hey—" the caller's voice lingered—"long time no talk."

Abby's heart caught in her throat. Months and years had passed since they'd been together, and John had been right—the offers had been plentiful. But none of the boys had ever made her feel the way John had that long-ago summer night, their bare feet touching in the sand. And now there was no doubt in Abby's mind that the deep voice on the other end of the phone belonged to him. "John . . ."

There was a chuckle that warmed Abby's heart. "Don't tell me the cute kid from all those summers ago has grown up?"

Once again she'd been thankful he couldn't see her blush. "Yeah, I guess so."

"Okay, I have a question for you." He was teasing her, taking his time, and Abby couldn't believe it. *He remembers me . . . after college, after everything he's done since then . . .*

"I'm listening." *Do I sound older . . . more mature? More—*

"Every year your parents come all the way to Ann Arbor to see me play . . ." he interrupted her thoughts, and she could picture the way his eyes danced, just like they'd danced that night on the beach, the last time she'd seen him. "And each time I ask 'em where you are, and you know what they say?" He hesitated for effect. "They say, 'Oh, Abby . . . she's busy with her friends, busy with school.' I mean, come on, Abby. Not a single game . . . you couldn't make it out for even one?"

Abby felt her confidence growing. That fall she was just a few months shy of her eighteenth birthday, and with John on the line everything felt right with her world. "Hmmm. Let's see, now . . . If I'm remembering right, I don't recall you ever inviting me. Not that I blame you—I mean I'm just a *cute kid.* What would a big-time Michigan QB like you want with a punk little girl like me, anyway?"

John allowed a silence, and she could practically see him grinning through the phone lines. "So how old are you now, anyway, Abby?"

"Almost eighteen." She tried to sound official, mature, but as the words escaped her mouth, she was struck by the fact that they sounded downright silly. He would have just turned twenty-one. *He's not interested in me. He's just playing with my—*

"So, was I right?"

At first she'd been confused. "About . . ." She let her voice trail off.

"About the guys lined up at your door."

That was the moment when it had all started feeling like a dream. *Why's he doing this? He couldn't really care, could he?* "There've been a few."

"Okay, okay . . . so who's the lucky guy?" He was still teasing, still playing with her and making it impossible for her to tell if he were even a little interested.

She giggled out loud. "You're crazy."

"No, I'm serious. I want details . . . I warned you, Abby. Don't forget that."

"No one. Just friends, that's all."

"Oh, sure . . ." His words were drawn out and playfully sarcastic. "I know your type. String along some poor fool, make him think he has a chance."

"No, really." She was laughing harder now. "There's no one. I don't have a boyfriend. Besides, you should talk. Mr. Hot Stuff on Campus. Your line probably wraps around the stadium."

"Oh-hooo. Very good." He paused a moment, and his chuckling faded. "Actually, I'm still seeing the same girl, the one I was dating the last time I saw you."

Abby stifled a giggle, picturing the way he'd cradled the football that night on the beach. "Paula Pigskin, wasn't it?"

He laughed. "Yep. Me and my ball, together forever." His voice grew more serious. "Like I always say, girls can wait."

Her heart soared with hope, and she chastised herself. *Be real, Abby. He's too old for you.* "So, your motto hasn't changed much since high school, huh?"

"Not much."

Neither of them said anything for a beat, then John picked up the conversation. "So what's your answer?" He was upbeat again, having fun with her. But the teasing was gone, and Abby knew instinctively that he was serious.

"You mean it, don't you?"

He huffed in mock indignation. "Of course I mean it. You haven't seen me play once. And I know for a fact that your parents are coming out again this season—mid-November."

Mid-November. The idea was suddenly very appealing. "Serious?"

"Sure." John's tone was light. *He probably sees me as a little sister.* "I'll show you around the campus. Introduce you to the real big men on campus."

"Your offensive line?"

"You got it." They both laughed. "So, what's your answer?"

The memory of how she felt that day warmed her heart even now. "Okay, okay. I should be done cheering for football by then, and if I'm not too busy . . ."

"Oh, right. I wouldn't want to cramp your style or crowd your schedule." He was still teasing her, and she decided to be serious.

"No, really. I'll come." She paused. *Should I tell him?* Abby closed her eyes and plunged ahead. "I've always wanted to see you play."

"Oh, sure." John's voice grew quieter as he continued talking. "I can tell by the effort you've made."

A giggle made its way to the surface. "I watch television, you know. You've been doing great, John."

"What? Miss Too-Busy-to-Come follows Michigan football?"

"Not like I have a choice. It's like a national holiday around here when the Wolverines are on TV. My dad gets the Ann Arbor paper delivered by mail so he can follow it each week. He's so proud of you, John."

He cleared his throat. "And you . . . ?"

Why was he acting like this? He couldn't possibly be interested in her as more than a family friend, could he? "Yes, John—" she bathed her words in a protective, teasing sarcasm—"I'm proud too. I'm sure that makes your day."

There was a hesitation. "Actually, it does." He waited again, almost as though he wanted to say something else. Instead, he wrapped up the conversation. "I'll see you in a couple months then, right?"

"Sure." She felt her eyebrows lower in confusion. "Did you want to talk to my dad or something?"

"Nope. Just you. Figured I'd never get you out here for a game if I didn't ask you myself. What with your busy schedule and all . . . well . . . I thought I better give you plenty of notice."

The months of waiting were unbearable. Everything about the high-school football season that year seemed dull and unimportant compared with the idea that John Reynolds wanted her to watch him play college ball. Better yet, he wanted to show her around campus.

A cold blast of winter wind startled Abby from her memories, and she snuggled deeper into her coat, picking up her pace. John had been bigger than life back then. A hero, really. Someone talked about in homes across the country, an athlete known for his physical talent, good looks, and high moral character. His name was mentioned in connection with college football's most prized award— the Heisman Trophy. Yet there she'd been—all of seventeen years old—believing that he really wanted to see her. Her, of all people.

Abby blinked, and the past disappeared. She stared straight ahead and felt the pull of gravity on her lips, realized how it tugged her mouth downward, giving her a perpetual frown. It wasn't just the passing of time that had aged her. It was her relationship with her husband, as well. When was the last time she'd laughed at one of his jokes? The ridiculous ones that left a new batch of high-school students in stitches every semester. She forced a smile, sad that it felt so foreign on her face. A farm and a frozen pond came into view on her right, and she stopped for a moment, trying to picture the way she'd looked that November day as she and her family took their seats at Michigan Stadium.

They'd arrived two hours early with plans to meet John on the field before the game. She could see her dad, still robust and healthy back then, waving his arm at the rest of them. "Come on, I know right where he'll be."

Abby had tossed her long hair over her shoulder and followed her father, determined not to let her nervousness show. Besides, what did she have to worry about? The whole thing was probably more her imagination than anything else. But just in case, she had worn her new black jeans and a form-fitting white turtleneck sweater. Her mother had commented on the drive over that Abby had never looked prettier. She had no reason to be nervous, but as they approached the entrance to the locker rooms, Abby thought she might faint from the uncertainty of it all.

John appeared almost immediately, wearing Wolverine sweats, his short dark hair combed neatly off his face.

Abby sucked in a quick breath. He was gorgeous. Much better looking in person than on TV or in newspaper photos. And much more a man than he'd been the last time they were together at her house that summer.

"Hey, how're you doing?" He was breathless, his face filled with energy, and his eyes quickly moved from her father's to hers. "Abby . . ." His eyes grew wide, and he moved closer so he was only a few feet away, his six-four frame towering over her. Even with her parents and younger sister standing around them, Abby could see the admiration in John's eyes. "My gosh . . . you've grown up."

She'd expected him to tease her, since that was the side of John Reynolds she knew best, but his eyes held pure admiration and not a trace of humor. Unsure of how to respond, she laughed lightly and cast him an exaggerated upward glance. *Lord, don't let my heart fall out of my chest.* "Not as much as you have."

He grinned. "Yeah, I shot up a bit."

She was still studying him when her father stepped up and put his arm around John's broad shoulders. "Perfect size for a Wolverine quarterback. And I believe it's true when I say never—not before or since—has Michigan had a quarterback like you, son. You're one of a kind."

Abby savored the chance to study John's face, his pronounced cheekbones, and she found herself agreeing completely with her father's assessment—even if all he threw were interceptions.

John's cheeks reddened slightly. "Thank you, sir. Did you find my folks?"

"Not yet." Abby's father glanced at the rest of them and nodded toward the field. "Let's take a walk around. I wanna show you the spot where the greatest play in history took place." He waved at John. "Go get suited up. Beat 'em good now, you hear?"

Abby and her sister had seen the famous spot—marked on the field only by the memory of the play—on trips to Ann Arbor when they were little. They'd heard the stories again and again. But still they turned to follow him, thriving on the memories every bit as much as their father did.

"Hey, Abby, wait." She turned around, her heart still pounding loudly.

"Yeah?"

The rest of Abby's family stopped and turned also, waiting expectantly for whatever John was about to say. He shifted his weight and hesitated, looking from Abby's father to Abby and back again. "Uh . . . can Abby and I catch up a bit? She can meet you back in the stands, maybe?"

Everything about Abby's world tilted crazily. *He wants to talk to me?* Wasn't it all just a joke? His way of trying to be nice to a family friend? Suddenly it seemed much more serious, and Abby could hardly contain her excitement. After a slight pause, Abby's mother took her father's hand and answered for him. "That's fine, John. You two go right ahead and catch up."

When her family was out of sight, John turned back to Abby. "Thanks for coming." His voice was gentle, tender, and though his eyes sparkled in the ice-cold early morning sun, there was not even a trace of teasing or silliness there.

Abby adjusted her scarf and grinned at him. "I told you I would."

John shrugged, his eyes still locked on hers. "I was afraid you'd think I was joking."

What's he mean? Where's all this going? Abby swallowed and angled her head curiously. "You . . . you weren't?"

"No, I wasn't." He hesitated and ran his thumb gently along the curve of her cheek just below her eye. "You're so beautiful, Abby. Do you know that?"

For all the times when she couldn't seem to stop talking, Abby was absolutely speechless. She stood there, soaking in the nearness of him, trying to convince herself she wasn't dreaming. When she said nothing, he continued. "Go out with me tonight after the game. We can get pizza or just walk around the campus."

Go *out* with him? Again the shock nearly knocked Abby to the ground. She felt suddenly shy with him. "Okay. If my parents don't mind."

A smile filled his face, and he glanced over his shoulder. "I better go get ready. Meet you at my folks' house after the game, okay?"

"Okay."

Then without any hesitation, he hugged her the way old friends hug at a class reunion. "It's good to see you again, Abby Chapman." He pulled back and smiled at her. "Really."

In an instant he was gone, taking with him all that remained of her heart.

She laughed out loud now, remembering the innocent, carefree days of seventeen and how smitten she'd been with John Reynolds, how sure that even if the world stopped spinning nothing would ever change the way she felt about the young man who stood before her that Saturday morning.

Abby's smile faded as she saw their house a hundred yards up the road. It was more fun walking down yesterday's trails than taking this very real one. Blinking back tears Abby dug her hands deep into her pockets, imagining the cool reception she would receive from John in a few minutes. An image came to her. She and John two years into their marriage, nestled close together on a threadbare sofa watching a suspenseful movie.

"I hate this part!" she whined and buried her head in John's shoulder. Stifling a grin, he took her hands gently in his and laid them across her face so she couldn't see.

"There. That better?" She remembered feeling safe and sheltered with John's arm around her.

"Yeah. Just one more thing." Her voice was muffled, filtering through the cracks in her fingers.

"For you, love, anything . . ." He leaned down and kissed her on the cheek.

"Tell me when I can open my eyes, okay?"

"Always, Abby. Always."

What had happened to that man, the one she'd fallen in love with that Saturday morning outside the Wolverine locker room? For the first time in years, against all her better judgment or reasoning abilities, Abby missed what they'd been, ached for the loss of what they'd once shared.

"Always, Abby . . . always, Abby . . . always . . ."

She was only a dozen yards from the front door and she stopped, feet buried in a foot of snow as tears pricked at the inside of her eyelids. *I hate this part. Help me through this, God; it's more than I can bear. I'm terrified of being alone, and the scary parts haven't even started yet. But this time I have no one to turn to, no shoulder to hide my face in.*

And no one to tell me when I can open my eyes.

Ten

THERE WAS NOTHING QUITE LIKE THE RELIEF of silence echoing through a high-school classroom ten minutes after the final bell.

It wasn't that John Reynolds disliked teaching. In fact he was one of the handful of teachers on campus that truly relished arriving at school each morning, greeting his classes, and alternating between educating and entertaining them. His classroom was his personal domain where he ruled supreme, the place second only to the football field where he felt completely in charge of his destiny.

Still, there was something he cherished about the solitude that came after every student had cleared the campus. Oftentimes it was the first chance all day for John to work on lesson plans for the coming week or ponder his personal life. Especially on days like today when everything about his existence outside the classroom seemed to be caving in around him.

The image of Abby's face earlier that day flashed in his mind. She'd been on the Internet, no doubt, probably e-mailing the editor she swore she wasn't involved with. But even with all the distance between Abby and him, John knew guilt when it flashed across his wife's face. And Abby was definitely guilty of something. He closed his eyes and remembered the exchange as though it had happened only minutes ago.

The tension between them had gotten worse since Nicole's engagement announcement, and he'd been determined to find a neutral zone, a common ground where they could set up camp and coexist for the next six months. With ten minutes to spare before leaving for work, he'd popped his head into her office.

Immediately she moved her computer mouse across the pad and clicked twice. "You scared me." Her tone was filled with accusation, and a dark shadow of wrongdoing shrouded her features.

"Sorry." He struggled for the right words as he entered the boxy room and shut the door behind him. Why was it so hard to talk to her now? Were they really that far gone, unable even to carry on a conversation? He knew the answer as surely as he knew that divorce was the only option they had left, the only way either of them would ever find happiness again. "Can you talk for a minute?"

She had sighed loudly and closed down her America Online application. "What is it?"

Her attitude caused his entire mind-set to change. If she couldn't be civilized first thing in the morning, what hope was there that she might be willing to reach some sort of combat-free agreement? *Never mind, Abby. Who needs your moodiness anyway?* "Forget it." He spat the words and turned to leave, but she cut him short.

"Listen, don't come in here interrupting my work and think I'm going to turn somersaults about it, okay? I have a life, too, you know." She remained in her office chair but turned it to face him. John hated the contempt in her eyes, the way they seemed to belittle him and everything he might have wanted to say.

"Why do I bother?" His arms hung at his sides, fists clenched. "I came in here to see if we could maybe work out some kind of deal, some way we might actually survive the months between now and July. But like always your attitude is too big to get around."

Anger pinched her features tightly together. "*My* attitude?" She didn't pause long enough to let him respond. "When you won't stay away from Charlene even now after I've asked you a dozen times to give it a rest. I mean really, John. Six months? Can't your teenage hormones wait that long?"

John chuckled once and shook his head. "I don't have to listen to this."

"Well, maybe you do. I'm finding notes, counting hours. Don't you think I know when you should be home? I've been married to you twenty-one years, John. I'm not completely stupid. I mean, you're either leaving early to be with her or staying late for it. Even now, when you promised me you'd back off."

"I absolutely refuse to make this a discussion about Charlene!" He was raising his voice, no longer worried about whether it might catch the kids' attention from upstairs, where they all were getting ready. "I've been keeping up my end of the deal, Abby. But you . . ." He let his voice trail off and stared at her dumbfounded. "You're so downright hateful I don't even see the point anymore."

Don't do it, My son.

He closed his eyes now, remembering the holy warnings, how they'd echoed through him . . . but they hadn't mattered. After years of ignoring them he'd become an expert at blocking them out. Besides, they were so infrequent these days he wasn't even sure anymore that they were holy warnings. *I can say what I want . . . she deserves it.*

"The point of what?" Abby stared at him as if he were a stranger demanding entrance to her house.

"If I spent more time with Charlene, at least I wouldn't have to be around here."

Abby shot him one more daggerlike glare, then spun around and anchored her gaze on the computer screen. "Get out of here, John. I have nothing to say to you."

Resignation worked its way up from John's chest. "What else is new? Isn't that where this all started? Back when you found your own little writer's life and stopped having anything to say to me?"

She refused to even shift her eyes in his direction. "Oh, here we go. Let's blame the whole thing on my writing. That's so you, John." She released a laugh that was completely devoid of humor. "You discouraged me about writing from the get-go, refused to read my work, and left me with the job of raising the kids. Now you blame me for the fact that our marriage is in cardiac arrest. That's really good. Perfect."

Her sarcasm stung at his nerves like so many fire ants. "Just once why don't you get off your high horse and look at the bigger picture, Abby? I wanted you to write articles. It's a great outlet for you. But you let it take on a life of its own, and whether you want to see it or not, after you started writing I fell down the list to about fifth or sixth in importance. Somewhere after the kids and your dad and e-mailing that—" he waved at her computer—"that *editor* friend of yours."

She jerked ever so slightly at the mention of her editor, and again John was sure that the darkness in her eyes was guilt. "I didn't realize you were so needy, John. I mean, did it ever occur to you I might need a little help, that I had a lot on *my* plate? Would it have killed you to do a load of laundry or fold your own socks?" She tossed her head in mock amazement. "You expected me to fawn over you when I was too tired to spell my own name by the end of the day?"

Her words were dry and biting, and he was suddenly sure he'd had enough.

"I'm leaving. And if I'm late tonight I'm sure you'll be too busy writing to notice."

John had replayed the scene a dozen times throughout the day. Now he reached for a paper clip from the organizer on his desk and bent it mindlessly. Had it really come to this? Was it impossible for them to even get along? If so, then how in the world was he supposed to stay away from Charlene? Especially now when Abby's mandate that he keep his distance only made him think of Charlene more.

He planted his elbows on his desk and hung his head. If Abby had been this way back in their dating days, he'd have dumped her after their first night out. She was arrogant and rude and downright mean. No wonder their physical relationship had been the first thing to go. Clearly she had no good feelings for him whatsoever and hadn't for years.

Maybe it's my fault . . . maybe I stopped loving her the way she needed to be loved . . .

Almost as if in response to his musings, Charlene opened the classroom door and peered inside. "Hi. Got a minute?"

She was dressed in navy slacks and a blazer, which she wore unbuttoned over her tight white T-shirt. John forced himself to keep his gaze from falling below her neck. "Sure." He sat up straighter, and all thoughts of Abby vanished from his mind. "What's up?"

"It's the kids in fifth period again." She moved into the room and sat across from him, her forearms resting on his desk so that their hands were only inches apart. "No matter what I do they test me. Don't you ever get sick of it? The way kids have changed over the years?"

"Sure." John studied her, fairly sure she hadn't come to talk about unruly students. Her perfume filled his senses, and suddenly it was nothing short of work to keep from thinking about how good she made him feel.

Flee! What God has joined together let no one separate.

The scripture felt like a bucket of cold water, and John blinked, trying to focus on what she was saying.

"So, what's the answer? You never struggle with control in your classroom."

I'm struggling now . . . "They know I'll make 'em run laps if they act up." He was teasing her, enjoying the relief she brought from the heaviness in his life.

She pushed at his arm in mock frustration. "Come on, I'm serious. You're supposed to have all the answers." With those words something changed in her eyes, and her gaze locked onto his. "Are the answers any clearer these days, John?"

Without a doubt she was no longer talking about classroom control. He ached with the desire to walk around the desk and take her in his arms. It wasn't her fault. She cared for him, clearly. And now the two of them would be forced to wait another six months before anything could be decided.

What God has joined together—

I didn't divide us, Lord; Abby did. His silent comeback was swift and sure. Besides, it was way too late for Bible verses now. Their decision to divorce was already set.

Charlene remained motionless, waiting for his answer, her head cocked, her face full of questions about his feelings for her. John released a hiss of air through clenched teeth. "I told you, Nicole's getting married in July. I won't know anything until she's back from her honeymoon."

Her face flooded with defeat. "So you're really going to wait?"

John hated the way her innocent questions underlined the fact that he was trapped, stopped against his will from doing the one thing he wanted to do—start over again with the fun-hearted, beautiful woman sitting across from him. "I have to. We owe it to the kids."

Abby would have fought him on the issue, but not Charlene. She settled back in her chair and let the information sink in. "What if . . . what if Abby wants to work it out?"

John chuckled sadly. "The only thing Abby and I are going to try and do is not kill each other." His eyes met hers again. "Lately we can't say two sentences without it getting ugly."

Charlene angled her head in a pretty gesture that always tugged at John's heart. "I'm sorry. I . . . well, I wish there was something I could do to help."

Yeah, you could convince me to run away with you and never—

Flee, My son . . . Flee.

I'm not doing anything wrong! The voice in his heart fairly shouted at the whispered warning echoing in his soul. He tried to keep his thoughts on a more honorable level. "It's just one of those things. We'll get through it somehow."

Questions continued to flash in her eyes. "What you asked me . . . you know, about giving you space . . . is that true for the whole time, the whole six months?"

She looked so young and lovely, so lonely and in need of someone to take care of her. John tightened his fingers into fists and forced himself to answer her. "I have no choice."

For a moment she said nothing, but John was sure she was wrestling with her emotions. Clearly she wanted to be with him, and finally, after nearly a minute, she reached out and wrapped her hands around his. "I'll stay away." She paused, allowing her thumb to rub small patterns of empathy across the back of his hand. "I didn't really have to talk about fifth period today." She dropped her gaze. "I just missed you."

John tightened his grip on her hands and lowered his head so he could connect with her gaze once more. "I miss you too. And once in a while we're bound to spend time together. But otherwise it has to wait until—"

At that moment his classroom door swung open, and Kade walked in carrying a notebook and a stack of papers. His eyes fell to the desk where John's and Charlene's hands were still linked. "Dad? What's going on?"

Charlene was immediately on her feet. "Your dad was

praying for me." There was an uncomfortable silence. "I was just leaving."

Praying for her? Charlene's words hit John in the gut like a prizefighter's fist. Charlene was not a praying woman; they'd never even discussed his faith. *What kind of witness have I been to her, Lord . . . what am I doing here?*

Kade stepped aside as Charlene hurried across the room and out the doorway. "See you later," she said, casting John a pained look before she disappeared down the hall.

"What was *that* all about?" Kade's face was still flooded with confusion. "Since when do you and Ms. Denton pray together?"

John's throat was suddenly thick, and he struggled to find his voice. "She, uh . . . she needed someone to talk to. She's having some trouble at home."

"Isn't she divorced?" Kade moved into the room, set his backpack down, and took the chair Charlene had been sitting in. The boy wasn't accusing, just curious and more than a little bothered.

"Yes, for a while now."

Kade shook his head as though the situation didn't make sense. "Weird." He reached into his backpack, pulled out his notebook, and set it on the table. "Do you think it's a good idea to pray with her like that, Dad?" He leveled his gaze at his father. "Might give her the wrong idea."

John laughed, but it sounded tinny and forced even to him. "Son, Ms. Denton and I have been friends for a long time. I don't think anyone's going to get the wrong idea."

Kade studied him a moment longer. "Okay. But what would Mom think if she walked in and saw you two holding hands like that? It's kind of . . . I don't know, just weird, you know?"

God, give me the right words here.

Repent! Remember the height from which you have—

"Everything's fine between me and Ms. Denton," John interrupted the scripture flashing in his heart. "Besides, your mother knows we're friends. Don't worry about it, okay?"

"Sure . . . whatever." Kade shrugged, and John was struck by how much the boy looked like himself twenty years earlier. Almost like history repeating itself. "It just didn't look good."

John shifted positions, desperate for Kade to change the subject. "I'm sorry. She needed someone to talk to." He fingered his son's notebook. "Did you want something?"

Kade opened the book and took out a bundle of stapled papers. "I had to pick a topic for my senior project." He turned the paper so it faced his father.

John let his eyes scan the sheet. "Habits of Eagles? That's your topic?"

A grin spread across Kade's face. "Yep. You know, like kicking tail all season long, winning the big games, standing up to adversity. Habits of Eagles. Marion Eagles, get it, Dad?"

John laughed and hoped it didn't sound as hollow to Kade as it felt. The memory of Charlene's hand in his still burned deep in his belly, stirring feelings he desperately wished he could control. *She's like a drug, God . . . get her out of my system.*

Repent! Flee immorality! Remember the height . . .

It was like a broken record. Wasn't there anything more comforting God could whisper to him? Something about how he and Charlene could be together when this unbearable time with Abby was over and Nicole and Matt were married and on their own? He shut out the warnings and focused on his son's paper. "I like it, Kade. A study on eagles."

Kade eased back in his chair, confident and comfortable, all signs of his earlier concern gone. "Yeah, only not the Marion Eagles, Dad. I don't think they'd let me do a report on that. I'm gonna study real eagles. I can go on-line and read books, and then I have to put together a graphic display. Mr. Bender said someone did a report on eagles last year, and the stuff he found out was amazing. Like, listen to this . . ."

He rustled through his notebook until he found a slightly crumpled sheet of paper. "The eagle is the only bird that doesn't run from trouble. Instead, it uses the storms of life to take it to a higher place."

John nodded, trying to seem interested. *Is Charlene waiting for me down the hall? Has she gone for the day? When can we finish our conversation . . . ?* He forced the thoughts from his head and focused on his son.

"Isn't that tight, Dad? It uses the storms to take it higher. Just like a Marion Eagle." Kade waited for his father's response. "Remember . . . when Taylor Johnson went down with a torn ACL and everyone thought we'd fall apart? But we didn't."

John worked to see the connection. "We rose above it; is that what you mean?"

"Right!" Kade's eyes sparkled. "And know what else? Eagles are in the Bible a lot too."

Just the sound of the word "Bible" put John's innards into knots. "The Bible?"

"Right . . ." Kade rustled through his papers once more until he found what he was looking for. "Here it is.

We shall mount up on wings as eagles. See, Dad, God didn't say we'd be like chickens or crows or parakeets. He said we'd be like eagles."

John smiled at his son's enthusiasm and tried to ignore the conviction strangling his heart. "Marion Eagles, no doubt."

A look of mock humility flashed in Kade's eyes. "Well, I wasn't going to make the connection, but since you brought it up . . ."

John pushed his fist into his son's shoulder playfully. "Sounds like the report'll be a winner, son. Just like . . ."

They finished the sentence in unison. "The Marion Eagles."

Kade grabbed his dad around the neck with the crook of his elbow. "That's my dad, sharp as a whip."

"Sharp as a tack . . . quick as a whip." John rubbed his knuckles against his son's head. "That's my boy, the dumb jock."

Kade was giggling now, sounding more like the little boy he'd been ten years earlier than the full-grown man-child he'd become. "Whatever." He rubbed his father's head until they were both locked in the embrace, laughing and struggling to get free.

John pulled away first and inhaled sharply, catching his breath. "Are you on your way home?"

"Yeah, wanna join me?" Kade sat back, not even breathing hard despite their roughhousing. "Mom's making homemade pizza."

The thought of Abby made John lose his appetite, and he struggled to keep his expression neutral. "Better not. Tests to correct."

Kade loaded his belongings back into his bag and

swung it over his shoulder. For an instant he leveled his gaze at his father, as though there was something he wanted to say but couldn't. "Hurry, okay." His grin faded some. "Mom likes it when we're all home for dinner."

John nodded, grateful Kade couldn't read his mind. "Okay, tell her I'll be there."

When Kade was gone, John exhaled and realized he'd been holding his breath since Kade's comment about dinner. If they were going to survive the coming months, Kade was right. He should make an effort to be home once in a while. Otherwise the kids were bound to figure out something was wrong.

He pulled out the papers from sixth period and began grading them. *Don't think about Abby or Charlene or any of it. Just work. Get it done so you can go home.*

Though he successfully fended off thoughts of the women in his life, he couldn't shake his mind of one very powerful image: an eagle midflight, climbing higher and higher while storm clouds brewed in the background. The harsher the storm, the higher the eagle flew, and John couldn't help but realize that regardless of the embroidery on his coach's shirt, he was not an eagle.

Not even close.

Eleven

As was often the case these days, Abby's father was asleep, and she sat alone in his room, no longer repulsed by the medicinal, nursing-home smell or the way the man she'd once thought bigger than life had wasted away to little more than skin and bones. She held his hand, stroking it gently with her thumb and wondering how long it would be now. Parkinson's did not keep a schedule, and the doctors had told her he could leave her this year or not for another five.

Abby's eyes fell on a wooden sign hanging near the foot of his bed: "I'm only passing through . . . this world is not my home."

Oh, but the passing through can be so painful, God. Like watching Dad disappear before my eyes . . . or seeing John with Charlene.

There was no whispered assurance or instant scripture to fill her mind, and Abby sighed, leaning back in her chair. She'd been busy most of the week, absorbed in household details, cleaning bathrooms, and folding laundry. And of course her writing assignments. She'd had three major pieces that needed finishing by Friday, and she hadn't submitted them via e-mail until after midnight the night before.

Now, for the first time since her walk in the snow, she actually had time to herself. Time when she didn't have to worry about where John was and what they might say to each other and how best to avoid him in the house they still shared. The entire week they'd done nothing but fight with each other, either about Charlene or about her writing or her editor. They hadn't said a kind word to each other, and Abby realized only now how draining it had been.

Six months of this, Lord? How am I going to survive?

What God has joined together let no one separate.

Abby sighed. God's warnings were like a broken record. They were trite and forced and lent no application whatsoever to her life today. Clearly there was nothing left between John and her. Why did God insist on bringing to mind scriptures of idealistic behavior? She and John were separating. Period. Now they had to find a way to survive the process.

Closing her eyes, Abby remembered her walk the week before and how good it had felt to spend time in the past, in the place where she and John were in love beyond anything she could have dreamed. A time when just waking each morning offered more excitement and promise than young Abby could bear.

Where had she left off . . . ? Abby concentrated, and her mind filled with the image of herself, black jeans, white turtleneck, sitting with her family watching the game—the first time she'd seen John play for Michigan. With every play she'd held her breath, desperately praying he wouldn't be hurt and at the same time mesmerized by the way his body moved. The Wolverines won handily that day with John throwing for three touchdowns and running for another.

"Show-off," she told him later as they strolled along the campus just before dusk. The temperature had dropped, and he had lent her his lettermen's jacket. Snuggled inside it, she felt like Cinderella at the ball, afraid that midnight would strike at any moment and she'd be forced to wake from the dream.

He had walked alongside her, as comfortable as if they'd spent every day for the past three years together. "Did I have a choice? You blow me off all those years and now . . . finally . . . you make it to a game. I mean, come on, Abby. The pressure was on big time."

His grin warmed her insides so that it felt like midday deep in her heart. For two hours they talked about his classes and hers, their goals and dreams. "It wouldn't surprise me if I end up coaching someday, when my playing days are over . . ."

His father was a successful banker, and Abby tilted her head thoughtfully. "Not going for the big bucks like your dad?"

She was teasing, and it was obvious he could tell. He smiled and shrugged. "There's more to life. I think if Dad had it to do over again he'd coach too. Like your dad." John gazed at the sunset through the trees, keeping his steps in time with hers. "It's a hard game to walk away from."

Abby thought about how intricately the game had been a part of her life growing up. "I know."

They had made their way across campus to a bench under a shady, ancient oak tree, and John stopped, turning so he faced her squarely. "You really do know it, don't you? You understand, Abby. Football, I mean. How important it is to guys like me and your dad."

Abby basked in his nearness. *Is this really happening? Am I here a million miles away from home and inches from John Reynolds?* She nodded shyly. "Yeah, I do."

John shook his head, his face incredulous. "And the best part is, you actually like it. A lot of girls could care less."

She grinned. "Well, now, I've only made it out for one game."

He laughed at first, then gradually his smile faded and his eyes locked onto hers. "I've thought about you a lot, Abby. Do you know that?"

Something in her wanted to bolt, wanted to protect her heart before it became too lost to ever find again. Instead she nodded, unwilling to break the connection between them. Then, with the winter wind sifting through the leaves around them, John placed his hands on her shoulders and leaned close, touching his lips to hers. He kissed her so sweetly, so simply, she was certain she was floating a foot off the ground.

It was not a seductive kiss or one that demanded more of her than she was ready to give, but it was a kiss that made his intentions crystal clear. She had pulled away first, breathless, scanning his face for the answers she suddenly needed more desperately than oxygen. "John?"

His gaze never left hers as he ran his thumb tenderly over her eyebrows. "I know you're young, Abby. But there's something between us. Something I've felt ever since I met you." He hesitated, and for all his fame and glory and cocksure athletic ability, he looked utterly vulnerable. "Do you . . . can you feel it too?"

A giggle rose from Abby's throat, and she threw her arms around his neck, allowing him to hold her close, savoring how his body warmed hers in a way she'd never known before. With his question still hanging in the air, she pulled back and angled her head, sure her eyes were sparkling with all she was feeling inside. "Yes, I feel it. I thought I was the only one who did. You know, because I was too young for you."

A grin broke out across his face. "No, it was never just you. But back then you were too little to talk about it; I even thought maybe I was imagining it. But over the years, it didn't go away. I would get home from a game and wonder where you were, what you were doing. Like . . ."

Suddenly confident in all she'd ever felt for him, she finished his sentence for him. "Like we were meant to be?"

He nodded and kissed her again. This time there was a fire between them, and when he pulled back he distanced himself from her. "Abby, I don't know how everything's going to work out. We won't even see each other much this next year. But there's one thing I've never been more sure of—I've never felt like this with anyone before."

She spread her fingers across his chest and met his gaze once more. "Me neither."

He trembled, and now she knew it had been with desire. She hadn't understood back then, but she was certain of it now in light of a lifetime of experience. How many times had she known that same trembling in their first ten years of marriage, felt him that way as his limbs spread out across hers, beneath hers, up against hers.

Yes, he'd felt deeply for her back then, their first night together, and she for him. But it would not be until after their wedding that either of them would act on their feelings.

As they made their way back to his dorm that night, Abby remembered the way he held her hand, treating her like the rarest of gems, precious and unique, convincing her with every step that his words were sincere. He had never felt this way about anyone else.

Abby's father stirred in the bed beside her chair, and she let go of his hand, instantly back in the present. Without warning, his eyes flashed open, frantic as he looked about the room until he found Abby. "Where's John?"

The question pierced the silence, and she felt her heart sink. "He's home, Dad. With the kids." Her words were loud and measured, the way people talked to the aged.

"He should be with you." There was wild fear in her father's face, and his hands shook uncontrollably.

"It's okay, Dad. He's with the kids." Abby took his fingers in hers and tried to still the shaking.

The sleep was wearing off. Her father's expression was less shocked and fearful. For a long moment he looked deep into Abby's eyes; then for the first time he voiced the thing that probably lay heaviest on his heart. "There's trouble, isn't there?"

Abby's first thought was to lie to him, the same way she lied to everyone else these days. But then the tears came, and she knew it was impossible. She was too close to this man, this giant-hearted father and friend, to hide from him the thing that was killing her. She nodded, squeezing his hands gently in her own. "Yes, Dad. There's trouble."

He seemed to shrink beneath the bedcovers, and his eyes grew damp. "Are you . . . have you prayed about it?"

Abby felt a gentle smile play across her lips. Her father meant well. *Dad, if only you understood how bad things were* . . . "We have."

Her father's emotions played across his face as clearly as if they were written on his forehead. Sorrow and confusion, followed by frustration and deep, boundless pain. "It's not . . . you aren't getting a . . ."

The tears spilled onto Abby's cheeks. Had it really come to this? Wasn't she the same girl who had stood beneath the oak tree with John, barely able to think while he kissed her for the first time? Wasn't she the only girl he'd ever loved? Her tears came harder and the words lodged in her throat. She opened her mouth but nothing came out.

Now it was her father's turn to comfort. He held her hands close to his heart and ran his frail fingers over the tops of them. "Oh, Abby, you can't, honey. There's gotta be a way . . ."

Abby shook her head and struggled to find her voice. "You don't understand, Dad. There's more to it."

Darkness clouded her father's eyes. "That woman? The one on the field after the state title game?"

So even her father knew the truth. John had taken up with Charlene and in the process left everyone but Abby's blindly devoted kids aware that he was cheating on her. She hung her head, and a fresh wave of tears spilled from her eyes onto her father's bedsheets. "He says they're just friends, but it's a lie, Dad. I've found notes."

With all the effort he could muster, her father raised a single hand and wiped the tears from her cheeks. "Have you tried counseling? Christian counseling?"

Abby exhaled and caught her breath, lifting her gaze to her father's questioning one. "We've tried everything. It's more than a faith issue, Dad."

Her father's hand fell to his side and he stared sadly at her. "Nothing is beyond God, Abby. Maybe you've forgotten."

She met his gaze. "Maybe we have."

Questions flashed in his eyes, and he cleared his throat, probably trying to stop himself from breaking down and crying. After all, John was the son of his best friend. The news was bound to be devastating, regardless of his earlier suspicions about Charlene. "Have you . . . told the children?"

Abby leaned back in her chair. "We tried, but the morning we were going to tell them, Nicole announced her engagement. We decided to postpone it until after the wedding."

"So it's final; you've made your decision?"

Again Abby hung her head. "We've talked to each other, talked to counselors, tried everything, Dad. We don't see any other way."

There was silence for a moment as her father took in the news. When he didn't comment, she continued, desperate to fill the space between them with something that might help him understand. "Maybe it'll be better this way."

Anger flashed in her father's eyes for the first time since she was a small child. "It can *never* be better to divorce, Abby. Never. That's a lie from the pit of hell; mark my words."

The tears came harder now, and Abby felt her own anger rising. It wasn't her fault, after all. "Don't blame me, Dad. I'm not the one seeing someone else."

Her father raised an eyebrow enough so that she noticed. "That right? What about your writing friends, your editor?"

Alarm raced through Abby's veins. *How in the world . . . ?* "Who told you that?"

Her father waited a beat. "John. Last time he was here. I asked him how the two of you were, and he said something about you spending more time e-mailing your editor than talking to him." Her father stopped to catch his breath, and Abby realized the conversation was draining him. His arms and legs were trembling harder. "He made light of it, so I didn't think it was a problem. Until now."

Abby stood up and folded her arms, staring at the ceiling. "Oh, Dad, I don't know how it all got so ugly." She lowered her gaze to him again and wiped fresh tears from her cheeks. "I need my friendship with Stan. Sometimes he's the only one who understands what's happening in my life."

Her father's anger was gone, and in its place was a sadness unlike anything Abby had seen before. "The only thing you need is faith in Christ and a dedication to each other. If you have that . . . everything else will fall in place."

He made it sound so easy. "He's having an affair, Dad. He admitted to kissing her. It isn't as simple as you think." She made her way back to the chair and sat down again, taking his hands in hers. "Go back to sleep. I didn't mean to get you so worked up."

This time the tears that filled her father's eyes spilled onto his cheeks, and he wiped at them self-consciously. "That boy's part of our family, Abby. Don't let him go. Do whatever it takes. Please. For me, for the kids. For God."

You don't understand, Dad. She hesitated, not sure how to answer him.

"Please, Abby." He looked so pained, so earnest in his request, that she knew she had no choice but to tell him what he wanted to hear.

"Okay. I'll try harder. Really, I will. Now you get some rest before they kick me out of here for good." She held tight to her father's hands, and in a matter of minutes he was asleep again, leaving her to wrestle with the knot of emotions that made up her insides.

Losing John would be like losing a part of who she was, a piece not only of her history, but of her father's as well. Abby's heart hurt as she watched her father sleep. She'd told him the truth; it wasn't her fault. She and John had let time come between them, and now he was seeing someone else. It was simply too late to undo the damage, too far into the process of breaking up to patch things together.

Her thoughts drifted back again to their first kiss, the way John made her feel like she was the most important girl in the world, the way he'd promised to write and call, and the way he surprisingly kept his word in the coming year.

She would never forget the look on her friends' faces when he showed up at the prom with her. The dance took place in the spring, just weeks before her high-school graduation. There he was, a junior at U of M, a nationally known quarterback, dancing by her side in front of all her classmates. She wore a light blue chiffon dress and he outdid every other girl's date with his black tuxedo and pale blue vest. "They're all staring at you," she whispered during one of their slow dances. Abby loved the way he held her close but not too tight, secure enough to show the world she was his girl, but respectful of her purity at the same time.

"They're not looking at me; they're looking at you. I've never seen anyone more gorgeous than you are tonight."

He was singly devoted to her throughout the year, and the following fall she enrolled at Michigan. If there was a period in her life she would never forget, a time that would never dim in its brilliance, it was the 1978–79 school year. John led the Wolverines to a championship season, and though he lost out on the Heisman, with two games to go, it still looked like he'd be drafted. She was at every game, every practice, soaking in everything about him.

Then, in his final game that season, John dropped back to pass and couldn't find an open receiver. A linebacker spotted his vulnerability and leveled a blow against his knees that buckled his legs and caused his head to ricochet off the artificial turf. He was knocked unconscious and lay there on the field for ten minutes while team doctors worked on him from every angle.

Abby still remembered how desperately she'd prayed for him from her place in the stands. "Please, God . . . please . . ." She'd been too terrified to voice the unimaginable, to consider that he could be paralyzed or that he might even die out there on the field. Suddenly everything about the game she loved became ugly and cheap. *What's the point?* she recalled thinking. *Give up your legs, your life . . . for a football game? Please, God, let him get up . . .*

Finally John moved his feet, and Abby began breathing again. *Thank You . . . oh, thank You, God.* She couldn't bring herself to imagine how different things would have been if . . .

A medical cart took John to the locker room where Abby met him after the game. The news was better than it could have been, but it wasn't good. John had suffered a serious concussion when his head hit the cement-like turf. And worse, he had torn a ligament in his knee—an injury that would require surgery and most likely end his football career.

The doctor had been brutally honest with John. "You might find a way to get that leg in playing condition again, son, but your head can't take another blow like that one. It would be a risk for you to play."

The knee surgery took place later that month, and by March John was running sprints and getting ready for NFL scouting combines. "I can do it, Abby. My head doesn't hurt. Really."

She knew there was nothing she could say, nothing that would take away his love for the game, a love that had been in his family and hers for as long as they could remember. But in the end, she hadn't needed to say anything. He never regained the speed and mobility he'd once had, and the NFL scouts wrote him off as too slow. By April it was clear that he no longer had a career in professional football.

For a week, John was devastated. He stayed in his dorm, saw little of Abby, and said even less. But at the end of that time, he took her out for pizza and walked with her to the same spot where he'd first kissed her more than a year earlier. "I've been thinking up a plan, Abby." He touched his fingers to her cheek and studied her eyes in a way that even now made her insides melt at the memory. "If I can't play the game, I have to coach it." He drew a steadying breath. "I'm going to take another year and earn my teaching credentials. Then I can go anywhere, teach, coach. Follow my dream."

As the moon made its way up in the sky, he held out a glistening diamond ring. "Marry me, Abby. This summer. That way we can live together next year and never be apart again."

Abby glanced at the ring now, still on her finger but dulled from the years. She had been stunned back then, shocked that he had asked her so soon. But she had never been more sure of anything in her life.

She closed her eyes now and remembered again what it felt like to lose herself in John Reynolds's arms and know without a doubt that it was the place she was born to be, the life she was created to live.

"Yes! I'll marry you."

She almost said it aloud again, as she'd said it back then. John had lifted her off the ground and swung her around, setting her gently on the old wooden bench. Then he sat beside her and took her face in his hands, holding her gaze in a way that no one had been able to do before or since. "I promise, Abby, I'll never let you down. We might have hard times, sad times. But I'll be by your side forever. There could never be anyone but you for me, Abby Chapman."

Yeah, me . . . and Charlene. Abby let the cynical words simmer in her mind for a moment. *Don't do this to yourself, Abby.* She heeded her own warning and banished the thoughts. No matter where time had taken them, she and John had been beautiful together back then. Their parents had been surprised and thrilled by their announcement, and that July she and John married in a church just off campus before a crowd of several hundred. The local Ann

Arbor paper carried a picture of the two of them on the front page of the Society section with the caption "Dream Come True—Childhood Friends Make It Official."

Never in her wildest imagination had Abby ever thought for a moment that things would not work out with John Reynolds. They were together constantly that first year, whispering softly to each other in a crowd and strolling the campus hand in hand. When other people looked at them, it was with that jealous longing, that certainty that even if *they* lived a hundred years they would never experience the magic that existed between John and Abby Reynolds.

Six weeks after their honeymoon they were excited to learn that Abby was expecting, and while she freelanced articles for the university paper, John located a teaching and coaching position for the coming fall. Nicole Michelle was born April 16, 1980, and that summer John took a job teaching at Southridge High School outside Marion, Illinois. Both their families were happy for them, and his father set them up with enough money to buy a small house near the high school.

What happened to our storybook finish, Lord?

An image appeared in Abby's mind and burned itself into her conscience: John holding a three-month-old Nicole on the sidelines during football practice not long after they moved to Illinois. Abby remembered capturing the scene and storing it in her memory for another time, aware even back then that their days would fly all too quickly and that before either of them knew it, their little girl would be grown.

John had been a wonderful father, every step of the way. When Nicole was five and rode her bike into the oncoming path of a Buick while Abby was at the market, John was the one who calmly, quickly scooped her into his arms and got her to the hospital. Nicole had escaped with a broken leg and five stitches above her forehead, but John refused to let go of her hand until Abby and Kade met them there an hour later.

Even during their darkest days of parenting, the desperate moments of unimaginable grief, he'd been a pillar of strength, a beacon of love and concern for all of them.

She thought her tears had dried up long ago, but they welled once more as her father's recent words played over in her head. *"That boy's part of the family, Abby. Don't let him go . . . don't let him go . . . don't let him go."*

Abby wished with all her heart there were some way she could fulfill her father's request. But no matter how many happy memories she had, no matter if John had long ago been the man of her dreams, and even though he'd been the most amazing father through every stage of their parenting, there was nothing she could do to keep him now.

Abby kissed her father's cheek and stood to leave. How could she hold on to John when he was already gone?

She walked through the front door twenty minutes later and saw Kade sprawled on the family sofa, NFL highlights playing on the television screen.

"Hey, honey, how was your day?" Abby did her best to sound upbeat. With a lifetime of memories rushing through the channels of her mind, she was bound to look preoccupied, even deeply depressed, unless she made a concerted effort to appear otherwise.

Kade sat up and stared curiously at her. "Come here for a minute, will you, Mom?"

Abby caught a note of concern in Kade's voice, and she

felt her heart skip a beat. Had John done something at school? Made a scene with Charlene maybe? She hated this life of pretending, not knowing when someone might discover their secret. *Please, God, help me say the right thing . . .* "Okay, I'm all yours." She plopped down beside him, her tone light and playful while her heart beat up in her throat.

"Mom, how did you and Dad get such a cool thing between you?"

Something inside her relaxed. "A cool thing?"

Kade smiled and for a moment looked like the young boy he'd once been, quizzical and absorbed with love for her. "Yeah, you know. The way you aren't all jealous and everything. Maybe that's why you guys have such a good marriage."

There was a lump in Abby's throat, and she swallowed, struggling as she uttered a forced laugh. "Where did all this come from?"

Kade leaned back and crossed his arms across his chest. "Well, like Ms. Denton. The other day I came into Dad's room, and she and Dad were holding hands." Kade's eyes flashed with concern. "Not like anything was happening between them, you know? Dad was just praying for her, which at first I thought was kind of weird."

Abby's insides suddenly hurt, and she slumped over a bit. *Act normal, Abby. Don't think about it; don't cry. Keep listening.* "Yeah, I could see that."

"Anyway, now that I've had time to think about it, maybe that's why you and Dad have such a great thing between you. There's no jealousy. I mean, the trust between you guys is something else." He shook his head. "I asked Dad what you'd think of him praying with Ms. Denton, and he said you already knew Ms. Denton was having trouble, and it was no big deal that sometimes he prayed with her."

Kade's face lit up into a grin again. "The more I thought about it, the more I realized how cool it was."

Abby uttered a pinched laugh, but Kade didn't seem to notice. "I want my wife to be just like you. That way, she won't freak out every time I talk to another woman."

Her voice was missing again, and Abby struggled to find it. "Well, that's good, son. I'm glad it made a good impression on you."

She stood and stretched, desperate to find a place where she could sort through her feelings, someplace away from the curious eyes of her children. Sean entered the room and walked up to her, throwing his arms around her neck. "Hey, Mom, how's Grandpa?"

"Good. He sends his love."

Sean nodded and continued across the room to an oversized sofa chair. It wasn't yet two o'clock in the afternoon and already the sun seemed to be setting, as if the whole world was in mourning for all that Abby was going through. Her anger at John was raging just beneath the image she was trying to maintain, and she needed to be alone before she exploded into a heap of fury and tears. Her sons were caught up in the television again, and she gazed out the front window, doing all she could to appear normal. "Is Nicole home?"

Kade stretched out his feet. "No, she's out with Matt. She'll be home after dinner."

Abby nodded and held her breath. "Dad?"

"He's at the club with Joe."

Good. He'd be gone awhile. Joe was one of the assistant football coaches, and the two could spend hours working out and playing pickup basketball with the guys at the club. Abby kept herself from racing out of the room, instead making her way slowly up the stairs into the guest room. There, curled on the bed, she buried her face in a pillow and gave way to the rage that welled within her.

Waves of tears assaulted her, and she hit the mattress with her fist over and over again. He had promised not to make a scene! Swore he would stay away from Charlene for the next six months. Yet there he was, holding the woman's hand in his classroom for the whole world to see. Who else besides Kade had walked in on them that afternoon? Abby could barely breathe, but she didn't care. She dug her face deeper into the pillow and allowed another onset of sobs. Poor Kade. How would he feel when they told the kids the truth? He would know that his father had lied about praying with Charlene, lied about many things.

"Great example, John," she whispered, easing back from the pillow and reaching for a tissue on the nightstand, "way to go."

Time wound back, and she could see herself walking down the hallway of Marion High, humming a happy tune, bringing John dinner since he'd had to work late grading tests. Their relationship had been badly strained back then, too, and the dinner was Abby's way of taking her counselor's suggestion to look for ways to be kind to John. She remembered actually feeling sorry for him because he was putting in so many hours on the football field and then relegated to overtime in the classroom as well. It had been eight o'clock, long since dark, and the rest of the school was deserted. Abby finally reached the end of the corridor and opened the door to John's classroom without knocking.

Her breath had caught in her throat at the sight of them. John and Charlene, standing near his desk, locked in a full-length embrace.

They pulled apart immediately, of course, and Abby—desperately unsure of how to respond—refused to run away. Instead, she kept her angry feelings inside and wandered into the classroom. "Hello, Charlene. Hope I'm not interrupting." She remembered smiling intently at the woman and then at John.

"Uh, no . . . I was just saying good-bye."

Charlene tripped over a few sentences, alternately trying to explain herself and voice reasons why she needed to leave.

Abby would never forget the anger and pain she'd felt when only she and John remained in his classroom. It was exactly how she felt now. Suspicions were one thing; facts were another. Her gut ached from crying so hard, but buckets of tears wouldn't ease the rage that burned within her.

There was a sound in the hallway outside, and before Abby could prepare herself, the guest-room door opened and John walked in. She faced him like a child caught in an act of disobedience, and he stared at her strangely, his eyebrows knit together. "Abby, what's wrong? The boys said you were making dinner."

She wanted to punch him, shake him, make him wake up to the pain he was causing her. Instead, she blew her nose and let her eyes bore into him, infusing him with some of the hate she felt. "Kade told me about your little . . . *prayer* meeting." Her words were barely more than a hiss, and she noticed that her arms were actually shaking from the fury that welled inside her heart.

John's face went blank. "Prayer meeting?"

Abby huffed. "Hard to keep all the lies straight, isn't it, John?"

He entered the room and shut the door behind him. "Abby, I have no idea what you're talking about. What prayer meeting? And why are you crying?"

He honestly didn't remember. How much must have been happening between Charlene and him if Kade's discovery wasn't even something he had logged in his memory. "Think back. The one with Charlene, remember? Kade walked into your classroom and found you and that . . . that woman holding hands." Every word was a dagger, but instead of diffusing her emotions, they intensified as she spoke. "And you told him the two of you were *praying*. Sound familiar?"

A tired breath escaped from John's lungs, and he lowered himself onto the foot of the bed. "I didn't know what else to tell him."

Abby clenched her fist and punched it with all her might into the headboard. Three of her knuckles started bleeding, but she didn't care. She wiped the blood on her jeans and glared at her husband. John's eyes were wide. "That's right, I'll punch the bed if I want to!"

There was a beat where John seemed frantically to search for something to say. "It wasn't like that. I was—"

"Spare me."

From downstairs came Kade's voice. "Hey, everything okay up there? I thought I heard something break."

John cleared his throat and yelled, "Everything's fine. Your mother dropped something, that's all."

Abby shook her head and stared at him in disbelief. "Is that what we're going to do for the next six months, John?

Lie to the kids every time one of them sees you with Charlene?"

He was on his feet and began pacing, rubbing the back of his neck. "What do you want to do, Abby, tell them the truth? That I'm trying to stay out of a full-blown affair with Charlene, and that you're so mad at me you're punching holes in the furniture? Is that a better option?"

Abby shook her head and stared at him. *He doesn't comprehend what he's done wrong . . .* "Look at me."

John stopped pacing and met her gaze. "What do you want from me, Abby? I didn't know Kade was going to walk in on us."

"I asked you to stay away from her. Six months, John. *Six months.*"

He sighed, no longer trying to defend himself. "I'm trying, Abby. I didn't invite her in; she came on her own. So I told her I needed time, told her to give me space until after Nicole's wedding. And whether you want to believe it or not, she actually understood. She was just telling me she would do whatever she could to make it easier on me when . . . when Kade walked in."

Every word that came from John's mouth was like an assault. How *dare* Charlene even *need* to be told to stay away? Who had led her to believe John would want her help to get through the next six months?

The answer hung in the room like an executioner's sword: John, of course.

He had allowed himself to get that close to Charlene, and now Abby could picture the scene in his classroom as if she and not Kade had been the one to discover them. Charlene would have been almost inconsolable at the thought of a six-month silence between her and John. Of course he'd taken her hands to comfort her. If Kade hadn't walked in, who knew what else might have happened?

John was waiting, staring at her, a man at the end of his rope and out of options. "I'm sorry, Abby."

Abby hated the way she felt, the way the anger ripped at her heart and made her feel like a monster inside. "John Reynolds . . . I hate you." Through gritted teeth, she fired each word with as much venom as she could muster. "Get out of here before I walk down those stairs and tell the kids the truth."

John's gaze narrowed as he studied her. "I can't believe what you've become, Abby. What we've become . . ." His expression softened. "I don't know what to . . ." He released a heavy sigh and shrugged. In all her life she'd only seen him look that sad one other time. "I'm sorry, Abby." Then without saying another word, he left the room.

As he shut the door and made his way down the stairs, she hurt in places she hadn't known existed. *Come back, John. Don't you care? Can't you tell me you'll forget about her, that she's not important to you and that you still love me?* She balled up her aching, bleeding hand again, and this time punched the pillow. Again and again and again . . . until the rage inside her subsided and gave way to an ocean of sadness.

Help me, God . . . I don't know what to do anymore. Make the time go fast, please. I can't bear to live with him, knowing he's in love with her.

Love bears all things; love never ends . . .

For most of her adult life, Abby had taken one thing for granted: if the Bible said it, she believed it. But as she lay there sobbing in a way that threatened to consume her, the scripture that came to mind made her consider that perhaps God's Word wasn't truth at all.

The verse played again in her mind. *Love bears all things . . . love never ends . . . never ends . . . never ends.*

It was a lie; it had to be. The love between John and her could not possibly bear this. While their daughter dreamed and planned about love's beginning, she and John were plotting and planning love's end. Either they had never loved at all—and Abby knew without a doubt that they had—or this time Scripture was wrong.

Because the love they'd once shared, the love that had shone like a lighthouse among the shipwrecks of other marriages, was absolutely, undoubtedly over.

Love ended, all right.

She cradled her swollen fingers close to her chest and allowed another wave of tears. The terminal illness their bond was suffering had grown for years, and in the end their love had died a predictably painful death. In a matter of months they'd have the proper documentation, the paper grave marker to prove it.

Abby sat there a long while until she began to drift off, the same words, same feelings playing over and over in her mind.

I hate you, John Reynolds . . . I hate you . . . I hate you. I hate you.

Twelve

It was Super Bowl Sunday, a holiday that ranked up there with Christmas and Easter in the Reynoldses' house, but Abby and Nicole had agreed to spend the morning and early afternoon looking for wedding dresses. The day out with Jo Harter had produced nothing but endless conversation, so this time Nicole was determined to find at least one gown she liked.

They were in the dressing room, and Abby was closing the zipper on the fifth dress in an hour when Nicole's mood seemed to darken. Ever since the comment from Kade, Abby had been extrasensitive to each of the children, aware that they might hear something about their dad and Charlene or pick up on the tensions between their parents. "You okay, honey?" Abby fluffed Nicole's hair over the back of the dress and stood back. "Oh, Nick, it's gorgeous."

Abby only used her pet name for her daughter once in a

while anymore. Nicole tilted her head and looked intently at Abby. "Dad's been quieter than usual lately. He's happy about me getting married, right? I mean, he likes Matt, doesn't he?"

Every inch of Abby's body was on instant alert. "Yes, sweetie, of course he likes him." She paused, searching for the right words. "He's been busy with school, that's all."

Nicole studied her reflection in the mirror and tugged at the dress a few times until she was satisfied with how it fit. "The sleeves are too plain."

Abby took in the details on the sleeves of the dress and thought them simple, but lovely. But this wasn't the time to argue with Nicole. "You're right. Let's see if we can find a few more."

Nicole hesitated and stared at Abby once more. "Kade said Dad's been praying with Ms. Denton." Nicole's pained expression gave Abby the sense that her daughter was uncomfortable, as though she were opening a deep, dark topic. "That bugs me, Mom. Doesn't she know he's happily married?"

Alarms sounded in Abby's heart and soul, but she worked to keep her face from showing it. *See what you've done, John? Why couldn't you stay away from her?* Abby angled her head and crossed her arms. "Well . . . I can understand how you feel. It bugs me too." *Pick your words here, Abby. In a few months she'll know the truth . . .* "Your dad's doing his best; that's all I know."

Nicole thought about that for a moment, then shrugged. "Yeah, I guess. There's just something about Ms. Denton I don't like. She's always flirting with Dad, giggling around him. It's obnoxious."

If only John could have seen through Charlene as easily as Nicole had. Abby uttered an appropriate laugh. "Your dad can take care of himself."

Nicole smiled and bent her neck as Abby unzipped the dress. "So everything's okay with you guys?"

Abby knew her daughter well enough to know that this was the heart of her concern, the fear that every child lives with but rarely voices. And even now, with Nicole grown and about to begin a marriage of her own, the childlike antennae were still up, her concerns still deep and frightful at the thought of her parents in trouble.

"We're fine. Don't worry about us." She helped Nicole slip out of the dress and waited while her daughter donned her skirt and sweater once more. "This is supposed to be your day, remember? We have a wedding gown to find."

By the day's end Nicole had found the perfect dress, and Abby was grateful that in her excitement her daughter had forgotten all thoughts of her parents and whether they were having trouble or not. After they were home she holed away in her room while Abby cut up vegetables and made snack trays for the game. Like always, they would have a house full—several of John's coaches and their families, a few players, and the boys' friends. Abby didn't care who came over as long as she kept busy. The busier she was, the less she needed to find ways to avoid John.

Her heart still ached from their blowup the day before, and she wanted more than anything to get through Super Bowl Sunday without a conversation or time alone with him.

Just before kickoff Nicole bounded halfway down the stairs and stopped at the landing. "Is Matt here yet?" Her voice was brimming with excitement, and Abby guessed her daughter wanted to show off her wedding gown.

"Not yet." She placed a stack of carrot sticks on the platter and ran her fingers under the water.

"He said he'd be a few minutes late." Kade's voice came from the next room. "What're you hiding on the stairs for?"

"Ta-da! Mom, come here. I have my dress on. Quick, before Matt comes."

Abby dried her hands on a towel and headed for the TV room. Although the gown had looked beautiful on Nicole in the dressing room an hour earlier, now she had taken time to fix her hair and slip on a pair of heels. The sight of her elegantly posed before her father and brothers caused Abby's breath to catch in her throat. She stopped midstep and let her mouth drop open. *Lord, she looks just like I did at her age. Have twenty-two years passed since I modeled my own dress in the weeks before marrying John?*

Before she could speak, John muted the television and stared wide-eyed at their daughter. "Nicki, it's gorgeous. You look . . . all grown up." His gaze caught Abby's, almost as if by mistake, and what she saw there mirrored all the things she was feeling. *Did we really create this woman-child? Have the years flown by as quickly for you as they have for me? And how come when our little girl is celebrating love, we're finding new ways every day to destroy ours?*

Abby looked away, refusing the subtle intimacy of the moment, and turned her attention where it belonged. To Nicole. "Sweetheart, the dress is perfect."

And it was, as right as if it'd been handmade for her. The bodice clung to her in fitted white satin, marked by sequins and fine embroidery. Sheer and subtly decorated with additional sequins, the sleeves ended with a wide cuff edged in elegant lace that lay against the backs of her hands. The layered satin skirt fell away gracefully, edged in the same lace as the sleeves and barely skimming the floor in the front. At the back it extended into a breathtaking train and a series of sequins and more embroidery that ascended to the bodice and made Nicole's waist look beyond tiny.

"I remember when my waist was that small." Abby angled her head, gazing at Nicole. *Back when I was the only one who could turn John's head.*

Abby glanced in his direction and found him staring at her again. This time she scowled, doing her best to discourage him from making contact. They had nothing to talk about. Any nostalgic glances were only bound to make things more difficult. When she looked again, he'd directed his attention completely on Nicole.

"Matt's one lucky guy." John stood up and stretched his bad leg, the one that had suffered the injury two decades earlier. It was something he did often—something most people missed—but Abby knew how badly John's knee still bothered him, how it stiffened up on cold days and caused him to limp first thing in the morning.

John took Nicole in his arms and hugged her close. "When did you get to be such a beautiful young woman, Nicki?"

The sight of John and Nicole together was too much for Abby. *If you cared about her at all, you wouldn't be holding hands with another woman in your classroom.* She kept her thoughts to herself and turned back to the kitchen. "Matt'll be here soon, Nick."

She heard her daughter gasp lightly and kiss her father on the cheek. "Gotta run. Don't say a word to Matt." And with that she was back up the stairs, completely unaware of the tension between her parents.

John was caught up in the second quarter when the phone rang. Abby had long since locked herself into her office, so he grabbed the cordless receiver and clicked the talk button.

"Hello?"

John thought he heard a rustling sound, but otherwise only silence. "Hello?" He was about to hang up when he heard her voice.

"John, it's me. Charlene."

A dozen emotions tore into John's heart. Surprise, elation, guilt, anger. He waited a beat so he wouldn't say anything he'd regret. Especially with a roomful of people seated around him watching the game. "Uh . . . hi."

She released a heavy sigh. "I know I shouldn't be calling you at home . . . I shouldn't be calling you at all. I just . . . I feel so alone, John. I didn't know what else to do."

There were times when hearing Charlene's voice sent unspeakable feelings coursing through his body. But here, in plain view of his children on a day that had always been theirs alone, John was torn between wanting to help her and knowing he should hang up on her. "We're watching the game, of course. And you?"

"You can't talk; I knew it. I'm sorry, John . . . I'll let you go."

"Is everything okay?"

Kade cast him a strange glance as soon as he asked the question, but John wasn't worried. He was willing to lie about it if he had to. If Charlene was in some sort of trouble, he wanted to be available for her.

There was silence for a moment, and he heard Charlene crying. "I feel like . . . like I'm in limbo or something, like there's no hope or promises or future for us." She paused and John's heart lurched. *Why is she doing this now? When she knows my family is around?* When he didn't speak, she continued. "I love you, John. I wasn't sure until you asked me to stay away. But now . . . now I'm sure. I love you like I've never loved anyone else. But I can't wait around forever . . ."

Careful, watch your tone. "I understand that." What did she expect him to say? Already there were bound to be questions, at least from Kade.

Charlene sighed. "Oh, I don't know . . . I never should have called in the first place. I'm sorry."

Again John was at a loss for words. He could hardly make her flowery promises now, even if the kids weren't listening to every word. "Right, well, thanks for calling."

"John, wait . . . I know I shouldn't have called you, but do me this one thing. If you think we have a chance . . . after Nicole's wedding, I mean . . . tell me. Please. Tell me you think the Rams are the best team no matter what happens in the game. That way I'll know at least that you care, that you want to be with me as much as I want to be with you."

John thought about that for a moment.

Flee immorality, son. What God has joined together—

The voice that surely belonged to God changed and became Abby's from the other day. *"I hate you, John . . . I hate you."*

"John? Did you hear me?"

He closed his eyes and massaged the bridge of his nose with his thumb and forefinger. Too many voices for a Sunday of football. How was he supposed to know what he wanted? Abby's words of hate continued to play in his mind, and the image of her spewing rage took up residence in his heart. Why not make promises to Charlene? He cared about her, didn't he? And things were only going to get worse where Abby was concerned.

John cleared his throat. Charlene knew him well—knew that his favorite team was the Rams and that no matter who was in the room, the words he was about to say would not sound unusual. Especially as well as St. Louis had done in the play-offs. "I don't feel this way all the time, but right now I'd have to say the Rams had the best season all year."

There, he'd said it. It was true. If he and Charlene could make it through the next six months without spending time together, John had every reason to think he'd have his second chance at life with Charlene Denton.

"What do you mean you don't feel that way all the time?"

John clenched his teeth. Why was she pushing him? He exhaled deliberately and forced a laugh. "You know me; I've liked the Rams for a long time."

Charlene hesitated for a moment and then released a childlike shout for joy. "John Reynolds, you've made me the happiest girl in all of Illinois. I'd wait a lifetime for you now that I know how you feel."

"Okay, well I better go. The game's just heating up."

"All right, I'm sorry." Charlene was contrite, but her happiness still spilled over into her voice. "And what I said about being discreet, I still mean it . . . I'm here for you whenever you want me."

Her last words hit their mark, and John could feel his cheeks getting hot. "Right, well, I'll call you later."

He hung up and immediately Kade caught his gaze.

"Who was that?"

Even though he'd expected the question, John wasn't prepared. "A teacher."

One of the coaches turned to him. "Who?"

Way to go, Reynolds. Lie about a teacher in front of a room full of school employees. "Uh . . . Joe Jackson, track coach. Just wanted to see what I thought of the game."

Another coach joined the conversation. "Jackson called you? I thought he was in Palm Springs with his wife?"

Cold fear ran through John's veins, and he suddenly felt like everyone in the room knew he was lying. "Come to think of it, maybe he was in Palm Springs. He didn't say."

The questions stopped as the room gradually turned back to the game. Only then did John realize how desperate he'd become. He had just promised forever to a woman who was not his wife in front of a dozen family and friends, and now his heart was beating almost out of his chest as payment for his choices. *I'm a rotten excuse for a man.*

It was halftime already, and while John made small talk with his friends about the game statistics, Kade began rattling off facts about the eagle.

"Okay, listen to this." The men gave him their attention, and Kade cleared his throat, glancing at the rough draft of his senior paper. "An eagle almost never eats anything dead." He raised a single finger. "But if it does, if something happens to make it sick, it flies to the highest rock it can find, spreads itself across it, and lets the sun soak out all the poison."

The analogy was so strong John wondered if Kade suspected his father of deceit. *Or is this just Your timing, Lord?*

I'm here for you, son. Remember the height from which you have fallen . . .

John banished the thought and focused on Kade, who was standing now, enjoying the attention as he carried on with more eagle information. John was still thinking about the poisoned eagle, who after getting in trouble at least had the sense to take his pain to the rock and let the sun make him strong again. He had a Rock he could go to, a Son that would certainly make him strong like before.

Repent! Remember the height from which you have—

John blinked away the warning. The trouble was, he didn't want that kind of help. Not now. Not when his wife had turned into a shrew and his closest friend, a beautiful young woman, thought the sun rose and set on him alone. What would God know of trouble like that?

A pain worked its way through his chest, and he became completely unaware of the others, their conversations about eagles and whether they were or weren't involving him. *I'll probably have a heart attack and go straight to hell.* John wiped a thin layer of sweat from his forehead and tried to understand how his life had gotten so completely out of hand. And how come the love of his life, the woman he had longed for since his childhood days, not only didn't love him . . .

She hated him.

Abby had heard the phone ring and figured it was for one of the kids. Either way she wasn't coming out of the office, not today. Her job as snackmaker was over, and now she needed to send in a piece for *Woman's Day*. Her Internet connection was good on the first attempt, and the opening screen showed her she had mail. Two clicks later she was into a lengthy letter from Stan.

Everything about her editor was as surreal as the cyber-world itself. Stan was the divorced father of two and the senior editor at one of the largest magazines in the country, one she wrote for at least every other month. Though she had started her freelance career with bit pieces for small Christian publications, in time she'd worked her way up so that now the articles she wrote were read by more than a million readers and brought her thousands of dollars each.

Now and then she missed the chance to share her faith in print the way she had when she'd written for the Christian magazines, but then these days there wasn't much to share anyway. Besides, she would need the extra income once she and John were living apart.

Her eyes found the beginning of Stan's note.

Hey, Abby . . . maybe it's my imagination but something told me this weekend's been a little rough on you. John and the other woman, maybe? Just a guess. Anyway, I hope not. In fact, even though it sounds crazy, I really hope things still work out for you two. And if they don't . . . well, I can think of at least one man who will celebrate the day you're finally free.

She read his note again. Was there any doubt that this man was interested in her? At first his letters had been purely professional, but two years ago he asked about her marriage in a note that was clearly more personal than the others.

Abby had written back, "Let's just say I'm not ready to give you an article on marital bliss."

The next week Stan surprised her with a bouquet of flowers. The card inside read, "To the prettiest woman in Illinois . . . John doesn't know how lucky he is."

It had been easy to write even that off as professional

flirtation, the kind of transaction that happened in the business world, a way to convince Abby to write primarily for their magazine and not another. Then his e-mails changed. There would be the usual discussion of her articles and developing ideas, but then he'd add a line or two that went far deeper, into territories of her heart that had been unexplored for years.

People who feel the most and deepest become writers . . . and inevitably they marry those who can't feel at all.

Or another time: *In the depths of my soul is a place unlocked only by the prose of a wordsmith. And you, my dear Abby, are the most accomplished wordsmith I know.*

It wasn't long before Abby began looking forward to his mail, signing on to the Internet twice a day in hopes that maybe there'd be a letter from him. Of course the timing couldn't have been more perfect because that same season Abby began getting weekly reports from her friends.

"What's up with John and Charlene Denton?" Rosemary from the booster club wanted to know. Rosemary was a blonde busybody whose very life centered around the happenings at Marion High. Her report was the first in a long line.

Next it was Betty from the school office, calling to say, "I hate to be the bearer of bad news, but rumor is that Charlene Denton has the hots for your husband. You know that, right, Abby?"

And in the football stands, Jill, one of the coaches' wives, asked her, "Doesn't it bug you that Charlene hangs out at practice each day? If she was after my husband the way she's after yours, I'd get down there and tell her off myself."

One parent to another in the school office: "Is Mr.

Reynolds still married? I always see him with Ms. Denton. They sure make a cute couple."

"They're together every afternoon from what I hear . . ."

The comments continued like so many painful, pelting balls of hail until Abby would have had to be blind to miss the storm gathering in the not-so-far distance. Whenever she would bring it up, John would get frustrated and deny any wrongdoing.

"People want to see us fail, Abby," he'd say. "Let's not give 'em a reason, okay?"

After a month of knowing about Charlene and receiving more e-mails from Stan, Abby broke down and bared her heart to the man. She could still remember the letter she wrote the first time she let him see inside her soul. *It feels like all our lives John and I have been creating this intricate quilt, stitched together with a hundred colors and patterns from stormy grays to brilliant yellows. And now, when it should finally be taking shape, we're both standing by and watching it unravel.*

Suddenly life is all about him, his work, his career. He's too caught up in himself to notice that I'm balancing the house and the kids and my writing, all while picking up after everyone else. I feel like we're becoming strangers . . .

She had seen Stan's picture by then and knew him to be at least five years older than she with a full head of white hair and the average build of a professional. Certainly not the physical specimen John had always been, but then maybe that was better. Maybe beauty lasted longer when it came from inside a person.

Abby scanned the rest of Stan's note and allowed her eyes to linger on the last few lines: *I've been through it before, Ab . . . if things get really bad, don't hesitate to call.*

I'm here for you always.

Here for you always . . . here for you always . . .

Where had she heard those words before? Maybe a million years ago from John, but weren't they somewhere in the Bible too? Wasn't that one of God's promises, that He'd never leave His people, never forsake them?

"Ah, but those words are for faithful hearts," she whispered into the stillness of her office, barely aware of the enthusiastic cheers going up at the other end of the house where the game was probably heading into the fourth quarter. She closed her eyes and thought about the Lord, how sweet it had once been to meet with Him in private each morning and seek His plan, His way for her life.

She stared again at the note from Stan, and her fingers began typing out a response. *It was good to hear from you, good to know that someone, somewhere, cared enough to ask how I was . . .*

Her fingers continued to dance across the keyboard, baring her heart, her soul, the deep-seated feelings she could no longer share with John. Other than their children, she shared nothing at all with the man she had once loved, the man she married. Because no matter what lies John told her there was no denying the truth—he was having an affair.

Yes, things were different now. John had made a choice to love someone else; he'd chosen on purpose to be unfaithful. She stared at the note she'd written to Stan and hit the send button.

The moment the mail was gone, she was hit square in the gut with the reality of their situation. No matter what lies she told herself, no matter how badly she wanted to blame John, the truth was suddenly clearer than water: John wasn't the only one being unfaithful.

Thirteen

THE LAST THING ABBY WANTED TO DO THAT Thursday night was sit across the table from Jo Harter and listen to another monologue about Denny. But the idea of getting out of the house and finally finishing Nicole's scrapbook was too appealing to turn down.

"This is my first time scrappin', Abby. I've cut out pictures and done some thinkin' on it, but I haven't actually started Matt's scrapbook, so this is all brand new to me. In other words, I'm as wide open for suggestions as a great white at breakfast time. Just fire away any old time you have an idea, Abby . . ."

Not more fish stories, please.

Jo caught a quick breath and kept talking. It had been an hour of monologue while Abby painstakingly laid out the photos and news clippings and dance programs that made up Nicole's eighth-grade year. Despite the constant rush of wind coming from Jo's direction,

Abby was grateful for a night away from John. Being near him left her torn between detesting him and longing for some far-off yesterday when they still loved each other.

Abby had just applied the glue to the final photo in a layout when Jo asked the question. It was the one everyone knew was taboo, the one friends and family alike had avoided for nearly two decades.

"Matt tells me you lost a little girl; is that right?"

As soon as the words were spoken, Abby's hands felt leaden, unable to move, and her heart took an eternity to decide whether it might actually continue to beat. *Matt tells me you lost a little girl . . . lost a little girl . . . lost a little girl . . .* The words ricocheted in her heart, poking holes into a wound that had never quite healed.

Haley Ann.

Her face filled Abby's memory until all she could see was their precious second daughter. Even with all the pain their separation was causing, those were easily the darkest days of her life with John.

Haley Ann. Sweet little Haley Ann.

Abby didn't have to think about how old the child would be today if she'd lived. She knew it as surely as she knew her own name or the way home after a long vacation: Haley Ann would have been nineteen, as lovely as Nicole and more excited than any of them about her sister's wedding. She'd have been maid of honor, no doubt. Nicole's best friend.

Haley Ann.

The silence was deafening, and Abby realized Jo was waiting for an answer. She blinked back the tears that burned in her eyes and without looking up tried to think of the right words. "Yes. We did. She was . . . she was very young."

Even Jo had the sense not to rush into a monologue on the topic of young, dead children. Instead she waited nearly a minute, and when she continued, her voice was softer than before. "I'm sorry, Abby. It must be harder than the steel trap over a sewer drain."

Abby nodded, embarrassed that she was unable to control her tears. When Jo looked down at her photographs, Abby dabbed quickly at her cheeks, stopping the watery trail from landing squarely on her scrapbook and ruining pictures that would have been impossible to replace.

Haley Ann. Was that when Abby's faith had taken a turn for the worse? It hadn't seemed so at the time, back when her ties to the Lord had been her only assurance that one day she'd hold her daughter again, cradle her in her arms in a place called eternity. But really, now that she looked back, God could have given her second daughter more time on earth. What sense was there in allowing a precious angel like Haley Ann to be born into this world only to take her back four months—

"Was she older than Nicole?"

Abby wanted to curse at the woman, beg her to stop asking questions about the one place in her heart where no one trespassed. But logic told her Jo meant well. Abby summoned her strength, ignoring the way fresh tears blurred her vision, and without gazing up she searched desperately for her voice. "She was . . . she was younger. Eighteen months."

Jo squirmed in her chair. "I know you probably don't talk about her much, Abby, but since you and me's gonna be family from here on out, I hope you don't mind my questions. I never knew anyone who lost a child so young. Most people say it's the death knell for a marriage. But you and John, I mean, look at you two. Still going strong after all these years. You'd never know the two of you'd been through something awful like that."

Despite the photographs spread out before her, a different picture came into focus. She and John at the hospital emergency room saying good-bye to the lifeless body of little Haley Ann. SIDS, the doctors had said. Sudden death, a risk for any infant. And there was John, T-shirt and gym shorts, tears streaming down his rugged, handsome cheeks, cradling the baby in his arms as though he could somehow love her back to life. Abby could still see him, still feel the tears shaking his body, still hear his voice. *"Dear God, I loved her."* She remembered how he wrapped his arms more closely around their baby's lifeless little body, protecting her the way he hadn't been able to when she lay dying in her crib. "Haley Ann . . . my precious girl, Haley Ann . . ."

The image of John and their second daughter stayed in Abby's mind, burning its way into her consciousness until she couldn't take it another moment. "Excuse me." She pushed herself away from the craft table, hurried into a back bathroom, and dropped herself on the closed lid of the toilet. As real as Haley Ann been, there was no room in Abby's life for thoughts of her now.

"Why did you take her from us? Why?"

The whispered question bounced around the tiled bathroom walls and came back to her. There were no more answers today than there had been back when Haley Ann died. And though that secret place in Abby's heart kept Haley Ann alive, monitored her milestones and birthdays, she never allowed herself to drift back to the day when she found her baby girl facedown in her crib, motionless and not breathing.

Abby clenched her fists and the tears came with a force that was almost violent. *Why here, God? At the craft store?* Couldn't she have had a neutral response to Jo Harter's question? Would it take another twenty years before mention of Haley Ann didn't ignite a bonfire of emotions?

Five minutes passed, then ten, and there was a soft knocking at the door. Abby's heart rate doubled. *Don't make me explain myself, God, please.* She swallowed hard. "What?" Her throat sounded thick from the effects of her tears.

"Abby? It's me—Jo. You all right?"

If Abby had made a line of people she might choose to befriend in this, her season of letting go, Jo Harter would have most certainly been at the end. The woman was all frosting and no cake, too caught up in surface conversation to understand the workings of the heart. Still, they were about to be linked by the marriage of their children, and Abby would not be responsible for doing anything that might alienate her. Even now, when all Abby wanted was to disappear through a crack in the mortar and find herself under the covers of their guest-room bed.

"I'm fine. I'll be out in a minute."

There was a beat. *Make her believe it, please . . .*

"All right. I was getting a little nervous out there by myself. Wasn't sure if you were sick or something."

Sick of your questions . . . "I'm fine. Really. I'll be right out."

When Jo had moved away from the door, Abby stood and splashed cold water on her face. There was no hiding the fact that she'd been crying, but most of the women would be too involved in their scrapbooking to notice her tear-stained face. Drawing a deep breath, she refused to think another minute about Haley Ann and the time in her life when she had needed John Reynolds just to make it through the day.

She looked at her reflection in the mirror. "Focus on the here and now, Abby." Her heart seemed to toughen some in response. She could do this, go back out there and face Jo and whatever other questions she had, finish an evening of photo layouts, and make it home. She could do it all without giving in to the pressing urge to go back in time, back to Haley Ann's birth and all that their lives had been that year.

Forget about it, Abby. Think about today.

With a resolve she hadn't known she was capable of, she drew a deep breath and returned to the craft table. The rest of the night, despite Jo's questions and well-meaning attempt to steer the conversation back to small talk, Abby hid behind her heart's iron gates and refused to let herself feel.

Not until she came home at half past ten that evening and found her entire family asleep did she do the thing she'd wanted to do since Jo first brought up the topic. Moving quietly so as not to wake them, she bundled into a parka that would protect her from even the most frigid temperatures. Then she wrapped scarves around her neck and head and donned a pair of thermal gloves. Grabbing a folding chair from the garage, she trudged outside through the snow to the pier, opened it, and sat down, gazing out at the moonlit reflection on the icy lake.

Had it really been nineteen years?

The cold made its way through a crack in her scarves,

and she pulled them more tightly. Whenever she needed time alone, space to think and dream and remember how to be again, Abby came here. To the pier: winter, spring, summer, or fall. The weather made no difference.

She remembered the dates like it was yesterday. Haley Ann, born October 24, 1981, an hour after the league football game against Southridge High. Dead just four months later, February 28, 1982. Nights like this it seemed as though Haley Ann had never really died at all, as though maybe she was asleep upstairs in the room next to Nicole, as much a part of their family as Kade or Sean or any of them.

Abby's body adjusted to the cold, and she relaxed. Across the backdrop of the shimmering lake she watched pictures take shape, saw scenes come to life again as though they were happening for the first time. Her pregnancy had been a dream, and more than once John had whispered to her that this child, this second baby, would certainly be a boy.

"You know, Abby . . . to carry on the tradition."

He'd been teasing of course, and as her due date neared he no longer even joked about having a boy. "I'm sure it's a girl. As precious as Nicole and as perfect as you. What could be better than being surrounded by princesses?"

And sure enough, when he arrived at the hospital after the football game in time to join her in the delivery room, they learned together that he'd been right. There was nothing difficult or remarkable about the delivery, nothing that might lend even a shadow of foreboding that this little girl was anything but the picture of health. Her skin was pink almost from the moment she was born, and her cries came in short bursts that sounded more like the tinkling of her older sister's laughter than the wailing of a lusty newborn.

"I knew it, Abby girl; she's perfect. Another precious princess for the Reynolds castle."

She could still hear him, see him holding his tiny daughter, cooing at her, welcoming her to the world. "Only the very best princesses have the good sense to be born after a football game is over . . ." He sang to her and whispered silly nothings to her while Abby fell asleep exhausted.

The next morning when Abby woke, there was John, long legs stretched across the hospital room, one hand on Haley Ann's back as she lay in the bassinet beside him. Abby remembered well the feeling of joy that grew in her heart that morning, the way she'd imagined only sunshine and rainbows for all the days that lay ahead. Her mother was down from Wisconsin watching Nicole, and later that day the group held an informal birthday party for the newborn with cake and streamers and balloons and a song that Haley Ann slept right through.

"She's *my* sister, right, Mommy?" Nicole angled her head lovingly, putting her nose so close to her baby sister's the two were almost touching.

"Yes, she's all yours, Nicole."

Abby had imagined the fun these two would have, growing up together, sharing a room and secrets and clothes and friends. They would be inseparable, not like Abby and her sister, who was four years younger and too caught up in her own life to have much of a friendship with Abby.

Nicole and Haley Ann.

Not long after Abby brought the newborn home, she stenciled the girls' names on their lavender walls and bought them matching bedding. Abby closed her eyes and let the memory become real in her mind. She could see the white, swirly letters, smell the fresh paint on the walls, hear the infant cries of Haley Ann when she was hungry or needed to be held.

Football season ended in December, and that same week they sold their two-bedroom home and moved into the house on the lake—the home where they'd lived ever since. Each day afterward brought hours of family time, leisurely evenings with John spread out on the sofa, Haley Ann bundled in the crook of one arm while Nicole cuddled into the other. He was such a wonderful dad, gentle and loving with the innate ability to make Nicole and even Haley Ann giggle at will.

One night when the boxes were unpacked, not long after the girls had fallen asleep, John took Abby by the hand and led her outside to the pier. In the bustling activity of moving and having a newborn in the house, Abby had done little more than admire the pier from a distance. But that night, bundled in their winter coats, John wove his fingers between hers and gently turned her so she was facing him.

"Do you hear it, Abby?"

She listened intently, the winter night quiet like the moon across the water. John moved his hands along her arms, drawing her close, pulling her into a hug. "Close your eyes," he whispered.

As she did, she heard gentle sounds she hadn't noticed before. A subtle breeze in the trees that lined the lake, the simple lapping of water against the frozen shoreline. The heartbeat of the man whose arms surrounded her. "I think so."

He pulled back then and stared into her eyes, and she

sensed he loved her more deeply than before, if that were possible. "It's the music of our lives, Abby." A smile played on his lips, and he leaned toward her, kissing her in a way that made her feel safe and protected and wanted. Desirable, despite the circles under her eyes from late nights with Haley Ann. "Dance with me, Abby . . . dance with me."

Taking her hand carefully in his, John led her in small circles, dancing with her alone on the pier to the melody of life, while their angel girls slept inside. Never mind the areas where ice made the wood slippery, in John's arms she was safe and secure, a ballerina being led across the grandest dance floor of all.

It was something he did often over the next two months: swept her outside and danced with her on the pier. Something that made her forget the day's diapers and feedings and sleepless nights. With all her heart Abby believed those days, those feelings between John and her, would never end. It wasn't just the dancing; it was the way Nicole became tender and gentle around Haley Ann, the way they felt together as a family. Invincible, almost. As if no bad thing in all the world could touch what they shared.

Abby blinked, trying to contain a tidal wave of sadness.

There was nothing remarkable about February 28. Nothing during Haley Ann's morning feeding to indicate it would be the last time Abby would hold her little girl close or stare into her eyes as the two of them held a conversation only mother and child could understand. When the baby was finished eating, Abby kissed her tenderly and lay her down on her side.

Two hours later, about the time when Haley Ann usually woke from her morning nap, Abby was folding a load of laundry on her bed when she was pierced with a sudden sense of panic, a warning she could not explain. "Nicole?" Abby's voice rang urgently through the house, and her older daughter, nearly two that month, was quick to respond.

"Yes, Mommy?" Her voice told Abby she was where she was supposed to be. Situated in front of the television, watching *Sesame Street*. "Is it lunchtime?"

Abby tried to calm her racing heart. "No, sweetie, not yet. Mommy has to get Haley Ann up from her nap first."

She dropped the towel she'd been holding and hurried into the baby's room. "Haley, sweetie, wake up. Mommy's here."

The memory sent a shiver down Abby's spine. Haley Ann was on her stomach, a position she often wound up in, but even with Abby's singsong voice she showed no signs of movement.

Hot tears forged a trail down Abby's cheeks as she relived the moment, felt again the slight stiffness in her baby daughter as she swept her into her arms and saw the blue in her face and fingers.

"Haley Ann! Wake up!" She had shouted the words, jerking the tiny baby just enough to jump-start her breathing, to waken her from the terrible sleep she had fallen into. When there was no response, no signs of life, she grabbed the phone and dialed 9-1-1.

"Hurry, please! My baby isn't breathing."

For the next ten minutes she gave Haley Ann mouth-to-mouth resuscitation, oblivious to the way Nicole sat huddled in the doorway watching, singing the alphabet song to herself over and over again.

"A-B-C-D-E-F-G . . ."

Abby could still hear the fear in Nicole's voice, see the

way she was whisked to another corner of the house when the paramedics arrived and one of them reached out his arms for Haley Ann.

"Ma'am, we'll take over now."

And in that moment she'd been forced to hand over her newborn, desperate to believe there was still hope but certain deep in her gut that Haley Ann was dead. A police officer took information from Abby, what time the baby went down, what she'd eaten that morning, how long she'd slept. Finally he asked about the baby's father. "Is there a number we can call for you, Mrs. Reynolds?"

Abby had been beside herself, barely able to breathe. But somehow she pulled the number from the recesses of her mind. Everything that happened next was a blur. The police took Nicole to a neighbor's house, then escorted Abby to the hospital behind the ambulance. As soon as they arrived, John greeted them.

"Honey, what is it? What's happened?" His face—normally ruddy and full of life—was gray and washed out. Fear screamed from his eyes.

There was nothing Abby could say. Haley Ann was gone; she was sure of it. "Haley Ann . . . she's . . . she didn't wake up from her nap . . . Oh, John, pray. Please, pray."

They were the last words Abby could say, the final moment before she collapsed against John and gave way to the sobs that tore at her heart. Together they took up their position outside the emergency room, where doctors were shooting drugs into their baby, using every possible attempt to jump-start her heart.

But it was too late. God had taken Haley Ann home, and there was nothing anyone could do to change the fact. Before the hour was up, doctors left them alone with their baby so together they could say their good-byes. It was impossible to imagine that just four months earlier they had been celebrating at this very hospital, welcoming her new life into their hearts and home.

John was the first to hold her. Moving slowly, like a man trapped in quicksand, he positioned himself near the hospital bed and carefully lifted her to his chest. It was the same image Abby had seen earlier that night at the craft store, the picture of John holding his tiny, dead daughter, trying to find a way to say good-bye.

He said little more than their baby's name, speaking it over and over again as his tears splashed onto her cool skin. But when it was Abby's turn to hold her, he broke down and wept. "Oh, Abby, it's my fault. God's punishing me. I know it."

Abby held Haley Ann tight and leaned into John's shoulder, the three of them connected as they'd been so often in the previous weeks. "No, love, it isn't anyone's fault. No one could have known . . ."

He shook his head, the sobs coming harder, almost violently. "I . . . I wanted her to be a son, Abby. I never told you, but deep inside . . . I hoped she'd be a . . . a boy."

His words caused her heart to swell with compassion, made her own tears come even harder than before. Poor John. He had loved the fact that Haley Ann was a girl, even welcomed his second daughter with open arms. But truly he'd longed for a son. And there in the hospital room . . . with Haley Ann's body locked in their embrace, he was blaming himself for her death. "No, John, don't do that. This was God's choice; He called her home. Don't you see? It has nothing to do with you wanting a son."

Somehow her words breathed strength into him, and though his tears continued to fall, he became the rock once more, the pillar of strength as they lay her down, fixed the blankets around her still body, and kissed her good-bye.

They made the decision to cremate her, and two weeks later they crept out to the pier together and spread her ashes on a breeze that blew over the lake. She and John cried silent tears that night, and when Abby was unable to say anything, John bowed his head and prayed aloud.

"Lord, we know that You are sovereign. You alone give life, and You can call us home, any of us, at any time—" His voice broke, and Abby reached her arm across his shoulders. The gesture gave him the ability to continue. "Take care of our little Haley Ann, please, God. And know that our love for You, for each other, has only been strengthened because of her brief time here, her sudden passing. We dedicate our lives to You again, Lord. And beg You to bless us with more children in the years to come."

After thirty minutes had passed, when the ashes of their infant daughter had settled into the depths of the lake, John wrapped his arms around Abby and whispered words she would never forget in a million years.

"She will always be a part of us, Abby. Right here. Whenever we take the time to stop and remember."

After losing Haley Ann, the bond between Abby and John seemed stronger than ever before. Friends and family offered condolences and words of comfort, but the only real peace, the only healing to be had, was found in each other's presence. They were best friends who had survived a devastating blow and come out stronger on the other side.

Because of their faith, yes. But because of each other,

most of all. They needed no words, no explanations, only the way it felt to stand at the edge of the pier, hand in hand, and look out across the lake. It was a loss that seemed possible only because each had the other. As if after losing Haley Ann they could survive anything life handed them so long as they were together.

Abby drew a deep breath that pulled her from the memory as she allowed the winter air to fill her lungs, washing away the sadness. She wiped her wet cheeks and remembered something else.

Haley Ann's death had been only the beginning.

Three months later a tornado ranking four on the Fujita scale ripped through Marion, missing the Reynoldses' house but killing 10 people and injuring 181 others. The Southridge High kicker—a lighthearted young boy responsible for a majority of locker room pranks—was among the dead, along with one of John's coworkers, a biology teacher with a wife and two young children.

As with losing Haley Ann, John and Abby needed no words that afternoon when the storm had passed. They left Nicole with the neighbor again, rolled up their sleeves, and worked side by side helping bandage victims in the temporary hospital ward set up in the Southridge gymnasium. Again that night they drew strength from each other, finding that together they could handle the unimaginable. In the wee hours of the morning, John drifted off to a private alcove, rested his head against a brick wall, and finally allowed the tears. Abby was instinctively at his side, covering his back with her body, telling him in a way that needed no words that she was there, she understood.

It was no wonder they so greatly appreciated their vacation that summer, celebrating life in the aftermath of all they'd lost. And neither of them was surprised when Abby learned early that fall that she was pregnant again.

Beauty from ashes, just like Scripture promised.

When Kade was born in April 1983, they figured that maybe, just maybe, the trials of life were behind them. Kade was their proof that life goes on, that regardless of the future, each day was precious all by itself. Nicole was three that spring, and though she still occasionally mentioned Haley Ann, her new brother quickly filled the empty places for them all.

"They'll be best friends one day, Abby; I can feel it." John had made the statement while they huddled together in the family room not long after Kade came home from the hospital. Abby appreciated the way John projected Kade's life, assuming that their son's days would not be cut short the way his sister's had.

And in the end John was right. A year later they celebrated Kade's birthday, relieved and grateful beyond words that this baby had never stopped breathing in his sleep.

"We're survivors, John, you and me." Abby had uttered the words against his chest while he held her close on the pier one evening a few weeks later. Summer had seemed to come early that year; already there were crickets singing in the background.

"The music never changes . . ." John stared wistfully out at the lake. "But it's up to us to keep dancing." Then he met her gaze, and she knew she would never feel connected to anyone the way she did with him. He was a jock, a football coach given to short sentences and barked commands, but she knew another side of him, the man who could look straight into her soul. He held her gaze. "Dance with me, Abby. Don't ever stop dancing."

Abby blinked and felt the memory fade into the winter wind. For all the times when John seemed utterly wrapped up in football, for the days and weeks and months when he seemed little more than a gridiron guy with no feelings beyond his drive to win, Abby knew differently. The heart of the man John Reynolds had been was deeper than the lake behind their house, deeper than anything Stan Jacobs might offer in an e-mail.

That was especially true on June 7, 1984.

A sigh escaped Abby, and she knew she could not truly leave the places of the past without revisiting one last memory. Along with the early summer that year came a rash of severe storms that culminated in an outbreak of tornadoes that June 7. Since most of them were developing in Wisconsin and Iowa, Abby had called her father that day, anxious for their safety.

"Everything's fine, honey. We've only had a few in our area, and they've all been small. Besides, your mother's completely out of danger. She's visiting her sister this week."

Abby remembered the surge of relief her father's words had brought. Aunt Lexie lived in Barneveld, Wisconsin, at the far west end of the state. Her father was right. None of the tornadoes that day had been near Barneveld. Abby assured her father she would keep praying and, after tucking Nicole and Kade into bed, she and John watched the news until after ten o'clock.

"Looks like it's easing up," John said. He flipped off the television, and together they turned in for the night. It wasn't until her father called the next morning that she learned the devastating news.

Just before midnight, an F-5 tornado ripped through

Barneveld destroying nearly all of the small town. Nine people were killed, nearly two hundred injured. Abby's mother and aunt were among the dead.

"I'm sorry, baby, I never wanted to have to tell you something like that." Her father, longtime football coach and perennial tough guy, wept on the other end. By the end of the day, John, Abby, and the kids were at his side, helping him cope and planning a funeral for Abby's mother.

Looking back now Abby knew there was only one reason why she'd survived that time in her life. God, in all His mercy, had given her John. And with him at her side, she could survive anything. The ferocity of a tornado. The loss of her mother. Even the death of precious Haley Ann. With John there were no words needed. She felt comforted merely by being in his arms, basking in his presence.

The years had brought other hard times, but nothing like the string of tragedies they survived in the early '80s. Abby felt the tears once more and moved closer to the edge of the pier, removed her glove, and bent down so that her fingers connected with the icy water below.

Haley Ann. I miss you, baby.

John's voice echoed on the breeze. *"She will always be a part of us, Abby. Right here. Whenever we take the time to stop and remember . . ."*

John's words faded into the night, and silence—icy-cold and terrifying—worked its way through Abby's veins. *What if we aren't a "we" anymore, John? Who will remember Haley Ann when we're just two people, separate and alone?*

She removed her hand from the water and dried it on her parka before slipping it once more into the glove. As she did, she realized how deep and great and overwhelming was the loss of what they shared together. How this pier, this spot where she stood, would not only be the place where Haley Ann's ashes lay, but also the ashes of their love, the burial ground of all they'd been together.

In the tender places of their hearts, the single heart they once shared, Haley Ann still lived. But now . . . without the two of them taking time to remember, everything about her would fade into the cold night.

Haley Ann, baby, we love you. No matter what happens, Mommy and Daddy love you . . .

Tears spilled onto her cheeks, and Abby reached her gloved hand out toward the water again, trying to somehow grasp their tiny daughter and everything they'd lost since then. Everything including each other.

"I can't hear it, John . . ." Her choked, whispered words hung like icicles in the air above her. "The music isn't playing anymore."

She had always known she could survive the darkness because something about being near John gave her strength to go on. But now she was just a woman in her forties with a head full of memories of a little girl that no longer existed. A woman cold and afraid and alone in the night, sitting on a pier by herself where once, a very long time ago, she was loved.

Fourteen

RUNNING WAS GOOD FOR THE SOUL, AT LEAST THAT'S what Coach Reynolds always told his players. But it was a brisk afternoon in early February, and this time John wasn't sure he'd survive the workout. His breathing was hard and labored, as though he were jogging with the stadium bleachers fixed to his back. Even worse, there was an occasional tightening in his chest, much like the feeling he'd had on Super Bowl Sunday . . .

John wasn't really worried; he knew there was nothing wrong with his heart. Not physically, anyway. He was too fit, too careful about what he ate. No, the pains were purely stress-related, the result of being married to one woman while falling in love with another.

He rounded the corner of the Marion High track and considered using this time to pray like he'd done in his younger days, like he'd done for a while even after he stopped going to church.

You wouldn't like much of what I'm thinking about these days, God.

Repent! Flee immorality, My son . . . draw near to Me and I will draw near to you.

The verses rattled around in his heart and drifted off like birds in flight. There was truth in the Bible words; John knew it as surely as he knew his name. But nothing about them applied to his current situation. Nowhere in Scripture was there wisdom for a man who was making promises to a woman other than his wife.

A passage from Proverbs flashed across the screen of his mind. *Avoid the harlot; stay clear of her doorway.*

Ridiculous. John shook his head, trying to clear his mind of the idea. Charlene was a beautiful young woman without a friend in the world. A fun-loving woman who admired everything about him and was willing to wait patiently while he and Abby worked out the details of their divorce.

She was hardly a harlot.

John picked up his pace and in the distance, in the trees that lined the creek adjacent to the school, he saw a hawk hanging in the wind. Bits and pieces from Kade's report on the eagle came to mind and seemed to hit him for the first time.

"The eagle allows the storm to take him to a higher place . . . the eagle finds a rock when he's in trouble and lets the sun cleanse him from any poison. The eagle doesn't flap around like the chickens and crows and sparrows. It waits patiently on the rock for the thermal currents, and only then does it take flight. Not by its own effort, but by the effort of the wind beneath its wings."

Again the analogies nearly screamed at him. With Christ, he soared like an eagle, not by his efforts but by the strength of the Holy Spirit. On his own . . . well, he was barely more than a chicken. Flapping and scuffling about in the dirt and never getting off the ground.

I want to be an eagle again, Lord. Show me how. When this mess is behind me, help me be the man for Charlene that I wasn't able to be for Abby.

Stay clear of the harlot, My son.

It wasn't the answer John wanted, and he shifted his gaze. Forget about the eagle. If he was doomed to the chicken pen, at least he'd be a happy chicken. The idea of fighting with Abby all his life was unimaginable. Unthinkable. Divorce was the only option left, even it meant he might never soar again. Besides, his flying days with Abby were long over. At this point they needed separate chicken coops if they were going to survive.

Together they were pecking each other to death.

John rounded another corner, appreciating the way the fresh air cooled his sweaty skin. In summer the track would be busy with people all day long. But now, months before spring, it was often just him. He cleared his mind and let his thoughts wander.

Oddly enough, the person he missed most these days wasn't Abby, but his father, Sam Reynolds. Invincible both on the field and in his faith. John drew a deep breath and kept running. *Dad, if only you were still alive, I know you could make sense of all that's happened.*

His father had been there through the tragedies of losing Haley Ann and Abby's mother in the early '80s. And again in '85 and '86 when Marion High opened and he left Southridge for the job as the Eagles' head football coach. There were days when John hadn't thought he'd survive the trials of building a program from the ground up. But his father had always been there, ready with words of wisdom, willing to lend balance to a life that seemed out of control.

Thoughts of eagles and harlots and an angry God faded as John drifted back to his first seasons as head coach at Marion—but instead of memories of his father, there was image after image of the one who had been there in an even more tangible way.

Abby.

Football reigned in Southern Illinois, where the magnetic pull of the pigskin was, for most people, greater than any other. The idea of Southridge's successful coaching staff giving up their top assistant to head the brand-new program at Marion High was at first welcomed by the townspeople. Especially since many of them still remembered him as Michigan's Miracle Man, the quarterback who could do no wrong. But when the varsity team went 0-11 its first season, a rumbling of community voices made their feelings known. Editorials appeared in the local paper questioning whether a young assistant with no head-coaching experience was the right choice for the prized new program at Marion.

The long-ago voices of discontent still rang clear in John's mind. The school board had seen to it that the students at Marion had the best of everything: science labs, computer rooms, and teachers. On top of that, the school had a half-million-dollar stadium; it was better than any in the state. Why, then—the editorials asked—had the school district hired the first guy looking for a coaching job? Why not search the state for a man who could make Marion High the winner it deserved to be? Forget this building-a-program business. The Eagle parents and boosters wanted a winning tradition. Now. Not next year or the year after.

The frustration of that season and the one that followed burned in John's gut. Didn't they know it took time to develop tradition? Couldn't they see that the moment the doors opened at Marion, every boy who didn't have a chance of playing varsity at Southridge transferred to the new school?

Up front John had predicted it would take every bit of three years to acquire talent that could match up with that at Southridge. He couldn't worry about the fact that the brand-new booster club and overanxious parents at Marion wanted results overnight—especially in games against the now rival Southridge Chieftains. He was only human, after all.

One day midsummer between his first two seasons, Abby found him at practice and waited patiently until the last player and coach had left the field. He'd been alone on the bench, unaware of her presence, when she came up behind him and eased her arms around his shoulders. "I got a baby-sitter," she whispered in his ear. "Let's take a walk."

They spent an hour strolling the track—the very one he was running on now—and in that time she told him a dozen different ways that he was a gifted coach. "The parents don't know a thing about play calling or creating a defense. They have no idea what type of dedicated athletes you need in order to compete with Southridge."

He listened, hanging on to every word. It wasn't so much that she shared any deep revelations that evening, but as she spoke he realized he'd forgotten the truth. He'd allowed the criticism of the community to tear at his confidence and heap upon him the pressure to make a better showing that fall than the previous one.

At the end of their walk, she faced him, brushing a section of hair off his forehead. "Everyone in town, everyone in the world for that matter, might overlook your talent as a coach, John Reynolds." She leaned into him, kissing him on the mouth in a promising way. "But I never will. What you have out there—" she waved her hand toward the field—"is nothing short of magic. A gift from God. Don't ever let anyone convince you otherwise."

Abby's pep talk restored his belief in himself and carried him through the off-season and into fall practice. But his second year proved to be even more disastrous than his first. Midway through the season they played Southridge and came up on the wrong end of a 48-0 beating.

The next day's headlines read "Marion High's Only Chance—Dump Reynolds?" In the article, the press blamed him for passing too much, not knowing his personnel, and not having his team prepared.

"You're playing with Southridge's bench, for goodness sake," Abby cried when she saw the newspaper. "None of your kids would have made the team if they'd stayed at Southridge. What do they want?"

It got worse before it got better. By the end of the season, John found an anonymous typed note in his box warning him that the parents were circulating a petition to have him fired. Another note, signed by the overbearing father of one of the players, said, "I've never seen a more worthless coach than you, Reynolds. You might be a nice guy, but you're hopeless out on the playing field."

John's father offered advice that had helped him in the banking business: "There will always be naysayers, son. The key is to listen to God's calling. If you're doing that, then everyone else's opinion amounts to little more than hot air."

John tried to keep his focus, tried to remember the words of wisdom from Abby and his father, but the season became unbearable as the weeks wore on. One night, after another lopsided loss, John stayed in the locker room an hour later than usual. The game had been a disaster, his players were bickering, and even his assistant coaches had seemed to disagree with the plays he called. Now that they were all gone, he dropped to his knees and gave his coaching game to the Lord, begging God to show him a way out. At the end of that time, he felt there was only one option: quit. Step down and let someone else give the people of Marion the winning program they wanted.

It was after eleven o'clock when he locked up and walked out onto the field that night, but regardless of the late hour, Abby was there, waiting for him like she did after every game.

"Honey, I'm sorry. You didn't have to wait." He took her in his arms, rocked by how good it felt to be held and loved and supported on a night when it seemed the whole world had been against him.

"I'd wait a lifetime for you, John Reynolds. Remember?" Her voice was soothing, a balm to his wounded spirit. "I'm the girl who's loved you since I was ten years old."

He pulled away and looked deep into her eyes. "I'm turning in my resignation tomorrow."

John remembered the anger that flared in Abby's eyes. *"What?"* She backed up several feet and faced him squarely. "You are *not* turning in your resignation." She paced nervously, her mouth open, eyes locked on his. "You can't do it. God brought you here to do a job. You can't let those . . .

those ignorant parents push you out of the very thing you were created to do. I won't let you quit. Think about the hours of . . ."

She had gone on that way for five minutes until finally she ran out of words.

"That's my Abby, shy and reserved." He tousled her hair and smiled sadly. "I still think it's time. They want someone else. Let 'em have their way."

Abby's eyes had filled with angry tears. "Those people are wrong, John. A couple of them are nothing more than frustrated, bitter old men who never amounted to anything in life. My guess is they couldn't play sports as kids and they can't coach sports as adults. So what do they do? They pretend to coach from the stands, making their sons and people like you miserable in the process." She paused and John remembered the sincerity in her voice. "They want you to quit, John. Can't you see that? They don't know the first thing about coaching, but still they've spearheaded this . . . this entire community into a frenzy to have you fired." She clenched her fists and swung at the air. "Don't let those crazy parents win like that, John. You have a gift; I've seen it. Besides, you're forgetting the first rule of being a Christian."

John could hear himself silently agreeing with her on every count. "What rule is that?" He moved closer to her, tracing his finger along her cheekbone, loving her for the way she believed in him.

She stared deep into his eyes, her voice softer than before. "The enemy doubles his efforts when a breakthrough is right around the corner." Leaning up, she kissed him long and slow before pulling back. "Don't give up, John. Please."

Indeed, the enemy attacks had doubled that year. Both he and Abby received angry, anonymous letters—some even sent to their home address. "Why do they hate us?" she had cried that afternoon, ripping one of the letters into a hundred pieces.

"They don't hate you; they hate me. Don't you get it, Abby? If they can hurt us bad enough, then maybe they'll get their way and I'll step down."

But every time he was tempted to scrap his efforts, Abby helped change his mind. In those early years she'd always known just what to say or do when he was hurting or tired or lonely for her touch. It was an art that had taken years to perfect.

He remembered how quickly the team's atmosphere had changed once that second season was behind him. That summer he could hardly wait for fall and the chance to show the town of Marion the fruits of his hard work. John hadn't thought about that summer for years . . . but it felt right to do so now, as though by drifting back in time he might find some of the strength and reason and guidance that was missing in his life.

He remembered one hot afternoon when training had been going better than ever, and he'd called his dad to talk shop.

"Sounds like you're doing everything right, son." It was a ritual, talking football father-to-son: a part of life John had known would always be there, the same way winter followed fall. "What're your chances?"

"This is the year, Dad," he'd been quick to answer, the misery of the previous season all but forgotten. "You gotta get down here and see these guys. They're bigger than most college players."

"Just as long as I'm there when they hand you the state trophy." His dad chuckled confidently on the other end. "That's a moment I wouldn't miss for the world."

"It may not be this year, but it'll happen, Dad. You heard it here first."

The news that rocked his world came the next day. He was in the weightroom with temperatures sweltering outside at just under a hundred and the humidity not far behind. Custodians rarely ran the air conditioner in summer, and John and the other coaches didn't complain. It was good for the guys to work out in a hot gym. Made them tough, ready for competition.

John was going over a player's routine, making sure the young athlete's training regimen was increasing on schedule, when Abby appeared at the door. A darkness in her eyes told him two things. First, the news was not good; second, whatever it was they would get through it together. The way they'd gotten through all the hard times they'd faced.

Without words, she used her eyes to suggest that the conversation they were about to have should take place behind closed doors. John excused himself from the player, and in seconds he and Abby were alone, face to face.

"What is it?" His heart was thudding so loud he wondered if Abby could hear it too. "Are the kids okay?" After losing Haley Ann he never assumed that his children would be alive and well at the end of the day just because they'd appeared that way at the breakfast table.

He held his breath while Abby nodded. "The kids are fine. It's your dad." She moved closer, placing her hands on his shoulders. "Your mother just called. He had a heart attack this morning. Oh, honey . . . he didn't make it." The news cut through him like a hot knife, but before he had time to react, he noticed tears in her eyes. It was her loss too. Feeling as though his heart were in his shoes, he circled his arms around her, strangely comforted by that fact.

For twenty minutes she stayed there with him, holding him, assuring him that his father was with the Lord, in a better place. Promising him that the few tears that slid down his cheeks were okay, even there in the Marion High weightroom. When the news had sunk in, she left him alone and told the other coach on duty that John needed privacy, that his father and mentor had died that morning.

When John was ready to leave, there were no students hanging around, no well-meaning teachers or staff members wondering what had happened. Abby had seen to that.

He thought back now and realized how different the day might have gone. Abby could have left a "call home" message with the secretary or waited until after dinner to tell him. Instead she'd gone the extra mile, bore the brunt of the bad news, forced herself to grieve later, and immediately found a way to be with him.

He tried to picture Charlene in that situation . . . but it was impossible.

Charlene had never known his father, never loved him or respected him or looked forward to his calls. Charlene hadn't borne his father's grandchildren or lived with the knowledge that her father and John's were best friends as far back as the beginning of time.

What could Charlene possibly have said that would have touched him the way Abby's presence had that afternoon?

It's a new day, Reynolds. Give the girl a break. You'll make memories with her in time.

The thought should have comforted him, but instead he felt the oddest chill run down his spine. He shook off the feeling and remembered Abby again—Abby whose father lay ill in a nursing home . . . a man who had been his father's best friend.

"I need to see him, talk to him."

John whispered the words and slowed his pace. He'd logged in five miles that day, but the relaxing sense of euphoria that usually accompanied his workouts was missing. In its place was a sense of confusion, uncertainty.

In the end, of course, the state title had come. Less than six months after his father's death, the Marion Eagles finished their season undefeated. It was as though the terrible seasons in the mid-eighties were only a bad dream, for there John stood, high on the winner's platform, accepting a trophy that was half the size of six-year-old Kade.

John remembered the moment like it was yesterday. He leaned over, stretching the muscles in his legs as he closed his eyes. Everything about that night was as sweet now as it had been back then. When it was his turn to speak, his message was simple. "I wanna thank God for giving me a wife who never once stopped supporting me." He gazed into the stands, knowing she was there somewhere, crying no doubt, cherishing the moment as deeply as he was. "I love you, Abby. I wouldn't be here without you." Then he raised the trophy into the night sky and stared up toward heaven. "This is for you, Dad!"

The memory faded. John stood up, wiped his brow, and headed for the car. How could he spend the rest of his life with Charlene, a woman who'd never met his father? A woman who hadn't ridden out the Marion tornado with him, or stood beside him while the ashes of his baby daughter danced in the wind and settled across the lake he loved best. A woman who was in love with a man that Abby Reynolds helped create.

If there's another way, God, show me . . .

The silence told him there was none. They were down three touchdowns with less than a minute to play. It was simply too late in the game. But even though that was true, John couldn't deny what he'd finally come to realize: taking up with Charlene would be like allowing a part of himself to die.

The part that still belonged—would always belong— to a blonde, blue-eyed pixie who had captured his heart on the sandy shores of Lake Geneva the summer he was just seventeen.

Fifteen

THE IDEA OF A COUPLES' WEDDING SHOWER HAD been Matt's. He reasoned that since Nicole Reynolds was the daughter of the famous Coach John Reynolds, she was very nearly royalty—at least by Marion's standards. So certainly there ought to be at least a barbecue to celebrate the fact that she was getting married.

Abby wasn't about to disagree since the whole reason they'd postponed telling the kids about their divorce was to give Nicole this season of happiness.

"Absolutely!" She'd looked expectantly at Nicole the moment Matt brought it up. "We could invite half the town of Marion."

Nicole's eyes had sparkled at the thought, and Abby's heart ached for her. Regardless of how happy these six months were, they would never make up for the hurt she and John were about to cause Nicole and the boys.

"Can we really, Mom? You wouldn't mind?"

"Not at all, honey. Invite whoever you want."

"Sort of like a couples' wedding shower." Nicole nudged Matt. "Like your friend Steve had last year, remember?"

"Right. Something like this can take the place of another wedding shower later on." He grinned at Nicole, teasing her.

"Now wait a minute—" Nicole poked him harder this time, giggling—"I never said anything about that."

Abby watched them. *They look like us twenty-two years ago, Lord.*

Love does not fail . . . love never ends, My daughter.

The words were dim at best, but they were there all the same. A constant reminder of how she and John had missed the mark.

Nicole cast a smile at her mother. "I can't help it if my friends throw me an all-girls' shower later on, right, Mom?"

With that the idea had taken root. They invited John's coaching staff and a dozen of Nicole's longtime friends, girls she had cheered with at Marion High and with whom she still kept in close contact. Matt asked several of his law school buddies, and Nicole insisted on inviting three families who had been closer than relatives as far back as she could remember.

John agreed to the party, but privately he didn't like the idea from the beginning. "It's hard enough pretending around the kids," he told Abby one evening. "Let alone with the world watching us."

Abby felt hatred bubbling to the surface again. "Don't talk to me about pretending. I'm not the one parading around with a lover on my arm." She disappeared into her office before he could return fire.

They got along best when they avoided each other, and

in the days that led up to the party, they managed to do just that. John spent more time working out or grading papers at school, and she kept busy helping Nicole make guestlists and pick out wedding decorations. Afternoons were spent with Sean, hauling him to indoor soccer games and baseball practice and lap swimming at the club.

When Abby was absolutely forced to be home with John, she found reasons to be in her office. And in that way they survived the first two months.

It was pouring rain the evening of Nicole's and Matt's party, and Abby glanced at the table. Cheese and crackers, fruit and cookies, everything was in order. Even the wrapped family Bible from John and her.

A Bible was the standard Reynolds family wedding gift, and even though John had argued with her about buying it, Abby had decided on a leather copy engraved with the couple's names.

"That way Nicole can always look at the Bible and remember how we lied to her during her engagement." John had tossed out the comment from where he sat in the living room, flipping between ESPN and Fox Sports. "Great gift idea."

"Maybe if we'd read ours a little more often we wouldn't be in this mess."

The barbs between them were getting more frequent, and Abby had no idea how they were going to survive until July. She laid a stack of decorated napkins on the kitchen table. It was no wonder John was more irritable than before. *He wants to be with Charlene, not us.* The thought pierced Abby's heart, and she pushed it away.

This was Nicole's and Matt's day, and she'd promised herself she wouldn't wallow in pity for herself.

Just get through it, Abby. Keep smiling and get through it.

John had dreaded this day since he'd first heard about it. It was one thing to honor Nicole's season of happiness. But this . . . this couples' shower idea was a joke. Let someone else throw them a party.

The doorbell rang, and John rose to greet the guests, helping them with their raincoats and stashing umbrellas in the entryway. At this point he had no choice but to put on a smile, go along with the plan, and pray he could steer clear of Abby for the next five hours.

Nicole's friends arrived first, but within a half-hour the house was full of dozens of familiar faces. As was usually the case when coaches gathered together, the Marion Eagles staff congregated in the living room not far from the television and a sports news program. But with thunder clapping outside and the banter of so many other people in the room, the coaches finally gave up and turned off the set.

John studied his buddies, guys he'd been with through long hours of training and planning and celebrating. Joe and Sal and Kenny and Bob. The best friends a man could ever hope to have. Maybe if he could keep his thoughts on football, the night would fly by and no one would notice anything different between Abby and him.

"How long's it been, guys, the five of us?" John leaned back in his easy chair, feet up, grinning at the men around him.

Joe stroked his chin and cocked his head. "You know,

I was just asking Alice that the other day." He gazed toward the ceiling in deep concentration. "The five of us weren't together until 1987, right?"

"Yeah, I waited until Rod Moore's kid graduated before applying." Kenny laughed hard at his own joke and patted his round stomach. "There's only so much the old ticker can take."

"I think that was it, 1987. First year we were all Eagles." John shook his head. "So it's been fourteen years. Where in the world did the time go?"

"Think about it . . . all the highs and lows." Bob grinned, his eyes glistening with a million memories. "That first state title . . . Tell ya what, there's never been nothing like it except this last one, watching you and Kade. Now that was something else."

Kenny chuckled softly and slapped John on the knee. "Yeah, the Reynolds family's always been something else. I mean, really, how many of us have wished over the years we had a marriage like John and Abby's?"

"Yeah, Abby's a kick all right. I wish my wife understood the commitment to coaching like Abby does." Bob tossed a pretzel at John and winked at him. "She's a one-in-a-million, John. If you hadn't kept her I woulda married her myself."

A tingling sensation worked its way from John's scalp down his spine. Did everyone have to put his marriage to Abby on a pedestal? Couldn't they talk about something else? He took small, steady breaths and tried to look natural.

Bob was still going on about Abby's many merits. "And just so you know, John, Kenny's next in line after me. Right, Ken?"

Kenny grinned and nodded once for emphasis. "She's a keeper."

Bob and Kenny were both divorced, and Sal had never been married. Only Joe had a wife at home, and from everything John knew they were happy together. He racked his brain trying to think of something else to talk about. "We've had our ups and downs like anyone else."

Joe laughed out loud. "That's right, like the time Abby tumbled down the stairs at Sea World." He looked at each of the faces around him. "Remember, guys?" He gestured his hand in a downward sliding motion. "Those must have been the 'down' moments."

Despite himself John smiled at the memory. He closed his eyes and shook his head slowly, still embarrassed for Abby after all these years.

"Come on, John, tell us again." Kenny leaned forward and took a swig of ice tea. "It's been a while since we've had a good laugh at Abby's expense. Besides, Sal's never heard the Sea World story, have you, Sal?"

"No, I think I missed that one."

"Yeah, well we used to get stories all the time." Joe grabbed another handful of chips and waited expectantly. "You know . . . Abby's latest driving story, Abby's latest shopping story, Abby's latest run-in with the neighbors . . ."

Joe's comment struck John like a blow. When had he stopped talking about Abby with his coaches?

"Come on, John." Joe stuffed several chips in his mouth. "Wasn't she carrying an ice-cream cone or something?"

The memory became clear and vivid. Sean had been something of a surprise baby, born the fall of 1990. It was the following spring and they'd taken a drive to Ohio to visit Sea World. Nicole was ten that year and Kade, seven.

The trip was a comedy of errors from the beginning.

They'd decided ahead of time that John would carry Sean in a baby carrier and Abby would tote the family's sweaters and belongings in a backpack. John glanced around the room and saw that the guys were waiting expectantly for a story. He grabbed a napkin and wiped his hands. "All right, all right. Most of you know the story. We were at the park, and Abby wanted to watch the sea lion show."

"Not the dolphins or whales, but the sea lions, right, Coach?" Joe was great for adding color whenever John told a story.

"Had to get to the sea lions . . . before we could do anything else." John hesitated for effect. "Anyway, we've got five minutes before the show starts and we see this ice-cream stand right next to the sea lion stadium. It's a hot day, the kids are hungry, so Abby decides why not? Let's get the kids cones before the show. That way they can eat them inside."

"Sounds like a plan." Joe had heard the story several times before, and he knew what was coming. He leaned back in his seat and grinned.

"Right, so we get to the front of the line and order three cones. There were two teenagers working the booth, so we thought we had a pretty good chance of getting waited on. But the guys just looked at each other real slow, then looked back at us, and back to each other again. 'Ice-cream cones?' the one guy says."

"These were linemen, no doubt." Joe elbowed Kenny in the gut. Kenny had been a lineman years earlier, and it was his specialty as a coach.

"Hey, don't pick on us linemen. We get a little goofy around ice cream."

"Yeah, well these guys were at least one crayon short of a box because they spent the next several minutes deciding between themselves whether we had actually ordered three cones." John was smiling now, enjoying the story, caught up in the memory of that summer a decade ago. "The whole time Abby's glancing at her watch and saying things like, 'I can't miss the sea lion show, John. We've got to get these people to hurry.' So I'm like, 'Yes, dear, I'm doing my best.' Because of course there was nothing I could do to make them move faster. So then—I'm absolutely serious here—the one guy goes to the ice-cream machine, takes a cone, and pulls the lever. The ice cream piles higher and higher until it flops over onto the floor. Without missing a beat the guy stares at the mess, tosses the cone in the trash, and takes down another empty cone."

"Ended up being about three for seven, isn't that right, John?" Joe chuckled at the thought. "Forget the fact that the line's out past the sea lion stadium now."

"Right. So finally we have the three cones, and Abby realizes we need napkins. The guys point to a service counter thirty yards away, and Abby takes off sprinting. I mean, Abby was quite an athlete in her day. Track, tennis. Even now she could take most of you guys in a footrace. But that day her footwork wasn't as smooth as it might have been and, with three yards to go, the ice cream toppled from the cone she was holding and landed splat on her foot."

Joe was laughing harder now, rocking slightly in his chair. "Eased right into her nice shoes. Can you see it, guys? Abby Reynolds? Dressed just so, with soft chocolate ice cream melting between her pretty toes?"

John began laughing at the picture. "People were staring at her, wondering why this woman had run so hard and fast with an ice cream cone in the first place. And there she was, a shoe full of ice cream, empty cone in her hand, the rest of us watching from the other side of the rest area, and the sea lion show just about to start. So Abby grabs a stack of napkins, wipes the ice cream out of her shoe, and sticks her foot back inside."

Kenny grimaced at the thought, and Sal began laughing so hard he had to set his drink down. "What about the sea lions?"

"So she runs back to the ice-cream booth, cuts in line, and tells the guy she needs another cone, only this time put it in a bowl. The guy does it, and now the music is playing for the sea lion show. 'Come on, let's get seats,' she tells the rest of us. And she's off . . ."

"Leading the way like a woman at a Nordstrom sale." Joe's face was red from trying to contain himself.

"We followed right behind, weaving our way through the crowd, determined to get seats before the first sea lion took the stage." John took a breath and chuckled harder at the images in his head. "So there we are at the top of the stadium, and Abby spots a row halfway down the stairs. 'Follow me,' she says. And those were her last words. The stairs . . ." He tried to catch his breath and realized how good it felt. Sitting here with his friends, barely able to breathe for the laughter and the way Abby had looked that summer afternoon. "The stairs were kind of like—" he gestured—"big, small, big, small. No idea why, that's just the way they were. But Abby must've only seen one size because the first step went just fine, but the moment she tried to get her foot to land on that second step, she wound up stepping on nothing but air, and she began to tumble."

All the men were laughing now, putting down their

food, bent over, struggling for air. John found his voice, and despite the way his body shook, he continued the story. "Not just any tumble, mind you. The backpack rode up onto the back of her neck and : . . and it pushed her down further and further . . ."

"She looked like—" Joe's voice was shrill from the lack of oxygen—"she looked like a turtle, right, John? Sliding down the stairs, one after another . . . the backpack . . . on her head."

"Right." John drew a deep breath and tried to control himself. "Her head was peeking out just a little from the backpack, and finally . . . finally a man put his hand out and stopped her."

Kenny was a big man, and when he laughed as hard as he was now, he began sounding like a sea lion himself. The realization made John chuckle even harder than before. Between breaths he was able to finish the story. "Of course the whole . . . the whole stadium was full of people and the show had already . . . started." He inhaled sharply. "At first the people thought it was part of the act . . ."

"A few women started clapping." Joe could still barely get the words out for the laughter that shook his body. "She actually stopped the show. Even the sea lions waited to see what was going to happen."

John nodded, the memory so funny he was starting to giggle like a girl. Abby had looked so pathetic. "Anyway, this man reaches out and stops her and . . . trying to look casual . . . she gets up all quick and waves at the people. Then she turns around and looks at me, and that's when I see the ice cream . . ."

"The bowl of ice cream she'd been holding." Joe was almost bent in half now, and the other guys were laughing so loud they were attracting the attention of everyone in the room. "Remember, the one she'd lost down her shoe the first time!"

"So there she is, knees and elbows all skinned and bleeding, backpack caught up in her hair, and ice cream smeared down the entire front of her shirt."

Sal hooted out loud. "I woulda bought tickets to that all right. Little Miss Perfectly Dressed Coach's Wife looking like that . . . with a whole stadium of people watching."

"We sat down and the show started up again." John caught his breath and forced himself to calm down. "She didn't say a word until the show was over, then she turned to me and said, 'Okay, how'd that look?' And I absolutely lost it."

"Somewhere someone probably got themselves a ten-thousand-dollar video moment." Joe slapped his own knee this time, and the group laughed hard again.

"Oooooeeee." John shook his head and exhaled long and hard. "That was something else all right."

Joe wiped a tear from his eyes. "I haven't laughed that hard in years." He shook his head. "And the thing about it is, to this day, Abby can laugh at it too."

Kenny got control of himself. "Yeah, that's the best thing about Abby. She doesn't take herself too seriously."

"Where is she, anyway? She should have been out here to tell us how it felt." Sal exhaled, still trying to catch his breath as he looked around the room.

A stabbing feeling cut into John's gut and erased all the silliness of a moment earlier. But before he could answer, Nicole walked up and grinned at them. "Okay, what's all the commotion over here?"

Joe shoved John in the shoulder. "Your dad was telling

us about the Sea World trip . . . you know, the actual 'trip.' When your mom made a splash at the sea lion show."

"Yeah, good thing Sean was on Dad's back, huh?" Nicole giggled and shook her head. "Poor Mom, we'll be telling that story until she's old and gray. At least she wasn't hurt."

Nicole wandered back across the room to her group of friends, and the guys began talking all at once. John felt suddenly sick to his stomach, Nicole's words punched around at his insides like perfectly delivered blows.

"Until she's old and gray . . . until she's old and gray."

The wife of his youth, his best friend and lifelong companion, would not grow old and gray with him. No, she would be married to someone else by then, spending the rest of her life with another man. In fact, there would be no stories about Abby in the years to come, no regaling the crowd with stories of how she'd talked herself out of a speeding ticket or burned the sweet potatoes on Thanksgiving Day. If he was honest with himself, the story he'd just told was probably the last he'd ever tell about his precious Abby girl. Once they were divorced, what sense would it make to sit around with the guys recalling the good times with Abby, the funny moments that no one in their family would ever forget.

And Charlene . . . well, John was fairly sure she wouldn't see the humor in their family memories anyway.

Abby managed to spend the first hour of the party in the kitchen, chatting with a number of Nicole's friends as they passed through. Abby's dad had wanted to join them at the house, but his nurses said the excitement would be too much for him. Instead Nicole and Matt had promised him a visit after church the next day. Abby stared out the window at Matt and his buddies anchored around a picnic table on the covered back porch. She felt the corners of her lips lift slightly. She liked Matt. He was strong and intelligent. There was a gentleness about him when he was with Nicole that told Abby he'd make a wonderful father. *I pray it lasts. Don't ever let the years get away from you, Matt . . .*

It was the first weekend in March, and though spring hadn't officially arrived, the thunderstorm that was blowing over assured them it was coming.

It won't be long now. Four months and the charade will be over.

She was alone in the kitchen freshening up the food platters when she heard John and his friends laughing in the family room. At first the sound made Abby angry. *He's sounding a bit too happy out there, God. Isn't he hurting even a little?*

Easing herself closer to the door, she caught pieces of the conversation. *Sea lion show . . . halfway down the stairs . . . tumbling . . . like a turtle.*

They were talking about the Sea World trip some ten years ago. By herself with no one to fool, tears filled Abby's eyes as a smile played on her lips. How long had it been since they'd laughed together over that story? And why was John telling it now?

She moved away, leaning against the refrigerator, eyes closed, heart thudding against her ribs. *God, how can we do this to each other? Why don't I go out there and laugh with him, sit with him. Love him again?*

Love never fails, daughter. Love never ends.

Well, it has for us, so now what, Lord? Where do we go from here?

It had been months, years even, since she'd held a discussion with God, allowed His thoughts to permeate her own, and given herself permission to respond. But now, tonight, with a house full of people she loved more than any in the world, she was desperate for answers.

I'm waiting, God. Tell me. What are we supposed to do next? I need real help here, Lord.

Silence.

Abby hesitated a beat, then wiped her tears. Fine. If God wasn't going to talk to her, she'd just have to make her way alone. It wouldn't be the first time. For all intents and purposes, she'd been alone since the day Charlene Denton set her sights on John.

Let he who is without sin cast the first—

That's not the answer I want . . . Abby spun around and forced herself to think of something else. She had guests to tend to, after all. This was no time to be wading knee-deep in guilt, not while everyone else was having a good time. John was the one to blame for the mess they were in, and she wouldn't let anyone tell her differently.

Not even God Himself.

The last of the guests were gone, and Nicole was stacking their opened gifts neatly in the middle of the coffee table. The boys and Matt were in Kade's room playing Nintendo, and Dad had turned in early. Only Mom was awake, but after finishing the dishes she'd excused herself to the office to finish up an article.

The party had been a huge success, giving Nicole and Matt time with their closest friends and family. There had been laughter and shared memories and good times for everyone until well after ten o'clock. But Nicole couldn't shake the feeling that something was wrong.

Deeply wrong.

She sat on the edge of the coffee table and slipped one leg over the other. *God, what is it? What am I feeling?*

The image of her parents came to mind, and she realized she hadn't seen them together once during the evening. *Is everything okay between them, Lord? Are they in some kind of trouble?*

Pray, daughter. The prayer of a righteous one is powerful and effective.

The answer was swift and almost audible. God wanted her to pray—but for her parents? Why on earth would they need prayer? Were they having money troubles, maybe? Was the wedding costing them more than they could afford?

Oh, Lord, my heart feels troubled beyond words. Father, be with my parents, and bring them to a place of togetherness. I'm afraid . . . I didn't see them near each other tonight, and . . . well, maybe I'm just looking too hard, but I get the strongest feeling something's wrong. Maybe money or something. I don't know. Please, Father, surround them both with Your angels, and protect them from the evil one and his terrible schemes. Where there's stress, calm them; where there's misunderstanding, clear it up. And use me, Lord, however You might, to help make things right. If they're wrong, that is.

She finished her prayer and studied the closed office door. Without hesitating she stood and made her way across the room, knocking once before turning the handle and easing herself inside. "Whatcha doing?"

Her mother looked up quickly, then stared briefly at the computer screen and clicked twice.

"Good-bye." The computer announced.

"I was . . . just checking my e-mail." Her mother smiled in a way that seemed a little too happy and turned her chair so that she faced Nicole.

Why did she look so nervous? "Hey, Mom . . . is everything okay? With you and Dad, I mean?" Nicole studied her mother, looking for signs that things might actually be worse than she imagined. Like maybe they were in a fight or something. In all her years growing up, Nicole could remember maybe three times when her parents had fought. Always it had been the most unnerving feeling she'd ever encountered. Her parents were like two rocks, the people everyone looked to when they wanted to know how a marriage was supposed to work.

The last time her parents had even raised their voices at each other was years ago, wasn't it? Nicole waited for her mother's response, aware that her own fingers were trembling.

"Yes, of course. Everything's great." Her mother angled her head, her features knotted up curiously. "What made you ask, sweetheart?"

Nicole swallowed hard, not sure if she should voice her concerns. "I didn't see you guys together all night, you know? It seemed kinda strange."

Her mother laughed once. "Honey, there were so many people here. Every time I started out to join your father, someone else came in to talk or brought me another food tray to fill. The night got away from us, that's all."

A warm feeling came over Nicole, and her whole body relaxed. It had just been her imagination after all.

The prayer of a righteous one is powerful and effective. Pray, daughter. Pray.

An alarm sounded again in Nicole's heart. Why was the Lord giving her thoughts like that if everything was okay? She cleared her mind and stared hard at her mother. "You're telling me the truth, right, Mom? This isn't about money or anything? The last thing I want to do is make things hard on you and Daddy."

Abby uttered a quiet chuckle. "Sweetheart, when your Grandpa Reynolds passed away, he left us plenty of money. Believe me, getting you married is not causing us any financial worries at all."

Nicole leaned her weight on one hip and surveyed her mother's face. "Honest? Everything's okay?"

A flash of something shadowy and dark crossed her mother's eyes, then just as quickly disappeared. "I told you, honey. Everything's fine."

Nicole reached out and took hold of her mother's fingers. "Come on, I wanna show you the goods."

Her mom stood up slowly and stretched. "I looked at them once already, Nick."

"I know, but I've got it all organized. You know, blenders and toasters on one side of the table, sentimental gifts on the other side."

"Oh, all right." Mom smiled and hugged her as they walked into the living room side by side. "Lead the way."

They were only partway there when Nicole stopped and held her mother tighter. "Thanks for the Bible, Mom." She pulled away, looking deep into her mother's eyes once more. "It's my favorite gift of all."

"Good. Keep it that way, and you and Matt will spend the next fifty years in love. Mark my words, honey."

Nicole smiled and linked elbows with her mother, moving happily beside her as they found the gifts in the center of the family room. They studied each item and chatted about the party and the coming wedding. Nicole knew that the prompting she'd felt from the Lord to pray for her parents was a good thing. Even the strongest couples needed prayer. But Mom and Dad were fine. Nicole felt certain that her strange feelings of concern were nothing more than an overactive imagination.

That and a good case of engagement anxiety.

Sixteen

DENNY CONLEY WAS TOO NEW AT THIS CHRISTIAN thing to know where else to go. He only knew he had a lot on his mind, and only one Person he wanted to share it with. Besides, taking his troubles to the Lord late at night like this had become something of a routine.

Denny knew one thing for sure: it beat the old routine, hopping from bar to bar and wondering every morning how in the world he'd made it home.

The church was small, not like the big chapels closer to the city. And that Monday night in late March it was almost pitch dark inside. Denny had a key because he'd been doing janitorial chores for them lately, and he kept it on his personal key ring, right next to the one that opened his apartment.

Quietly, so that even the church cat wouldn't be bothered, Denny made his way to the front row and eased himself into a pew. Like he'd done a dozen times in the past few months, he stared in awe at the life-size wooden cross.

Denny had been raised Catholic, and he'd seen his share of crosses. Crucifixes, really. The kind where a pained-looking Jesus hung from shiny brass beams. Nothing wrong with crucifixes except they put the focus on the suffering.

Sometimes that was a good thing, remembering the Lord's pain. In fact, it had been after coming home drunk one night a few months earlier that Denny had spotted the crucifix on his bedroom wall and moved in for a closer look. Was it true? Had an innocent man named Jesus really hung on a cross like that and died for Denny Conley's sins? He found it hard to believe. Why in the world would someone do something like that? For a person like him, no less?

By then it had been four years since his son had gone and found this personal relationship thing with God. It was all Matt ever talked about back then. Golly, it was all he talked about still. But Denny's encounter with the crucifix happened on a night weeks after the last time he'd talked to the boy. Denny had been wobbly and ready to pass out from the whiskey, but something in the way that Jesus hung there—taking all that pain and not complaining about it—all so people like Denny and Matt could make it to heaven.

Well, something about that was almost more than Denny could bear.

The next day he looked up churches in the phone book and found him a nice community-sized one with a picture of a friendly looking man named Pastor Mark. Denny had stopped in that afternoon and met with the guy, and sure enough, Pastor Mark told him the same thing Matt had been saying from the get-go. Jesus died all on His own, regardless of whether you were a good person or a bad person or some drunk hopping bars, halfway in-between. Either way, it was up to Denny to accept the gift of heaven or walk away from it and keep living life on his own.

Denny remembered the decision better than he remembered almost any other detail of his life. He had made some awful mistakes in the past. Walked away from Jo when Matt was just a little tyke, married another woman, and spent two decades drinking his life away. That night, drunker than a skunk, he was single again and looking for offers.

Never, though, had he been offered anything like what Pastor Mark offered him that afternoon. Eternal life. Already paid for. And all he had to do was ask Jesus to forgive him of his past sins and then grab hold of the gift that was already his for the taking.

It was too much to bear, really. An offer Denny simply couldn't refuse. He asked Christ into his life that night, and the change in his heart was almost instant. First thing he did when he got home was phone Matt.

"Your old man's a believer, Matt. Just like you."

There was a pause, and Denny wasn't sure but he thought Matt was crying a little on the other end. That conversation had been only the beginning. They'd talked more in the last few months than all their years combined, but they still hadn't seen each other. Not once since Denny had walked out on him and Jo, back when the boy was four years old. Matt had wanted to see him after Denny's first phone call, but Denny hadn't wanted the boy to see him drunk. And back then there weren't many days . . . well, there weren't many *hours* when Denny wasn't stone-flat plastered.

But the day he began believin', Denny believed for something else too. He believed that if God could raise Jesus Christ from the dead, He could certainly deliver Denny Conley from the demons of alcoholism.

Denny smiled up at the cross. It had been four months since then, twenty-four church services and fifty meetings with a Twelve-Step group designed to help break the addiction of drinking. He was gaining weight, losing the ruddy complexion he'd developed during the years of drinking. In fact, he might almost be ready to see Matt. Every day, every hour, found him clean and sober. And it was all because of Christ.

Which brought him to his current prayer, the one that had been drawing him to church late at night, the one he'd been laying directly at the foot of the cross. It was a prayer for Jo's salvation. Denny knew from Matt that his mother was cynical about the whole Jesus thing. She was probably bitter and angry and frustrated at having lived a lifetime as a single mother. It wasn't going to be easy for her to accept the truth.

That Denny Conley was a new man.

Denny sighed. Something about the coming wedding made the whole thing seem more urgent. He was going, after all. Sure as the sky was blue, he was going to be in church when his son married that young bride of his. And if God heard him good, he was going to take a few minutes and talk heart-to-heart with Jo.

Then maybe, just maybe . . .

Denny bowed his head and closed his eyes. "Lord, my Jo's hurting right now because of me . . . and because she doesn't know You yet. She needs to, Lord. But . . . well, I'm not really the one to tell her, know what I mean? I hurt her pretty bad all those years ago, and I'm awful sorry. You know that and I know it. But Jo . . . she thinks this whole Jesus thing is just a phase. Maybe my way of connecting with Matt after so much time's gone by between us.

"Anyway, God, You know what I mean. Reach down and touch Jo's heart, Father. Make her feel uneasy so that nothing gives her peace except You. Save her, Lord. And work it out so the two of us can have a talkin' to. Together, I mean, maybe at the wedding somehow. Make her ready to see me, God. Please." He thought for a minute. "I guess what I'm askin' for, Father, is a miracle for Jo. Just like the miracle You gave me and Matt." He hesitated. "In Jesus' name, amen."

When he was finished praying, he let his eyes linger on the cross awhile longer, grateful that Jesus no longer hung there but that He lived, that He was alive forevermore. With his gaze still upward, his thoughts on his Savior, Denny did the same thing he always did after these prayer times.

He sang.

Pastor told him the song had been around for more than a hundred years, but it was brand new to Denny Conley. As far as he was concerned, it could have been written for him alone. Like the hesitant notes from a dusty piano, Denny's voice rang out and lifted to an audience of One. It didn't matter if he couldn't carry a tune or if the cat woke up and thought he was crazy. All Denny cared about was the song.

The words to the song.

Great is Thy faithfulness, oh God my Father
There is no shadow of turning with Thee.
Thou changest not, Thy compassions they fail not
As Thou hast been Thou forever wilt be.

He hummed a bit then, because he didn't yet know all the words. But one day he would. Until then, he would sing the part he knew.

"Great is Thy faithfulness, great is Thy faithfulness
Morning by morning new mercies I see.
All I have needed Thy hand hath provided;
Great is Thy faithfulness, Lord, unto me."

It was Thursday night again, and the craft store scrapbooking class was empty except for Abby and Jo and two other women. Abby was midway through Nicole's high-school years and making good progress, despite Jo's ongoing banter.

There were two hours left in the session when Jo took a deep breath and leveled a new line of questions in Abby's direction.

"You think you're going to heaven, Abby? I mean really . . . like there's a place called heaven that some people go to when they die?"

Abby blinked and set down the photograph in her hand. It wasn't something she'd thought about much lately, but surely it was true. She'd given her life to Christ ages ago, and even though her personal life was a mess, that didn't mean God had rejected her, right? She gulped discreetly. "Yes, I'd say I was going to heaven."

"A real place called heaven? You think you're actually going there someday?" Jo rattled off the next question without giving Abby time to answer. "Not just a fantasy place, like an idea or a dream, but a real place?"

Abby sighed. It was enough to be racked with guilt where John was concerned, but being forced to think about heaven too . . . it was almost more than she could bear. They were halfway through the six-month prison sentence of pretending they were happily married, halfway to the day when they would file divorce papers. *What do I know about heaven?* "Yes, Jo, it's a real place. As real as anything here."

For the first time since she'd met the woman, Jo Harter had no response. She let Abby's comment sink in for nearly a minute before she thought of another question. "If you're right . . . if this heaven place is real, then that means hell's real too. Would you say that was so, Abby?"

Abby rested her forearms on the edge of the table and looked carefully at Jo. *I'm the most imperfect example here, Lord, but use me, please. Even as far gone as I've been lately, I know this much: her salvation is bigger than anything I'm dealing with.* "That's right, Jo. Hell's a real place."

"Lake of fire and the whole works? Torment and torture forever and ever?"

"Right, that's how Jesus describes it."

"But it's only for the bad guys, right? You know, murderers and people who fish without a license."

Abby was completely caught off guard. *Help me, Lord. Give me the words.* She brought her fingers together and tried to look deep into Jo's eyes, tried to exude the compassion she suddenly felt in her heart for this woman, her daughter's future mother-in-law. "Not according to Scripture." Abby paused. "The Bible says hell's for anyone who chooses not to accept His gift of salvation."

Jo released a tired huff. "Now that's the part that always gets me. Everyone goes on about how loving their God is, and then we get to this part about Him sending people to hell and I have to really wonder about that." She grabbed a quick breath. "What kind of loving God would send some-one to hell?"

I'm not up to this, Lord. Speak for me here, please. Her heart filled with words that were not her own. "People get a little mixed up when they think about God. See, when a person dies, God doesn't really *send* him anywhere."

Jo's face wrinkled in confusion. "There's only one God, right? Who else might be doin' the sending?"

Abby smiled. *Lord, she really doesn't know. Thank You, God, for the privilege of telling her.* "The way I understand it from Scripture, we make the decision for ourselves. When we die, God simply honors our choice."

"Meaning?" Jo had all but forgotten her scrapbook layout, her eyes wide with fascination.

Abby was consumed by a feeling of unworthiness, but she continued on, believing God for every word. "Meaning if we've admitted our need for a Savior and accepted Christ's free gift of salvation, when we die God honors that choice by welcoming us into heaven." Abby didn't want to give her too much at once. She hesitated, letting that first part sink in. "But if we've decided not to pursue a relation-ship with Jesus, if we've ignored the opportunities Christ presents for us, then when we die God honors that choice as well. Without the covering of grace from a Holy Savior, a person could not possibly gain entrance into heaven. In that case, hell is the only other option."

Again Jo was silent for a moment. "So you think the whole thing's true? And if I died tonight . . . I might not . . ." She didn't seem able to bring herself to finish the sen-tence. Instead she picked up her photograph and began cutting. Then without looking up she changed the sub-ject. "Did I hear Nicole right that we're planning a girls' getaway the week before the wedding? I can't think of a better idea, to tell you the truth. I mean a getaway to me suggests a cabin and a lake, and if there's one thing I love to do when I'm on vacation it's take in some good old-fashioned fishing . . ."

Jo was rambling again, running as fast and far as she could from the sentence she'd been unable to finish. Abby listened only partially, but focused most of her attention on the Lord, begging Him to let the seeds of truth take root in Jo's heart.

And in the process maybe ignite something new in her own.

"You know, Abby, I think I remember when it was things got bad for me and Denny. I mean, it was his choice to leave and all, but it was my fault too. I see that a lot clearer these days. It takes two to make a marriage work and two to make it fall apart. Those are words o' wisdom, for sure."

Abby nodded. "Sometimes, but not always." She thought of John and Charlene. "Sometimes one person finds someone else to love. That happens too."

Jo didn't seem to hear her. "You know what it was? I got busy. Busy with Matt, taking him to toddler classes and park outings and falling asleep beside him at night. I forgot about Denny pretty much, Abby. About that time the little things became big, know what I mean? Like him leaving the toothpaste lid off and forgettin' to put his dirty underwear in the laundry basket. We started fightin' about everything, and after that it didn't take long before we was only strangers walking around in a boxy little house in the heart of South Carolina."

"Hmmm. Where does he live now?"

"Boxy little apartment about an hour from here. At least that's what Matt says. I haven't talked to him in years."

The evening wore on, and Abby pondered the things Jo had said, things about heaven and hell and how it took two people to tear down what two people had built.

That night before she fell asleep, her last thoughts were of Jo Harter.

It's too late for me and John, Lord, for our marriage. But it's not too late for Jo. Tonight, Lord, please . . . let her fin-ish that all-important sentence before she falls asleep. Let her know that without You, she would have no chance whatso-ever of going to heaven.

Oh, and you do, right, Abby?

The voice hissed in her heart, and Abby refused to acknowledge it. She still loved Jesus very much, and she'd never rejected Him or willfully walked away, had she? A sinking feeling worked its way through her gut. Okay, but she hadn't rejected Him often. And though the choices she and John were making were bound to grieve God, certainly they wouldn't keep her from heaven.

Abby closed her eyes shaken by the truth. They might not keep her from heaven, but they would keep her from the paradise of growing old alongside the father of her children, from loving the man who once upon a lifetime ago was her other half.

Seventeen

SPRING FOOTBALL BROUGHT JOHN ANOTHER REASON to be out of the house—as well as the certainty that in three short months he and Abby could stop the charade and get on with the rest of their lives. Whatever that meant, John wasn't sure, but he found himself grateful beyond words for the hours when he stood planted on the sideline of the Marion High practice field, mindlessly barking correction and encouragement as the team walked through passing plays and prepared for a season still months away.

Brilliant afternoon sunshine beat down on the field, and the temperatures were unseasonably high. No wonder the team was having a hard time focusing. John crossed his arms and stood with his legs shoulder-width apart, knees locked. It was a stance familiar to his athletes, one that always seemed to convey his absolute authority.

His quarterback—a sophomore looking to take over Kade's position—dropped back and searched frantically for an open receiver. Downfield two players tripped over each other as the ball soared high above their heads.

"Line up again," he barked. "You look like a bunch of junior high players. Start over and do it right, or we can spend the next fifteen minutes running lines. Take it slow. We're learning the plays, remember?"

Next time through was smoother, and the ball settled easily into the hands of one of the tight ends. "Better! That's the way. State championship football, guys. Keep it up!"

He had yelled the same thing every spring for almost twenty years, and by now he could almost set himself on autopilot and coach an intense practice while his mind was miles away.

Four miles, precisely. Back at the house he still shared with Abby, the place where wedding plans were constantly at the center of every conversation and where the woman he was married to had figured out a way to make avoidance an art form.

So this is how it's going to end, huh, God? In a blur of busyness and wedding plans and promises of new love. The whole family was all worked up over the celebration of Nicole and Matt, and the plans left not even half an hour for Abby and John to talk about how they were supposed to do this, how they might cut ties that ran two decades deep. Was what they had, what they'd shared just going to fade into the distance?

Love bears all things, My son. Love never ends.

John clenched his jaw. "Shift right, Parker," he shouted. "The defense lines up the same each time. Football is a game of adjustments."

It wasn't about love; it was about letting go. Love had

long since left their marriage. Twenty years ago—ten even—this separation process would have been unbearable. But what he and Abby were losing now was a marriage of convenience. Two people who'd figured out a way to coexist, pay the bills on time, and celebrate their children's milestones together.

Love had nothing to do with it.

Remember the height from which you have fallen. Love as I have loved you.

John worked his worn-out gum and rubbed the back of his neck as he stared at the ground. He'd tried that, hadn't he? Back when Charlene first entered the picture, and he'd had the strength to walk out of her bedroom. Wasn't that an effort at remembering the height from which he'd fallen? He looked out at the players on the field once more.

It was Abby, really. It was her fault everything had fallen apart. She demanded so much, and she wasn't . . . well, she wasn't fun anymore. Always bossing him around and giving him that look that said he'd failed to live up to her expectations. Sometimes it seemed the only thing separating John from being just one more kid under Abby's control was the fact that his to-do list was longer than theirs.

She hadn't loved him in years. "Line up and do it again," he shouted. If she did, she had a strange way of showing it. "Get your seat down next time, Sanders. Linemen draw all their strength from their legs. Do it again."

No, she didn't love him. Not like she used to back when she would drop by at spring training or find a spot in the bleachers once in a while for summer two-a-days or wait for him at the end of every game—not just the big ones. Back when the kids and the writing and her father weren't more important than he was.

John huffed. That was the latest guilt trip she was laying on him: her father.

"He won't be around forever, John. It wouldn't hurt if you visited him once in a while."

Why did she have to word it like that?

"Footwork, Johnson," his voice bellowed across the field. "Catching a pass is all in the footwork. Find your rhythm, and let the ball come to you."

Couldn't she just have said that her father enjoyed spending time with him? John released a measured breath and shook his head. It wasn't her words exactly; it was her tone. Everything she said to him these days had an edge to it.

Not like the old days when she'd come up behind him and—

A delicate brush of fingers grazed the back of his neck and he spun around. "Charlene!" His players were watching, and he recovered instantly, regaining his stance and forcing an air of indifference. "I didn't hear you come up."

She wore a tight navy tank top and a jaunty skirt that clung to her in all the right places, stopping just short of her ankles. *I can't do this, God. Get her away from me.*

"I saw you out here and couldn't resist." She pouted in a way that made his insides melt. "Forgive me?"

He could feel a smile playing on his lips, but he shifted his weight and sidestepped her so that he faced the football field again. "Parker, try to hang back in the pocket five seconds this time. Under those Friday night lights every second counts. Let's go, guys, come on. Eagle pride!"

From the corner of his eye, he watched Charlene position herself next to him, standing close enough so their bare elbows touched, far enough away so as not to spark the curiosity of his players.

All her attention seemed focused on the field. "No answer, Coach?"

Why did she have to make him feel so alive, so good about himself? "Forgiven." He cast her a sideways grin. *Don't say it . . .* "You look good."

She angled her head so that her eyes were able to travel the length of him. "Yeah, you too." When her eyes reached his, her expression grew more serious. "I've missed you."

John clenched his teeth. *Flee this, My son. Flee!* He blinked back the warning. "Abby and I aren't talking anymore. Two strangers under the same roof."

She moved an inch closer, brushing her arm against his in a way that sent fire through his veins. "I'm taking some night classes . . . but I'll be home tonight." She slid her sandal closer to his shoe and tapped at him playfully. "Come by, why don't you? Tell Abby it's a coaches' meeting. Sounds like you need someone to talk to."

John stepped forward and cupped his hands around his mouth. "Run it again! That was terrible, defense. Key on the ball." He clapped three times. "Let's look like state champs out there."

Charlene waited a beat. "You're avoiding my question, Coach."

A breeze came across them and filled his senses with the fading smell of her perfume. *God, I can't resist this . . .* The idea of spending an evening with her, getting reacquainted after three months of intentionally staying away, was more enticing than he cared to think about. "Maybe."

Flee! Avoid the harlot, son.

The whispered words echoed through his heart and cooled his blood considerably. For reasons he couldn't understand, he suddenly regained much of his control. After all, he'd asked her to wait until after Nicole's wedding. Why was she here, anyway? "Actually, maybe not. I have a stack of tests to grade tonight."

Charlene's words were slow and measured, aimed deliberately at the place where John's passions were birthed. "You can't run from me forever, John Reynolds." She let her arm drag along his as she turned to go. "I'll be around if you change your mind."

Knowing she was walking away caused sharply contrasting feelings. A part of him wanted to blow the whistle, call off practice, follow her home, and stay with her all evening. Nothing physical, just a night of conversation with someone who actually liked him. But another part of him was experiencing relief like he'd never felt before. Strong and tangible. As though he'd just been spared a tumble into the darkest, deepest abyss.

Possibly into the pit of hell itself.

Matt's apartment was walking distance from Marion High, and with the weather nicer than usual, he'd taken to jogging back and forth to the campus each day after classes. His coursework was actually lighter than during any other semester, but what with studying for the upcoming bar exam and policing himself around Nicole, the stress was starting to get to him. Running did wonders to restore the peace.

That afternoon he figured he might do more than his usual three-mile jog. The Eagles would be practicing, and maybe Nicole's father could talk for a minute or two. It was strange, really. What with the wedding and all, he and Nicole needed to spend more time together than ever, but each day was more difficult than the previous one when it came to their physical relationship.

The night before was a perfect example. Nicole was at his house making plans about which songs the disc jockey would play at the reception, and before either of them knew it, they were on the sofa kissing. The hunger, the desire he felt for her was so strong that sometimes he felt like Esau—willing to sell his birthright for a single bowl of soup. Or in this case, a single night of . . .

Matt laced up his shoes and tied them with a ferocity that showed his frustration. Why couldn't he get a grip in this area? Twelve weeks. Eighty-four days, and they could love each other the way they longed to. But last night when she pulled away—her eyes clouded with a desire as intense as his—he literally had to ask her to leave.

"Not yet," she'd told him, still breathless from their kissing. "It's only nine-thirty."

He walked to the kitchen, ignoring her comment, and downed a glass of ice water. *Think of something else, Matt. Dirty fish tanks . . . bar exams . . . the ACLU.* That did it. His emotions cooled slightly.

"Did you hear me?" Nicole's tone was frustrated, and Matt realized he hadn't answered her yet.

He swallowed the last bit of water. "I don't care what time it is; you need to go. Believe me, Nicole."

Times like that had them on the verge of fighting, when all he wanted to do, all every part of his body wanted, was to love her totally and completely. *Lord, get me through these next three months without compromise.*

Honor one another above yourself . . .

Honor. That was the key. He'd read the verse earlier that morning, but it only now hit him. Why hadn't he thought of the truth there earlier? Victory could only be found by seeing Nicole the way God saw her, as a child of the King; not as the gorgeous, godly girl who was about to be his wife.

Honor one another . . .

Matt set out toward the school, still thinking about the idea. That had to be it, the reason God had guided him to that verse in the first place. By the time he got to school, he was determined to talk about it with Coach Reynolds. He knew from Nicole that her parents had avoided physical intimacy until after they were married. If there was one person who would understand what it meant to honor a woman, it was John Reynolds. And since Matt didn't yet have that kind of relationship with his own father, he could think of no one he'd rather talk to that afternoon than Nicole's dad.

The Marion High football field came into view. The team was spread out across the grass, and Nicole's father was on the sidelines with . . . was it Nicole's mother? The woman looked shorter, with darker hair. The closer Matt got, the easier it was to see that she wasn't Abby Reynolds, even though she stood arm to arm beside Nicole's father.

Matt studied the way Coach Reynolds seemed to be enjoying the woman's attention. The way they smiled at each other, their elbows touching . . . If he didn't know better, Matt would have been concerned. But she was probably just the girls' coach, someone he worked with.

He was still studying them, drawing closer, when the woman brushed past Nicole's father and walked purposefully across the field, back toward the school buildings. A few seconds later, Matt was at the older man's side, breathless and sweating from his run. "Hey, Mr. Reynolds."

Nicole's dad had been watching the brunette as she left, and he swung around, eyes wide. "Matt! Where'd you come from?"

Matt bent over to catch his breath. "Home. I jog by here every day. Thought I might catch you." He pointed at the kids on the field. "You whippin' these guys into shape?"

Nicole's father uttered a strange-sounding laugh and hesitated a beat. "Every year. Same routine." He took a step toward the playing field. "Get some air under the ball, Parker. Give your receivers time to get downfield!"

Waving in the direction of the woman, Matt cocked his head. "Is she one of the coaches here?"

Nicole's dad licked his lips and glanced over his shoulder. "The woman, you mean? The one I was talking to?"

Again, his reactions seemed odd. *Probably preoccupied with coaching* . . . "Right. A few minutes ago."

"She's a teacher here, a friend." He barked another command at his team. "What brings you by?"

Matt took up a similar stance as the man beside him, his attention focused on the playing field. "Honor, I guess."

He glanced at Nicole's father. Was it Matt's imagination, or had the man's face gotten paler since his arrival? Maybe he was sick.

"Honor?"

Moving his foot in small figure eights in the grass, Matt thought about his choice of words. "Nicole and I are fighting a lot lately. I don't know, I don't think it should be like this right before our wedding."

Coach Reynolds's brow wrinkled. "Fighting? You mean you're not getting along?"

Matt exhaled through pursed lips and shook his head. "No, it's the other way around. We're getting along too well, if you know what I mean." He leveled his gaze at Nicole's father. "It's like I can't even be near her. I'm so tempted I can't see straight."

There was a flexing motion in the man's jawline. *Great, now he thinks I'm a dog. Why did I want to talk to him about this? Give me the words, God. I'm sure this man has insight . . . if only I can get him to share it with me.* Mr. Reynolds looked like he was afraid to ask the next question. "But you've . . . I mean so far you haven't . . ."

Matt was quick to answer. "No, that's just it. We've stayed away from each other. We promised God, each other for that matter, that we'd stay pure." He shook his head and stared at the ground for a moment. "It's a lot tougher than I thought it'd be. Like there's this constant tension where we want to be together, but we know there's only so much we can take."

Nicole's father nodded. "Gotcha. Wish I could tell you it'll get easier."

"Maybe I need to change my thinking, you know?" Matt shifted his position so he could see the man better. "This morning I read a scripture about honoring others, putting them above yourself. I think there's truth there, something that might help me get through this without breaking my promises."

The coach swallowed hard and seemed to struggle with his words. "Honoring others, huh?"

The cheerleaders had been working out on an adjacent field, and two of them ran up, slightly out of breath and giggling. Their entire attention was focused on Matt. "Mr. Reynolds, you've been holding out on us," a tiny blonde said, tossing her ponytail.

"Yeah, who's the new coach?" The taller of the two blushed and giggled, elbowing her friend.

Matt contained a chuckle. It had been a while since he'd been on a high-school campus, but girls like these didn't affect him. There was only one girl who had power over him anymore. He held out his hand politely to one cheerleader, then the other. "Matt Conley, and I'm not a new coach."

Nicole's father cleared his throat and raised his eyebrows sarcastically at the girls. "Matt's marrying my daughter in a few months."

Both girls' eyes grew wide, and they repressed a bout of nervous laughter. "Oh . . . right. Okay." The blonde grabbed her friend's arm, and the two headed off, giggling over their shoulders. "Bye, Matt. Nice to meet you."

Coach Reynolds leveled a humorous gaze at him. "Is this a daily problem?"

Matt laughed softly and shrugged. "Sometimes, but that's true for most guys." He grew serious. "After meeting Nicole it's like they're not even there." He looked at the man beside him. "Sort of like you and Mrs. Reynolds."

Nicole's father crossed his arms more tightly in front of him, and Matt noticed that his fists were clenched. "Keep that feeling, Matt. Whatever you have to do, keep that."

"Was it, you know . . . did you and Mrs. Reynolds struggle with staying pure before you got married?"

A sigh slid out through the man's clenched teeth. He looked at Matt and angled his head as if caught up in a dozen memories. "It wasn't easy. I guess it was like you said: I honored Abby. I loved her for who she was, not what she could do for me. Not for the feeling I got when we were together." He paused. "When I had my focus right, it wasn't so bad."

He loved her for who she was, not what she could do for him. Matt played that over in his mind again and felt like someone had turned on a light. Hope filled him, and he knew that next time he saw Nicole, he would see her soul and not only her body. Maybe that's why God asked couples to wait. So they could learn to love each other. Because over the years it would take that kind of love to make their relationship a beautiful thing.

"You have the best marriage, Mr. Reynolds. I want you to know how much your example has helped me." Matt shook his head, amazed at the wisdom the years had developed in Nicole's father. "I want to love Nicole the same way you've loved her mother. The last thing I want is the mess my parents made of their marriage."

Nicole's father changed his footing. "Your parents split up a while ago, huh?"

"Back when I was a little kid. Mom was busy with me, and Dad . . . well, he had a hard time telling the girls no. Same thing with the bottle. After a while he took up with someone else and left us."

Coach Reynolds swallowed hard and stared at his football team. "He's, uh . . . been in contact with you lately, that right? That's what Nicole said."

"Yeah, it's amazing. He gave his life to God, and the changes have been something else. Still, he missed out on me growing up. Missed out on a lot." Matt let his gaze fall on the tree line in the distance. "Makes me wonder how different it might have been if he'd been a believer before. You know, like you guys. Then divorce wouldn't have been an option, and they'd have found a way to make it work."

Nicole's father took a deep breath and bellowed toward the field. "All right guys, bring it in." Immediately the players stopped what they were doing and jogged toward their coach. He looked at Matt. "Don't know if I was much help, son, but I need to talk with the team. You wanna hang around?"

Matt reached out and shook the man's hand. "That's okay. I gotta get back and study. Actually, you helped me a lot." It was all Matt needed, knowing that this man had faced temptation and succeeded by learning to truly love his wife-to-be. "See ya, Coach."

And with that Matt jogged off toward home, certain between God's help and Mr. Reynolds's example he could survive the next three months.

John had been trembling inside from the moment Matt walked up, deeply afraid his daughter's fiancé had seen something between him and Charlene, a nuance or glance or flirtatious look. A sign that John Reynolds was not the man he appeared to be, but rather a cheap, two-timing hypocrite.

He talked to his team briefly and dismissed them to the weightroom, where Coach Kenny would be in charge. By the time the last player had made it off the field, John's trembling had become full-blown shakes.

Liar, John Reynolds. Liar, phony, hypocrite.

He shook off the taunting voice and began making his way around the field, collecting cones and gathering equipment.

You're a snake, a worthless excuse of a man.

John gritted his teeth and forced his body to relax.

Nausea caused his lunch to well up somewhere near his throat, and he gulped several times to keep from losing it. *I need to talk to someone, get this off my chest.* Maybe Abby's father. He thought about the man as he had so often lately, his father's best friend, lying ill in a nursing home without the benefits of his son-in-law's regular visits.

He wouldn't want to see me now, anyway.

An aching filled his heart, and again John knew deep in his bones it had nothing to do with his health. Suddenly his words to Matt came back loud and clear, as if someone was shouting at him.

"I honored Abby. I honored Abby . . . honored Abby. I loved her for who she was, not what she could do for me. Not for the feeling I got when we were together. I loved her for who she was . . ."

He chided himself. *How could you talk to that boy as if you understood love? You don't know real love from lust anymore.*

An oppressive feeling settled over his shoulders, bringing with it a burden he could barely stand up under.

One after another, Matt's statements flashed in his mind.

"You have the best marriage, Mr. Reynolds . . . your example has helped me . . . I want to love Nicole the same way you've loved her mother. Makes me wonder how different it might have been if he'd been a believer like you guys. Then divorce wouldn't have been an option . . . wouldn't have been an option . . . wouldn't have been an option."

John hauled a bag of cones across the field. Without realizing it, everything Matt said had been wrong. All of it. *And you let him believe it was all true.* Suddenly he understood the nausea; he was making himself sick. He was so far gone he ought to get Charlene and leave town tomorrow. Forget about his family. They wouldn't want anything to do with him once they learned the truth. The burden in John's heart grew heavier until he dropped the equipment bag and eased himself onto his knees, falling forward, his face buried in the musty grass.

God, help me! I can't leave them now, not yet. Oh, Lord, how have I failed You so badly?

Hear Me, son. The voice was so strong, so real, John sat up and looked around. *Love one another . . . as I have loved you, so you must love one another.*

He glanced in a handful of directions, but there was no one else on the field, and a chill ran down his arms. God still cared, still heard his cries. Otherwise He wouldn't have answered that way. *I can't do it, Lord. She hates me. It's too late for love.*

Silence.

John turned his face to heaven. *Cure me of the desire I feel for Charlene, Lord. My body wants her like . . . like . . .*

Then it hit him.

He wanted Charlene the same way he'd once wanted Abby. The exact same way. But when he thought about the advice he'd given Matt, it simply didn't apply to Charlene. He didn't love her that way, didn't love the soul and spirit deep inside her. There was only one thing he loved about her: the way she made him feel. Emotionally and physically.

But definitely not spiritually.

It hit him there on the forty-yard line, as his heart pled for God's intervention, that what he sought in Charlene Denton was a shadow, a counterfeit. Because the real thing, the love he had longed for all his life, could only be found in Abby Reynolds.

The woman who had first taught him what it was to love.

Eighteen

THE PHONE CALL ABBY HAD DREADED ALL HER ADULT life came at 4:15 in the afternoon the first week of May. John was at practice; Nicole and Sean were playing catch outside; Kade was working on his senior project at the school library.

"Hello?"

There was a hesitation on the other end. "Mrs. Reynolds? This is Helen at Wingate Nursing Home. I'm afraid your father has had a stroke."

Abby's breath caught in her throat. *No, God. Not now. Not with Nicole's wedding so close. I need him, Lord. Please.* "Is it . . . is he okay?"

"It happened about thirty minutes ago, and he's been in and out of a coma ever since. He doesn't seem to have control of his extremities."

What? No control? The words rang like a series of

alarms in Abby's mind. "I'm not sure I understand. You mean he's too tired to move?"

The woman at the other end sighed. "The stroke may have left him paralyzed, Mrs. Reynolds." She hesitated. "I'm sorry to have to tell you this over the phone."

Dear God, no. A series of images flashed on the screen in Abby's heart: her father running the sidelines at one of his games, doing sprints alongside his players, playing tennis with her the year before his diagnosis. Her father thrived on being active. If his legs were gone, his spirit to live would quickly follow. *No, Lord . . . please. Help him.*

"I'm on my way." She thanked the woman and hung up the phone. Then, as if by being in control she could keep her dad from dying, she went outside and calmly explained the situation to Sean and Nicole. Next she called Kade on his cell phone.

"Grandpa's had a stroke."

Kade's voice reflected his shock. "Are you sure? I was just there last weekend. He seemed—"

"It's true." She forced herself to remain composed. "Your dad's at practice. Get him and meet me at Wingate." She swallowed back a sob. "Hurry, Kade."

There was one last phone call, to her sister on the East Coast.

"How serious is it?" Beth had not been close to their father since before her divorce twelve years earlier. Now, though, there was concern in her voice.

"It's bad, Beth. Get on a plane, quick."

Abby, Nicole, and Sean piled into the van, and the drive that usually took fifteen minutes took ten. They hurried inside, and Abby saw that Kade and John had not yet arrived. *Don't blow this one, John.* He hadn't been in to see her father in more than a month.

She banished the thought. There was no time for negative feelings now, not with her dad fighting for his life down the hall. "Nicole, stay here with Sean and watch for your dad and Kade. I'll go see Grandpa first."

Nicole nodded, her eyes, damp, face drawn and filled with sadness. She had always been close to her grandpa. Especially in the eight years since he'd given up his home in Wisconsin and moved closer to them. It was the same way with the boys. He'd been a part of their lives almost as far back as they could remember.

Abby hurried down the hallway and quietly opened the door to his room. What she saw brought tears to her eyes. Her father lay prone and utterly still, his face slack, hands motionless as though he'd aged twenty years overnight. A nurse stood nearby taking his vital signs.

"Should we call an ambulance?" Abby was at her father's side immediately, taking his hand, shocked at the way it hung limp in her own.

The nurse shook her head as she adjusted his intravenous needle. "He's stable now. There's nothing more they could do for him. We're giving him a medication to undo the damage done by the stroke. It'll take time, though."

"To work?"

"To know if it did any good. Sometimes a major stroke can set off a series of strokes. With someone as ill as your father, the chances of him recovering without damage are slim, Mrs. Reynolds."

She tightened her grip on her father's hand. "But it's possible, right? I mean he could come out of this and be the way he was before the stroke, right?"

The nurse looked hesitant. "Not very likely." She finished working on him and straightened, leveling a sympathetic gaze at Abby. "We think it'd be best if the family came now, Mrs. Reynolds. Another stroke could be the end for him, I'm afraid."

More tears filled Abby's eyes, and she nodded, unable to speak. The nurse took the cue and left them alone. Abby waited until the woman was gone before she found her voice.

"Dad, it's me. Can you hear me? We're all here, Dad. The kids are in the other room."

Her father's eyelids fluttered and his mouth, dry and cracked, began working without sound.

"Dad, I'm here. If you wanna talk I'm right here." Tears spilled down Abby's cheeks, but her voice was stronger than before. "I'm listening, Dad."

His mouth worked some more, and this time his eyes rolled back in his head three times, as though he was trying to focus on her, trying to see her one last time.

"Oh, Dad, I'm so sorry . . ." Her voice broke and she laid her head on his chest, allowing the sobs that had built in her heart. "I love you, Dad."

"John . . ."

The word startled Abby, and she lifted her head, searching her father's face for signs of life. His eyes opened slowly, and he caught Abby's gaze. Again his mouth worked, and he repeated the same word he'd said a moment earlier. "John . . ."

"You want John, Daddy?" Abby didn't understand. John hadn't been to see him in weeks. Why now, when he couldn't move, could barely speak, would he want to talk to John? Especially when he knew the truth about their troubled marriage.

There was a pleading in her father's eyes that was unmistakable, as though whatever he had to tell John was, in that moment, the most important, most pressing thing in his life. Abby remembered how strong her father had looked that day at the Michigan football game when her family had greeted John outside the team locker room. The year she was just seventeen. Later that week her father had winked at her and confessed something. "John's always been like a son to me, Abby. The only son I ever had. I kinda hoped he'd wait for you to grow up."

Abby looked at her father now and squeezed his hand. "All right, Dad. I'll get him." She started backing away. "You hang on now, okay. I'll be right back."

Tears still spilling down her cheeks, Abby rushed down the hall, relieved to see John and Kade with Nicole and Sean in the waiting room. John hurried to meet her with the others close behind.

"How is he?" John's face was a mask of concern, and Abby wanted to spit at him. *Sure, care about him now . . . now that he's dying.* She hung her head and squeezed her eyes shut.

"Abby, how is he?" John's voice was more urgent.

"He's . . . he's . . ." The sobs overcame her, and her body shook with the force of her emotion. *Don't take my dad, Lord. He's all I have. My only friend. Please . . .*

Her family circled in closer, and John put his arms around her, holding her in a loose hug that probably looked more comfortable than it felt. "Honey, I'm sorry. We're here for you."

Abby reeled at the feel of his arms around her. How long had it been since she'd stood in his embrace? And how come it still felt like the most right place in the world? She thought about his words, and she wasn't sure if she should hold onto him tighter or kick him in the leg. How dare he lie and call her honey at a time like this? Was it that important to look good in front of the kids? He hadn't been protective of her for years. Why would now be any different?

And why did it feel so good to have his arms around her? She cried softly, keeping her warring emotions to herself.

"He's . . . still alive . . . right, Mom?" Nicole's expression was racked with fear.

Abby nodded, realizing that she hadn't explained the situation. "He can't move; he can barely talk. He . . . he looks like a different man."

Nicole started crying, and John circled her and Sean and Kade into their hug. The five of them hung on to each other, and Abby realized that she wasn't only losing her father. She was losing this—her family's ability to grieve together, to suffer life's dark and desperate times under the strength of her husband. In a few months she would be on her own, forced to shoulder every major setback and milestone by herself.

From where he stood near the back of the huddle, Kade began to pray. "God, we come before You as a family asking that You be with our grandpa, Mom's dad. He loves You very much, Lord, and, well . . . You already know that. But he's real sick, God. Please be with him now, and help him not be afraid."

Abby tightened the hold she had on Kade's shoulder. He was such a good boy, so much like the man his father had once been. The thought of his leaving for college in the fall was enough to send another wave of sobs tearing through her gut. Then she realized that Kade had not prayed for healing.

Almost as if God was preparing them for the inevitable.

The sobs subsided after a few minutes, and Abby remembered her father's request. She lifted her head and found John's eyes. "He asked for you."

Was it her imagination or did John's eyes cloud with fear the moment Abby told him? "Me?" The word was barely more than a whisper.

Abby nodded. "It seemed urgent."

John drew a steadying breath and nodded toward the waiting room. "You guys wait for me. I'll be back."

Without hesitating, he led the way down the hall while Abby stayed close behind him. They entered the room together, and Abby took up watch on the far side of the bed. Her father's head was moving about restlessly on the pillow, and when he heard them his eyes opened, searching until they found John.

His mouth started working again, and finally the sound followed. "Come . . ."

John moved close to the bed and took her father's lifeless hand in his stronger ones. "Hi, Joe."

It broke Abby's heart to see her dad struggle so hard to speak. Clearly he couldn't move, and she realized the nurse had been right. The stroke had left him paralyzed—at least for now.

Once more he began opening and closing his mouth, but this time his eyes were more alert, more focused. Never once did they leave John's face. "Lubber . . ."

What was her father saying? Abby couldn't make it

out, and the expression on John's face told her he couldn't either.

"It's okay, Joe," John's voice was low and soothing. "Don't struggle. The Lord's here."

Oh, please . . . you of all—

Abby stopped herself. This wasn't the time to harbor resentment toward John. "Dad . . ." She spoke loudly so he could hear her from across the room. "Say it again, Dad."

Her father kept his gaze glued to John's face. "Lub-ber . . ." His words were slurred, running together so that it was impossible to understand. Abby closed her eyes and tried to hear beyond his broken speech. "Lub-her . . . lub-her . . ."

"Lu . . ." John tried to repeat the beginning of whatever it was her father was trying to say. "Can you say it once more, Joe. I'm sorry."

Abby willed her father the ability to speak clearly. Just this once when whatever it was he wanted to say was of such importance to him. *Please, God . . . give him the words.*

Her dad blinked twice, and his eyes filled with desperation as his voice grew louder. "Love her . . . love her."

"Love her." The words hit Abby like a tidal wave, washing away her determination to be strong. *"Love her."* In his most pained moment, when death itself might be only minutes away, his single message to his son-in-law was this: Love her. Love his daughter Abby for now, forever. Love her.

Abby looked across the room at John and saw that he, too, understood. Tears trickled down his rugged cheeks, and he seemed to struggle for the right words. When none came, he nodded, his chin quivering under the intensity of the moment.

Her father didn't let it rest. He blinked again—the only action he seemed to have left—and this time said it even more clearly. "Love her . . . John."

Guilt and remorse worked their way into John's features and he cocked his head, gazing across the bed at Abby. Then without speaking, he held up a single, shaky hand in her direction, beckoning her, begging her to come to him. Silently he mouthed the word, "please."

Two quick breaths lodged in Abby's chest, and she moved toward him. No matter that he'd fallen out of love with her, regardless of the ways in which he'd betrayed his wedding vows, despite Charlene and everything she represented, Abby came. John held his arm out to her until she was nestled underneath it, snug against him, side by side. A couple, facing her father as one.

Even if only to appease him in his dying hour.

"She's here, Joe. See . . . she's here." John's tears fell on her father's hand and bedsheets as Abby remained at his side, one arm clinging to her husband, the other stroking her father's kneecap.

Her dad's eyes moved from John to Abby, and his head began to bob ever so slightly, up and down, as if approving what he was seeing between them. He nodded this way for a while then let his eyes settle on John once more. "Love her."

"I will, Dad." John had never called him that before. But since his own father had died, he hadn't had a man to fill that role. Over the years John had grown too consumed with his increasingly separate life to spend much time with her father. And now . . . by calling him *Dad*, John was conveying his regrets.

"Love her . . . always." Her father's words were getting

weaker, but his message was exceptionally clear and repet-
itive. *Love Abby. Again and again. Love her now. Love her
forever.*

Two short sobs escaped from deep in John's heart, and
he blinked hard so he could see clearly. Tightening his grip
on Abby, he nodded again. "I'll always love her, Dad."

A peace came over Abby's father, and his entire body
seemed to relax. His eyes moved slowly until they found
Abby again. "Kids . . ."

John was quick to pull away, nodding to Abby. "I'll get
them." He returned with all three in tow in less than a
minute. They filed in, Nicole taking up her position
opposite the place where Abby stood, and Kade and Sean
falling in beside her.

Her father shot a questioning look at John, and in
response he immediately resumed his place at Abby's side.

"Hi, Grandpa." Nicole cried unabashedly, indifferent
to the way her makeup ran down her cheeks. "We're praying for you."

As if every bit of motion required the effort of a
marathon, Dad turned his head so that he could find his
grandchildren. "Good . . . good kids."

Sean started to cry, and Kade—his own eyes wet—put
an arm around his brother, pulling him close, letting him
know that tears were okay in times like this. Sean leaned
forward and threw his arms around his grandpa, holding
on as though he could keep Abby's father from leaving
them. "I love you, Grandpa."

The sounds of gentle sobs filled the room, and Abby
noticed tears in her father's eyes as well. "Jesus . . ."

Sean stood up slowly and crowded close between Nicole
and Kade.

Abby thought she understood, but it grieved her all the same. "Jesus . . . Dad . . . you want to go to Jesus?"

In response, another wave of peace washed over his features, and the corners of his lips lifted just a fraction. "I . . . love you . . . all."

A flicker of concern flashed once more in her father's eyes, and he turned with excruciating slowness back to John and Abby. Before he could say anything, John tightened the grip he had on Abby, fresh tears spilling from his eyes. "I will, Dad."

His shoulders sank deeper into the bed, and his smile grew until it filled his face. "God . . . is happy."

Abby's body convulsed with sobs, hating how they were tricking him into believing everything was okay, and yet wishing with all her heart that John meant what he said. That he actually might still love her, that he always would love her . . . that they would love each other. And that somehow by doing so they might actually make God happy again.

With the five of them holding on to him, each hoping that somehow it wasn't his time to go, he closed his eyes and breathed three more times.

Then he was gone.

It took five hours to say their good-byes, finish the paperwork, and watch while a mortuary attendant took her father's body to prepare it for burial. The funeral was set for three days later, and throughout the evening Abby felt as if she were wading through syrup, as if death had happened to somebody else's dad and not hers. As if the entire process of planning her dad's funeral was little more than a poorly acted scene from a bad movie.

John stayed by her side until they got home, then as all three kids headed for bed, he went to sit in the silent living room, dropping his head in his hands. Abby stared at him. *Are you wishing for more time with him, John?*

She kept her question to herself and headed upstairs to make sure the kids were okay. One at a time she hugged each of them again and assured them that Grandpa was at home now, in heaven with Grandma where he'd longed to be for years. Each of the kids wept in her arms as she made the rounds, but Abby stayed strong.

It wasn't until she headed downstairs that she felt the finality of the situation. Her father was gone. Never again would she sit by his side, holding his hand and listening while he talked about the glory days on the gridiron. Her mentor, her protector . . . her daddy.

Gone.

Abby reached the last stair, rounded the corner, and suddenly she couldn't take another step. Her back against the wall, she collapsed, burying her face in her hands, giving way to the sobs that had been building since her father's final breath. "Why?" she cried out softly in a voice meant for no one to hear. "Daaaad. No! I can't do this!"

"Abby . . ."

John's hands were on hers before she heard him coming. Gentle, strong, protective hands that carefully removed her fingers from her face, then eased her arms around his waist as he drew her to himself. "Abby, I'm so sorry."

She knew she should pull away, should refuse his comfort in light of the lies he'd told her father earlier that evening. But she could no more do so than she could force her heart to stop beating. She laid her head on his chest and savored the feeling, allowing him to absorb the shaking of her body, the stream of tears that worked its way into his sweaty coaching shirt . . . a shirt that smelled of day-old cologne and musty grass and something sweet and innate that belonged to this man and him alone. Abby savored the scent, knowing there was no place she'd rather be.

John tightened his embrace and let his head rest on hers. Only then did Abby feel the way his body trembled. Not with desire as it had so often in their early days, but with a sadness, with a wave of sobs deeper than Abby had ever known him to cry. She thought how her husband had missed his chance, how he'd chosen to be too busy to visit with her father in his dying days.

How great his guilt had to be.

She raised her head and swallowed back her own sobs, searching John's face, so close to hers. His eyes were closed, and grief filled his features. Abby allowed his forehead to rest against hers and felt his weeping ease some. His arms still locked around her waist, he opened his eyes and looked deeply into hers. "I loved him . . . you know that, right, Abby?"

Fresh tears forged a trail down her cheeks as she nodded. "I know."

"He was . . . he was like my own dad." John's words were little more than a whisper, and Abby savored the moment even as her heart shouted at her: *What are you doing, Abby? If things are over between you two, why does it feel so right to be here? Why did he come to you if he doesn't love you anymore?*

John let the side of his face graze up against hers, nuzzling her in a way that was achingly familiar. A roller-coaster feeling made its way across Abby's insides as her body instinctively reacted to John's nearness.

"My dad told me you were like a son to him . . ." Abby clung tightly to John, speaking the words inches from his ear. "He said he was glad you waited for me to grow up because you were . . . the only son he ever had."

A faint sense of hope filled John's watery eyes, and he pulled back a few inches, searching Abby's face. "He said that?"

She nodded, her hands still linked at the back of his waist. "When I was seventeen. A few weeks after that first game, remember? The first time I watched you play at Michigan?"

Instantly the mood changed, and John went still as his eyes locked on hers. Without saying a word their embrace grew closer, their bodies melding together. Wasn't this how he'd looked at her all those years ago, back when he had wanted nothing more than to be by her side?

John ran his thumb over her cheek. "I remember . . ." He framed her face with both hands and wove his fingers into her hair. "I remember . . ."

She realized what was about to happen seconds before it actually did. He brought his lips closer to hers, and she saw his eyes cloud with sudden, intense desire. Abby's heart pounded against his chest.

What are these feelings, and why now? When everything is over between us?

She had no answers for herself, only one defining truth: she desperately wanted John's kiss, wanted to know that he could still feel moved in her arms, even if it made no sense whatsoever.

He kissed her, slowly, gently at first . . . but as she took

his face in her hands, the act became more urgent, filled
with the passion of a hundred lost moments. His mouth
opened over hers and she could taste the salt from both
their tears. Fresh tears, tears of passion . . . tears of regret.

The urgency within Abby built, and she could feel
John's body trembling again—but this time in a way that
was familiar, a way that made her want to—

His hands left her face, and he ran them slowly up
and down her sides as he moved his lips toward her ear.
"Abby . . ."

What did he mean by all this? Was this really happening? Was he comforting her the only way he knew how? Or
could he be trying to tell her he was sorry, that no matter
what had happened in the past, it was behind them now?
She wasn't sure about anything except how good it felt to
be in his arms, as though whatever mistakes their hearts
and minds had made might somehow be erased by the
physical feelings they apparently still had for each other.

Abby kissed him again and then slid her face along his,
aware of the way his body pressed against hers. "I . . . I
don't understand . . ."

John nudged her chin with his face and tenderly
moved his lips along her neck as his thumbs worked in
small circles against her upper ribs. He found her mouth
once more and kissed her again . . . and again. He moved
his mouth closer to her ear. "I promised your father, Abby
. . . I said I would love you . . ."

What? Abby felt like someone had dumped a bucket of
ice water over her head. Her body went stiff. That's what
this was about? His coming to her now, his kisses and
desire . . . it was all part of some kind of guilt trip her
father had placed on him minutes before dying? Her

desire dissipated like water on an oil-slicked freeway. She braced her hands against him and pushed him.

"Get away from me." The tenderness in her voice was gone, and she spat the words through gritted teeth.

John's eyes flew open, his face awash with shock and unrequited desire. "What . . . what're you doing?"

"I don't need your charity, John."

His expression was frozen in astonishment. "My . . . what do you mean?"

Fresh tears filled her eyes and spilled onto her cheeks as she pushed him again. "You can't love me out of . . . of . . ." She searched for the right words, her angry heart racing in her chest. "Out of some kind of obligation to my dead father."

Abby watched as a handful of emotions flashed in John's eyes. Shock gave way to understanding, then shifted to intense, burning rage. "That is *not* what I'm doing!" His face grew red, and the muscles in his jaw flexed.

A wind of regret blew across the plains of Abby's barren heart. Why was he lying to her? He'd explained it perfectly a moment ago: he'd promised Abby's father that he'd love her, and this—*whatever* this was that had happened between them—was merely some dutiful way for John to make good on his word.

Strangely, his expression grew even more troubled, and Abby tried to make sense of it. Was that hurt in his eyes? Pain? How *could* it be? She was the one who'd been tricked into thinking he actually wanted her again . . . actually felt about her the way he had before they'd grown apart.

New tears built up in his eyes, and twice he started to open his mouth as if to speak, then once more he clenched his teeth together. The intense anger in his eyes was too much, and Abby looked away. As she did, he put his hands on her shoulders and jerked her close against him again, kissing her with a passion that was as much rage as it was desire. She kissed him back, her body acting with a will of its own.

"Stop!" She was crying harder than before, disgusted with herself for her inability to tear away from him. *How can I enjoy his kiss even now?*

In response to her own silent question, she yanked her head back and snarled at him, "Get away from me!"

His hands fell to his sides, and he took a step backward. His eyes were dry now, his words hard, lacking any of the emotion of the past ten minutes. "It's no use, is it, Abby?"

She shook her head. "Not if it's going to be like that . . . just a way for you to keep your promise to my dad." She fanned her fingers over her heart as another wave of tears spilled from her eyes. "You don't want me, John. You're in love with Charlene. I know that. Don't stand here and try to convince yourself you feel something for me when we both know you don't."

John sighed, and his head dropped in frustration. He looked up and gazed at the ceiling. "I give up, Abby." His eyes found hers again. "I'm sorry about your dad." He paused, the anger and even the indifference replaced by a sad resignation. "I loved him too. And about tonight . . ." He shook his head. "I'm . . . I'm sorry, Abby."

His last words were like a slap in the face. *Don't apologize, John. Tell me you meant that kiss . . . every moment of it. Tell me I'm wrong, that it wasn't because of your promise to Dad.* She wiped her hand across her cheeks and hugged herself tight. *I know you felt something with me, John. We both felt something! Tell me that . . .*

But he said nothing, and Abby exhaled as the fight left her. She didn't want to argue with John; she just wanted her dad back. "It's been a long day for both of us . . ." She was suddenly sorry she'd lost her temper with him. Even if he had kissed her for all the wrong reasons, somehow she knew he was trying to comfort her, trying to show her that despite their differences he still cared. The fact made her want to reach out and at least hug him, but there seemed no way to bridge the distance between them. She took a step toward the stairs. "Good night, John."

He stood there, not moving, watching her as something raw and vulnerable flashed in his eyes. Whatever he was feeling, he shared none of it with her. "Good night, Abby."

She forced herself up the steps to the guest room, peeled off her clothes, and slipped into a T-shirt she kept under the pillow. Then she tried desperately to remember every happy moment she'd ever shared with her father.

But it was no use.

As she drifted off to sleep, there was only one troubling thought that reigned in her head . . .

How good it had felt to kiss John Reynolds again.

It was the morning of the funeral service, and for John, the single feeling that prevailed in the days since Joe Chapman's death was not grief at the man's passing or the chasm of loss he felt at having missed the chance to know him better. Rather, it was the memory of Abby in his arms, wracked with tears, clinging to him, fitting next to him, beside him, the way she hadn't been in years.

The memory of their kiss.

No matter what Abby thought, his kiss hadn't been

out of obligation. His feelings had been stronger than anything he'd ever felt for anyone else. Even Charlene. But obviously Abby hadn't felt the same way. As always, she'd found a reason to fight with him.

Since then John had wrestled so strongly with thoughts of Abby that the morning of the funeral service he was running on only two hours' sleep. He had been up most of the night wondering what the feelings meant. Had Abby's father prayed some miraculous prayer, uttered some powerful words of healing? Was it possible that John Chapman's death might spark new life in their dying marriage?

It didn't seem like it.

After all, she hadn't said more than five words to him since then, and at night she still headed off for the guest room without so much as a good-night. But still . . . the possibility was there, wasn't it? Or maybe Abby was right. Maybe the kiss was out of some deep obligation to her father, something to make up for the fact that he'd made the man a promise he couldn't possibly keep.

Love her forever? When they were weeks away from being divorced?

John released a quiet, frustrated sigh and glanced around the church. There weren't many people, only a fraction of those who remembered the goodness of Joe Chapman. Abby's friends from school—mostly parents of the kids' friends. Matt Conley and his mother, Jo; Abby's sister, Beth; and a handful of nurses from Wingate. John's mother was too ill with Alzheimer's to leave her nursing home, otherwise she would have been there. Abby's father had been her friend too.

In his glory days, Joe had been every bit the well-known

football coach John was. Hundreds of people would have recognized him as he went about his day, greeted him in the markets, and counted themselves lucky to be among his friends. Yet here, at the end of his journey, Joe Chapman was only remembered by a handful, a remnant of the fan club that had once been his.

Is this all it amounts to, God? Live your life year in, year out, affecting the lives of hundreds of kids only to go out all alone?

This world is not your home, son . . .

The verse came to him as easily as air, and John knew it was true. But still . . . John wrestled with his feelings, not sure exactly how he felt about heaven. It sounded good, certainly. Talking about Joe Chapman being at rest, at peace, having a body that was healthy and would never wear out . . . assuring each other that he was in the presence of God and his wife and John's own father and a dozen others who'd gone on before him.

But still, he was gone. And right now that seemed like second best.

A preacher took the podium and unfolded a sheet of paper. "I didn't know a lot about Joe Chapman," he began. "So I acted on the suggestion of his daughter Abby and contacted the Christian church where Joe was a member for nearly thirty years." He paused and let his eyes fall over the small gathering of people. John liked the way the man talked, slow and friendly, as if he'd known them all for years.

"You might be surprised with what I found." The pastor shrugged his shoulders and smiled in a sad way. "I'm not sure he'd like me telling you, but I think it's okay just this once. So you might know what an amazing man Joe Chapman really was."

Peering down at his notes, he began. "Joe Chapman was a teacher, a football coach. He did not make a great deal of money. But every fall from the first year he taught until he retired, he purchased a complete Thanksgiving dinner and had the church deliver it to one of his players. A boy and his family who would otherwise have gone without."

John cringed inwardly. *What had he ever done for others? In that moment he could think of nothing . . .* Beside him, Abby cast a curious glance down the row at her sister. Abby's father had never talked about the dinners, never mentioned them at all. Obviously even Abby hadn't known about them. John focused his attention back on the pastor.

"Until Parkinson's disease got the better of him, Joe spent the early hours one Saturday each and every month raking leaves or planting flowers or doing whatever he could to keep the church grounds clean. Joe's pastor tells me even his family didn't know about those acts of service. Why? Because Joe didn't want anyone but his Lord knowing about it."

John felt his insides melting. *We wasted a lifetime talking about first downs and passing plays and missed out on the real victories. Why didn't I take the time to get to know him better, Lord?*

There was no response as the pastor looked down at his notes and shook his head once. "Here's the kicker, though. When Joe's wife died in the tornado of 1984, eight other people died too. Among them was a man with no insurance, no worldly means but to work by the sweat of his brow. He left behind a wife and four kids destined to spend the rest of their days on welfare.

"Joe found out about the lady at his own wife's funeral,

and the next day he called a banker friend of his in Michigan . . ."

A banker friend? John sat up straighter in the pew. That had to be his father. What other banker friend did he have in Michigan?

"Turns out the banker friend was the one who led Joe Chapman to the Lord years earlier, and now Joe wanted to give him another chance to invest in eternity. The widowed woman and her kids needed a place to live, he told his friend. And Joe combined half the money from his wife's insurance with a donation from his banker friend, and together they asked the church to buy that family a house. Maybe you don't know it, but money donated to a church for a specific cause is not tax deductible. In other words, the only reason Joe and his friend asked the church to be the middle man was because they wanted their act to be totally anonymous."

John heard Abby's breath catch in her throat. Neither of them knew anything about the woman or her orphaned children or the house that their fathers had provided. A house built with a kind of love John had all but forgotten about. The goodness of their act was too much for John to bear, and his eyes grew wet. No wonder he'd made such a mess of his life. When had he ever given that way, selflessly, at the expense of his own personal ease?

The pastor was finishing his message. "Until the day he died, Joe Chapman helped that woman, arranging his pension so that a hundred dollars went through the church into her bank account every month, year in, year out." He paused. "Anything else I could say about Joe Chapman—details of his coaching career or how he is survived by two daughters or that he had hundreds of students who loved him—all of it seems like an afterthought compared to the way he loved his Lord."

John felt hollow, as though he had failed to furnish a room in his heart reserved for Joe and his father. *God, why didn't I know before?*

"I do want to read one more letter. Abby found it in a drawer by his bed when he died. It's an essay written by one of his students." The pastor looked at the paper in his hands and hesitated. "'Mr. Chapman is my favorite teacher because he never forgets what it is to be a kid. He doesn't bark at us like some teachers, and yet everyone in class listens to him and respects him. A lot of us want to be just like him when we grow up. Mr. Chapman tells us corny jokes, and in his classroom it's okay if we make a mistake. Other teachers say they care about their students but Mr. Chapman really does. If someone's sad or lonely, he asks them about it and makes sure that when they leave his classroom they're feeling better. I'm a richer person for my time in his class, and no matter how long I live, I'll never forget him.'"

John felt like falling on his face, crying out that it wasn't fair, that God should have taken someone like him instead and let someone as good and generous as Abby's father live to be a hundred.

The pastor cleared his throat. "Now, just in case you're thinking that Joe was somehow robbed, that after a lifetime of giving he wasn't given a fair shake by God Almighty, let me tell you this. Some people store up treasures on earth . . . houses, cars, illicit relationships . . . and every day they wake, they move one day further from their treasure, one day closer to death." He smiled broadly. "Ah, but then there are people like Joe, people who wake every day one step closer to their treasure. One day closer to leaving this lobby and entering the main ballroom. Closer finally to being home in the place that was created for them. So don't grieve for Joe, people. Believe that, as C. S. Lewis once said, for Joe life here on earth was only the title and cover page. And now he has begun the greatest story of all, one that no one on earth has ever read in which every chapter is better than the last. Believe that, if given the chance, he would have agreed with D. L. Moody, who said in his dying days, 'In a little while you will read in the newspaper that I am dead. Do not believe a word of it, for I will be more alive than ever before.'"

John felt like the wind had been completely sucked out of him. The pastor's words, the picture he'd painted of heaven, was like none John had ever heard. It felt as though his entire perspective had shifted in a single sermon, and suddenly John grieved for the hundreds and thousands of sermons he'd missed over the years.

Jo Harter sat near the middle of the church hanging on every word the preacher said. For weeks, months really, she'd been feeling a calling, something stronger than anything earthly, stronger than her desire to fish or shop. Even stronger than her hope that someday she'd find new love with Denny.

It was the very thing Matt told her to watch for. A holy longing, he called it.

"It'll happen one day, Mom, wait and see. You'll wake up and have a feeling of want so big and bad nothing in the world'll be able to fill it. Nothing but Jesus."

Well, here she was at this funeral feeling a want every

bit as big and bad as Matt had described it. Throughout the service she fidgeted in her seat this way and that until Matt leaned over and whispered at her. "You all right?"

"Fine." She reached out and patted her son's knee, grateful he'd chosen to sit by her instead of Nicole just this once. "I'll tell you later." She didn't want to talk about it yet. Not when every word the pastor uttered seemed hand-written for her alone.

At the end of the service, the pastor did something Jo had never seen done at a funeral. He told them he had an invitation for them. At first Jo thought it was an invitation to the potluck at the Reynoldses' house after the service, but then the pastor asked them to close their eyes.

Okay, God, my eyes are closed. What's happening here, anyway?

Come, daughter. Come to Me.

Jo opened her eyes and sat straight up in the pew. She poked Matt in the ribs and whispered, "Who said that?"

He looked at her like she maybe needed a little more sleep and put his finger to his lips. "Shhh. No one said anything."

Fine. Now I'm hearing things. Jo closed her eyes again and listened hard to the pastor's invitation.

"Many of you may already have the assurance that Joe did, assurance that your name is written in the Lamb's Book of Life, assurance that you are saved from your sins because of what Jesus did for you on the cross. Assurance of heaven. But I believe there may be some of you out there who have never made the decision to trust Jesus Christ for life. You have a hole in your heart only Jesus can fill, and you want to know your future is safe with Him. If that's you this morning, could you please raise your hand? I'll make sure I talk with you after the service, give you a Bible, and help you get started on the right path."

He hesitated, and Jo could feel the longing grow with each passing second. There was a hole in her heart all right. No doubt about it.

"Anyone?"

It made no sense to wait. If walking with Jesus had filled the holes for Matt and Denny, then just maybe they would fill this one for her. It was time she stepped down from her high horse and did something about it. Without another moment's hesitation, her hand shot into the air.

I do want You, Jesus. I do. Show me the way, God . . .

Beside her, Matt reached over and squeezed her knee, and as the prayer ended, she hugged her only son. It was then that she noticed something she hadn't before.

For the first time since the funeral started, Matt had tears in his eyes.

Nineteen

BETWEEN THE SCENE AT HER FATHER'S DEATHBED and the way John had kissed her later that night, Abby had moments when she wondered if maybe, just maybe, John was having second thoughts about their divorce. Could a man fake the trembling she'd felt when John had his arm around her, promising her dying father that he would love her forever? Could he manufacture tears of regret for the hours and days he might have spent with the man who had been his own father's best friend?

Could he really have kissed her that way out of some obligation?

Abby didn't think so, but for all the emotion that surrounded them that week, time passed like always and nothing changed between her and John. The proof came just one week after the funeral, when Nicole burst into Abby's office, her face stricken.

"Why's Charlene Denton hanging out with Dad at

practice?" She was angry, and her mouth hung open while she waited for Abby's response.

Before Abby could come up with something witty and believable, she let loose the first thing that came to mind. "Why don't you ask Dad?"

The reaction on Nicole's face made Abby sure she had said the wrong thing. Nicole's eyes grew wide, and a flicker of raw fear flashed across her face, like heat lightning in a summer sky. "What's that supposed to mean?"

In that instant, Abby had the first glimpse of the nightmare it was going to be to tell Nicole and the boys the truth. She tried to cover up with an innocent-sounding laugh. "Relax, honey. I'm kidding."

"Well, Matt wasn't. He saw them together and asked me why." She shifted her weight, her eyebrows lowered. "What am I supposed to tell him?"

Abby released a controlled sigh. "Obviously they work together, honey. Ms. Denton's been friends with your father for years."

"Yeah, and I don't like it. She flirts with him." Nicole clenched her fists. "And Dad spends more time with her than he does with you."

Abby couldn't think of anything to say. She angled her head and resisted a shudder as she thought again of how hard Coach John Reynolds—father, hero, and friend— was about to fall in the eyes of the children who loved him most. "What do you want me to tell you, honey?"

Nicole huffed in response. "Tell me it's a coincidence; tell me it's my imagination; tell me Dad's acting the same as always." She hesitated and her eyes filled with tears. "Tell me everything's okay between you guys."

Abby's heart plummeted. She stood up and pulled

Nicole into her arms. "Oh, honey, I'm sorry." Nicole held on tighter than usual, and Abby desperately wanted to ease her fears. "Everything's—"

Don't lie to her, daughter.

The voice rang clear in the inner places of Abby's heart, and she stopped short.

"Everything's what?" Nicole pulled away slightly, meeting Abby's eyes, searching for any sign of the security she had always taken for granted.

God, give me the words. "You know how much we love each other." Abby hugged Nicole again as her insides contorted in a wave of sadness so deep and strong it shook her to the core. "Our family's always loved each other."

Nicole drew back again as though she wanted to say something, but before she could speak, Abby bent close and kissed her on the tip of her nose. "How 'bout some tea, huh? Why don't you go start a pot of water, and I'll join you in a minute."

The diversion worked, and Nicole smiled at Abby, clearly convinced that her comforting words were proof that everything was, indeed, all right.

Like enemy soldiers easing their way across a minefield, Abby and John survived the next several weeks without anyone bringing up Charlene's name. It was Monday night, the last week of school, and Abby was making brownies—part of a longstanding Reynolds family tradition. Every year just before school let out, the kids took plates of brownies to their teachers and shared them with their classmates. As they got older, the ritual became almost silly, but the kids still loved it. Even as a senior football player, Kade had asked her the night before if she was going to bake this week.

Abby pushed the wooden spoon through a bowl of wet brownie mix and thought how next year at this time the kids probably would have adapted to their new life, the one where their dad was no longer married to their mom. She dumped the batter into a buttered pan and slipped it into the oven. Abby gazed out the window across the expanse of green, rolling hillside and out over the lake.

Was it possible Kade was already graduating? Where had the time gone? Abby blinked back the tears that stung at her eyes. She was always fighting tears these days . . . and why not? She had a daughter getting married, a son graduating and moving away to college, and a husband who didn't love her anymore.

It was a wonder she didn't wake up crying.

The phone rang, and Abby inhaled sharply, switching gears. No amount of remembering could change the fact that every aspect of her life was about to change.

"Hello?" She pinned the receiver with her shoulder and wiped her hands on a paper towel.

"Uh, yes . . ." It was a woman, and she seemed nervous. Abby felt the color draining from her face. *It couldn't be . . .* The woman cleared her throat. "Is . . . is John Reynolds there?"

Abby's heart felt as though it had fallen onto the kitchen floor. Even when she tried she couldn't bring herself to breathe. "Can I . . . tell him who's calling?"

There was a heavy sigh on the other end. "It's Charlene Denton. I need to ask him a question about school."

A round of emotions exploded at strategic points throughout Abby's body, temporarily decimating her heart, soul, and gut. *Breathe, Abby. Breathe.* She felt sick to her stomach, and she closed her eyes. A dozen come-backs fought for position. *You have a lot of nerve, lady. What kind of an idiot do you take me for? Something about school? Give me a break.*

In the end, Abby couldn't speak over the pounding sound of her heart. She gripped the phone tightly, cover-ing the mouthpiece as her initial hurt and shock gave way to a burning rage. *How dare he have her call at the house!* Carrying the phone as though it were a weapon, she stormed through the living room and into the garage.

John was tinkering with a fishing pole, and he looked up when she appeared. He waited for her to speak, his expression slightly baffled, as though he could feel her anger from twenty feet away and hadn't a clue what he'd done to cause it.

She thrust the receiver in his direction. "It's *Charlene.*"

The surprise on his face seemed genuine, but his eyes were immediately flooded with guilt. He took the phone, turned his back on Abby, and spoke in a muffled voice.

It was as though she were drowning at sea, and John had made the decision to let her go under for the final time. He was choosing Charlene over Abby so blatantly she didn't know how to react, and she waited until she heard the sub-tle electronic tone indicating the call was over.

John held the phone but let his hand drop to his side, his back still to her.

"We need to talk." Abby's voice wasn't angry or fran-tic; it held none of the range of emotions that had assault-ed her since the phone rang. Why be angry now? It was all over but the paperwork.

A sense of finality hugged Abby close, bringing with it

an unnatural calm as John spun around and met her gaze, his back stiff, eyes narrowed and ready to fight. His voice was hot from the moment he started talking. "Look, Abby, I didn't tell her to—"

"It doesn't matter." She was businesslike, which clearly surprised him, as he stopped midsentence. "I don't want to fight, John. It's not going to change anything." She dropped down onto the garage steps and set her elbows firmly on her knees, her eyes still locked on his. Suddenly she felt too old and tired even to explain herself. "Charlene's your future. I can see it. I'm not going to scream at you and call you names because you're in love with another woman. It's too late for that."

John released a huff and rolled his eyes. "I didn't tell her to call me, Abby; you've got to believe—"

Abby held both hands up, and again John stopped short of finishing. "Don't give me excuses." Her tone was calm but resigned, and as she spoke John's posture relaxed. "I'll be honest . . . I don't want her calling here. But I'm not blind. I can read the writing on the wall and one day . . ." The last thing Abby wanted was tears, especially now when her heart no longer seemed linked to the issue at hand. But they came anyway, filling her eyes and spilling onto her cheeks before she could do anything to stop them. "One day she may be my children's stepmother. I'm tired of hating. I don't want to hate her or you or anyone else."

John hung his head for a moment and then came closer, leaning against their blue sedan and drawing a slow breath. "I'm sorry, Abby. I never meant to hurt you with any of this." He dropped his gaze once more, obviously unwilling to watch her cry.

As calm as Abby felt, she was rocked deep in her heart

by John's agreeing with what she was saying. *Fight for me, John. For us. Tell me you can't stand her, that you were out here thinking of how we might find a way to make it work* . . . But the truth was, at this stage of their marriage, they both knew the score. There were only minutes left in the game, and there were simply no winners anywhere. Except maybe Charlene. Abby wiped away her tears. "I have a favor to ask."

He stuffed his hands in his pockets, his head still lowered so that only his eyes made contact with her. "Anything, Abby."

Don't say it, Abby. Love bears all things . . .

The voice faded and she angled her head, willing John to see that this was the only way out for either of them. "Get the paperwork done. Make an appointment with an attorney. Someone we don't know. That way we can move quickly once the kids are married." She hesitated, trying to read his expression and failing. A devastating realization struck her: *I'm no longer the expert on navigating the deep places of John Reynolds's heart.*

His gaze fell to his feet, and nearly a minute passed before he spoke. "I'll call first thing tomorrow." Without looking at her or saying another word, he walked slowly past her into the house. After a few minutes, the automatic lights clicked off, and Abby peered into the black emptiness, realizing it was in some ways a sneak preview of her future without John.

Complete and utter darkness broken only by frightening shapes and vague, uncertain shadows.

The week sped by in a blur of final exams and yearbook signings and preparations for Kade's graduation. But John had kept his promise. It was Thursday, and his appointment with the attorney was set for four o'clock. He had finished entering grades into the computer and was taking down the posters from his classroom, an annual task required of all teachers. Like so often that week, as he worked he was haunted by the look on Abby's face when Charlene had called.

He rolled up a poster and sighed out loud.

Charlene.

He still wasn't sure why she'd called him at home. She'd said it was because she had a question about Marion High's computer grading policy, but John thought there might be more to it. Although she'd kept her distance as he'd asked, when their paths crossed she seemed more forward, less patient than before. The last time he'd seen her prior to the phone call, she'd asked if Abby knew about them.

"What's there to know?" John was still drawn to her, but her questions set him on edge. Whatever happened to the days when their friendship was fun and carefree? Didn't she understand how hard this was for him? How devastating it was to watch his son graduate and his daughter get married weeks before he would walk out on all of them and start his life over?

Charlene had pursed her lips in a mock pout. "I just mean in a few months we'll be together all the time. She has to know you have a life outside the family home. You're getting divorced, after all. It's not like you have to keep me a secret from everyone who matters to you."

Her words rang in his head still, and he figured they had more to do with her phone call than any excuse about grading policies or trouble with her classroom. He remembered the way Abby's face changed from anger to ice-cold indifference. *Is it that easy, Abby girl? Letting Charlene have her way? Wanting only divorce papers from me, nothing more?* He rolled the final poster and was slipping a rubber band around it when Charlene walked in.

She stopped in the doorway and grinned at him. "Do you know how gorgeous you look when you're working?" Her skirt was shorter than usual, legs tan and toned as she made her way across the classroom. She caught him looking and smiled when his eyes made their way back up to hers. "Hi . . ."

No question John was attracted to her, but her sudden appearance made him angry at her. What right did she have to violate his solitude? Besides, he wasn't in the mood for her questions. He thought about telling her to leave as he straightened and stretched his bad knee. "Hi."

"The school's a ghost town." Her eyes burned into his, the meaning of her words far from lost on John. Classes let out at one o'clock every day the last week of school, so she was right. There were no students anywhere. She crossed the room and perched herself against the edge of the desk. She was inches from him, and her perfume filled his senses. "I've stayed away as long as I can, John."

He cocked his head and thought of what he might say to hold his ground. *Give me the words, God . . . please.*

Flee, son! Return to your first love . . .

"You shouldn't be here. I asked you not to . . ." John wished he could speak with more conviction, but he didn't want to be mean. Charlene was one of his closest friends, even though she'd been getting on his nerves lately.

"I missed you . . ."

He kicked the empty poster box gently toward the edge of the room. "I'm still a married man, Charlene."

Suddenly, his frustration shifted. It was Abby's fault he was in this mess. She was the one he should be angry with, not Charlene. All Charlene had done was be his friend, listen to him, make him feel like he mattered.

Things Abby hadn't done for a long time.

He looked at Charlene, and suddenly he felt drawn to her again. He took a step toward her. "No matter how much I might wish I wasn't."

John thought about what he'd just said. *No matter how much I might wish I wasn't? Wasn't what? Wasn't married to a girl I waited years to marry?* Was that really him talking? John broke the connection between him and Charlene and let his gaze fall to the floor. Was he crazy?

Charlene seemed to sense that his thoughts had shifted. She angled her head and raised her eyebrows, her face the picture of sympathy. "It must be hard. Pretending all the time in front of the kids, I mean." She hesitated. "I wish there was something I could do . . ."

John leaned against his desk alongside her. This time Charlene's offer of help played over in his mind. When was the last time Abby cared about his feelings or wanted to help him? She hadn't been his best friend in years. Maybe the tensions with Charlene were just the result of his inability to spend time with her. After all, these days his best friend was . . . he looked up and caught Charlene's eyes again. "We need to take it slow."

As naturally as if they were the ones who had been married for years, she came to him, wedging herself between his knees as her arms went up around his neck. "I haven't waited this long because I want to rush things." Her voice was a whisper, her eyes probing his, and John was certain she could see how weak he was. Without meaning to, his knees tightened slightly, keeping her close, not wanting to let her go now or ever.

"I don't want to make the same mistakes again." Desire overpowered John so much it was frightening. It suddenly felt as though he might sell his very soul to have the object his body so intensely craved. He brought his hand to her face and traced her cheekbone. "Tell me we won't make the same mistakes, Charlene."

She didn't answer. A smile filled her face, but instead of smiling back, John felt something deep in his gut. Something hesitant . . . even resistant. He couldn't pin it down, but there was something in her smile he didn't like . . . something wrong.

Before he could think those feelings through, she moved closer, fitting up against him . . . and he readily accepted her kiss. At first it was slow and tender, but in a matter of seconds it became filled with blazing passion, intense beyond anything John could remember.

"Come home with me, John. I need you . . ."

He was still sitting on the desk, but as the kiss continued he slid closer to the edge, closer to her, digging his fingers into her beautiful, dark hair. *Help me, Lord . . . I've lost all control . . . it's like she's cast a spell over me.*

A burst of loud, tinny feedback filled the room. "This is a reminder that Mr. Foster has asked all teachers to have their classrooms ready for inspection by eight o'clock tomorrow morning."

The words rang loudly from the intercom at the front of the classroom, and John jerked back as though he'd been slapped.

"Also, graduation assignments have been posted on the main office door. Thank you."

Charlene's eyes were clouded with the intensity of their kiss, and the same smile that had bothered John moments ago returned. She nestled herself up against him again, framing his face with her fingers. "Where were we?"

He thought of Abby, of their brief but intense encounter after her father died, how the passion then had been far stronger than this, better somehow . . . more pure. Nausea at what he'd done racked his gut. *What kind of man have I become?*

He turned his face and squirmed free from her, moving three feet away and easing into one of the student desks. When his breathing was stable, he looked at Charlene. "I'm sorry; that was wrong." He rested his elbow on the desk and caught his forehead between his thumb and forefinger, rubbing his temples, praying that God would disperse the pent-up feelings he had for this woman. He closed his eyes as he spoke. "I'm not ready for this." He opened his eyes and peered over the edge of his hand at her.

She nodded once and moved to sit behind his desk, suddenly less the seductress and more the good-intentioned friend, and he shifted uneasily. It was as though to please him she could take on any role she wished. That thought, and her smile, set him even further on edge, and he felt his body cool. She met his gaze straight on and spoke gently. "I've missed you . . . but I didn't come here for that."

John was suddenly nervous, anxious to be on his way to the appointment with the attorney. Where could this meeting with Charlene possibly go, anyway? He waited for her to continue.

She crossed her arms, her face more serious than before. "I've been given a job offer."

John's heart lurched. She wouldn't move away, would she? Charlene had finished her administrative credentials the year before and had put out feelers in local school districts. Her goal was to take an assistant principal position somewhere in Marion. "That's great." He searched her eyes, looking for clarification.

Charlene's hands came together, and she dropped her gaze. "The job's in Chicago, John. Someone at the district office told the staff up there I was looking." She brought her eyes up again, and he could see how strongly she was struggling. "It's a good offer."

The muscles in his jaw clenched, and he fought with himself. Why were his feelings for Charlene all over the board? One minute he was wishing he'd never met her, the next wishing he could . . . "Is it what you want?" If it was, he could hardly stand in her way.

She exhaled through pursed lips, and a sadness filled her eyes. "I want you, John Reynolds. If I have to wash dishes for a living."

Well, there it was. So why did her words make his heart feel like it was being squeezed by a vice grip? There was something she wasn't saying. "But . . ."

"But if you don't see yourself . . . having a future with me . . ." Tears filled her eyes, and she pulled a neatly folded tissue from her purse, dabbing at the wetness before it could mar her perfect makeup job. "Then I have no choice but to go. To start life over somewhere without you."

Once, a long time ago, John had seen a movie where a man was trapped in a shrinking corridor, where both walls were moving slowly in on him. Now, with all that was looming in his life, John knew how the man felt. His shoulders slumped. "What do you want me to say?"

"Tell me you feel the same way I do, that you see us together when this mess you're going through is finally behind you." Her answer was quick, and he saw in her eyes that she cared enough for him to turn down any job, to call him at home even when it meant making him angry, to risk getting caught kissing him in his classroom—clearly a violation of school policy. The truth was simple. She thought she was in love with him, and if he were willing, she would gear the rest of her life around him.

She was young and pretty, bright and incredibly devoted to him. In her presence he felt loved and appreciated and full of life. So why didn't he jump at the chance she was offering him?

Was it the fact that he wasn't legally divorced yet that held him back? Was it his faith? Or was it the way she'd come across as manipulative and pushy lately? His feelings were so jumbled he had no answers for her. "You know how I feel about you."

"That's not what I'm asking." Her tone had gone from troubled and sincere to impatient. "Am I part of your future? *That's* what I need to know."

John thought about her question. He did care deeply for her . . . didn't he? Hadn't she been the one willing to put her life on hold while he sorted out the details of his divorce? Wasn't she the one who had been his friend, his confidante and ally, while Abby drew further away with each passing year? He thought about the pain in Abby's eyes when Charlene had called at the house the other day. Was that why Abby had stopped being his friend? Because she felt replaced by Charlene?

He suddenly wanted nothing more than to be away from her, by himself where he could sift through his emotions.

"When do you have to let them know?" He gathered his posters and felt her eyes follow him.

"The end of July."

The end of July. There wasn't any way the timing could be more perfect. *Like trading Abby's dreams in for Charlene's.* He winced inwardly and forced the thought from his mind. "Give me some time, okay? I'll let you know before the wedding."

"If you want me, John, I'm staying."

He had nothing more to say to her. Instead he glanced at the clock on the wall. "I have to run." Divorce attorneys charged by the hour. He stood and grabbed a few files and his car keys, leaving Charlene alone in his classroom without so much as a good-bye.

As John climbed into his truck, he caught a glimpse of himself in the mirror and wondered at the man he'd become. His older son was graduating the next day, and a few weeks after that he would walk his only daughter down the aisle and hand her over in marriage. But here, in the hours before the milestones his family had waited a lifetime for, he'd allowed himself to be swept into a wave of passion that but for his weakly uttered prayer would have led . . . where? Would he have cancelled his appointment and followed her home? Allowed his passions to dictate his actions as though he didn't have a responsibility in the world?

He thought of his prayer again and how the blaring office message had broken the spell, changed the moment so that he could think clearly again. A shudder went over him at the thought of what might have happened.

Then it hit him.

What was the difference? Whether he gave in to Charlene now or later, he was still destroying something he'd vowed to keep forever, burying for all time the dreams of Abby and Nicole and Kade and Sean. Who was he kidding?

The image of Abby's father and his final request filled his mind: *"Love her . . . love her . . . love her."*

He pushed the gas pedal down and felt the truck pick up speed. The plans were already in motion, too far gone to change despite distant holy whisperings or graduations or weddings or deathbed promises made about honoring his marriage. It was too late for any of it. His marriage was terminally ill, and in a few minutes he would take part in the only thing left to do.

Sit down with an attorney and draw up the death certificate.

Twenty

FOR THE MOST PART DENNY CONLEY WAS NOT A nervous man. After all, he'd found the nerve to stand in front of his Twelve-Step group and tell the whole wretched story of how he'd drunk away his early years of being a father, how he'd walked out on Jo and Matt when the kid was barely old enough to remember him. Not only that, but in the past year he'd been bold enough to tell a whole congregation that he, Denny Conley, was a sinner and needed a Savior.

The boldness, he'd learned, came from God and not himself, and that was a good thing. That kind of power would never let him down.

But none of that mattered now as he followed the final directions to Nicole Reynolds's house. He was shaking like a leaf, and only the grace of God kept him from flipping a U-turn and heading back home, an hour south.

The meeting had been Matt's idea.

"Dad, don't wait 'til the wedding." His son's voice had been filled with such sincerity that this time it was Denny who'd been choked up. "Come to the graduation party. There'll be lots of people; you'll fit right in."

Denny gulped. *Calm me down, Lord. Calm me down.*

He'd seen pictures of Matt, of course, but he hadn't looked into his son's eyes since the boy was four years old. Hadn't felt those young arms around his neck or wrestled with his son or brushed his fingers against the boy's hair. Hadn't loved him the way a father should. A gust of shame blew through his beat-up Ford, and he shook his head.

"Kid must be crazy," Denny mumbled out loud as he changed lanes. "Shouldn't be givin' me the time of day."

It was another one of the benefits of following after Jesus, the rewards Pastor Mark had talked about back when Denny first made his decision. The idea that he might actually have a second chance with his boy, a chance to know him and love him like he should have done at the start, was almost more than Denny could imagine.

No doubt it was the reason he was fighting the shakes. After nearly twenty years he was about to be a father again. Not only that, but he was going to meet the pretty little thing who was marrying his boy. She was a smart one, just like Matt, and she came from good people—parents who'd loved each other since the beginning of time.

Parents like he and Jo might have been if he'd done things differently.

Denny eased up on the gas pedal at the thought of Jo. With all the excitement of seeing Matt again, he'd done everything he could to keep from thinking about the woman to whom he'd once promised forever. He glanced at the directions. Right turn at the light, four blocks to the lake. Left, and the Reynoldses' house was third on the right. He'd be there in two minutes.

The best news of all, of course, was that Jo had actually given her heart to God too. Two decades after scattering into the world, the members of the Denny Conley family had each found their way home to the Savior. That fact alone was proof that God was real and that He listened to the prayers of His people—even those in the off-key voices of one like himself, those with so little to offer.

Denny was more nervous than ever before, if that were possible, but nothing could replace the deep-rooted joy that grew in his gut like an everlasting flame. He was going to see his wife and son again! Going to hold them, feel them snug in his arms. Denny's heart pounded so hard he was surprised he couldn't see it pushing its way out of his chest with every beat. He made the final turn and saw twenty or so cars gathered around one of the driveways.

The Reynoldses' home. *Here I go, Lord. Walk before me.*

He ran a hand over his slicked-back hair and moved quickly now, as though he were leaving everything about his old life behind and moving into some new, brighter existence with every step.

Jo Harter had been anchored in a chair by the front window, glancing out every minute or so and searching the street for the old beater Denny drove. Matt had described it, and then fiddlesticks if he wasn't able to let it go at that. None of this hanging-around-the-window routine for Matt.

The party was in full swing, people gathered in pockets throughout the house, celebrating young Kade

Reynolds's graduation. That boy had a real good future set before him for sure, and Jo had made a point of telling him so when she first arrived. After that she'd found Matt and asked for the tenth time when Denny was set to arrive.

"Mom, he said he wasn't sure." Matt grinned at her as though somehow their roles had reversed, making him the patient adult and her the pesky child.

Come on, get here, Denny . . .

She'd no sooner thought the words than she saw a car like the one Matt described move slowly past, turn around, and stop not far from the house. Jo held her breath as he climbed out and headed for the house. He looked just like she remembered him. Not much taller than herself, dark hair—what was left of it—and just enough bowlegged that she could pick him out in a crowd. A catch if ever she saw one.

Without another moment's hesitation, Jo nearly danced across the living room to the front door and swung it open. "Denny!"

He stopped in his tracks, his eyes locked onto hers while a full-bore grin spread across his face. It punctuated his cheeks with the cutest dimples Jo had ever seen, and suddenly she was in his arms, certain beyond words that the marvelous God they served had pulled off nothing less than a miracle.

He put his hands along either side of her face and studied her like a winning lottery ticket. "Jo . . . I've missed you, sweetie. I can't believe I'm here."

There were a hundred things Jo had hoped to say, but none of them was right at hand except a few simple words: "Welcome home, Denny Conley."

Once again his smile lit up the late afternoon. "Thank you, Jo. And now I believe I have a son to see."

Abby surveyed the dwindling party guests from the doorway of the kitchen, and her gaze fell on Jo and Denny, deep in conversation with Matt and Nicole. They looked awfully cozy. Was it possible that life was going to turn out right for Jo and her beloved Denny after so many years? She remembered Jo's monologue about her ex-husband and how she'd hoped to lose ten pounds in order to catch his eye at the wedding.

She watched Jo's eyes sparkle and saw the way she spoke to the man she clearly still loved. The woman might have lost weight in the past few months, but it wasn't what she'd lost that had Denny Conley hanging on her every word.

It was what she'd gained.

Abby sighed and turned back into the kitchen. *How come Jo's faith seems more real than mine, God? She's only believed for a few months.*

Silence.

Abby grabbed a stack of empty platters and began wiping them down in the sink. It wasn't fair. She and John had been faithful all their lives, teaching their children about walking with God, building a relationship with Him, worshiping Him. But now, when it mattered most, their faith was like a corroded, dead battery, incapable of giving off any power at all.

Washing dishes was mindless enough, and she listened to conversations in the adjacent room as she worked.

"So, Kade, tell me it isn't true about your sister." Abby recognized the voice of Dennis Steinman, one of Kade's football buddies. "She isn't really marrying someone else, is she?"

"Yeah, in four weeks." Kade's tone was light and full of laughter. The party was already a huge success, graced by the presence of friends, teachers, and townspeople who had been a part of Kade's life since he was a young child.

"Come on, I thought she was waiting for me. She loved me, man."

"No, Steiner, that wasn't love. It was pity."

Laughter erupted among the friends, and Abby thought back to earlier that afternoon and the graduation ceremony. John had been one of the teachers asked to stay near the student section, so Abby and the others sat together without him. She had glanced at him every now and then and knew his attention couldn't have been farther from the students. It was all focused on Kade, his older son, his star quarterback . . . and Abby's gut had ached at the loss John must have been feeling that afternoon. There was always pain in bidding good-bye to a senior player, someone John had worked with three, sometimes four years straight.

But losing Kade . . .

Abby pictured their son the way he'd looked a few hours earlier, decked in his cap and gown and ready to tackle the world. No matter what the future brought, she would never forget the image of him walking proudly across the football field to receive his diploma—the same field where he and John had built a lifetime of memories, a bond that would remain through all time. It filled her heart with misty, watercolored yesterdays and pictures of a happier time when Kade was just starting school and everything looked like it would go on forever.

She finished washing the last platter and began drying. This should have been a day when John would pour out his feelings to her, a day when they might have taken a walk or wound up on the pier, reminding each other of the times when they'd predicted this very thing. How Kade's school years would fly by, just like Nicole's had. No one, not even Charlene Denton, could know exactly how John's heart felt watching Kade graduate.

No one but Abby.

She stacked the dried platters and wiped her hands on the dishtowel as her ear picked up Matt's voice.

"Yep, we're completely ready. Flowers, bridesmaids, color schemes, matching plates and napkins, little minty things so the guests can spoil their dinner . . ."

Nicole laughed at that. "Matt's right. I can't believe the planning."

"Of course the planning's half the fun." It was Jo, and she sounded as though she were keeping a secret. Denny had been there little more than three hours, and already the two of them were brushing shoulders and making eye contact like newlyweds. Jo was going on about the trouble and cost of big weddings when she paused just long enough to catch her breath.

"Okay, kids," Jo said. "Don't you want to know the news?" Abby would have loved to move into the room and fall in place alongside Nicole, but she stayed in the kitchen. Something about Jo's tone told Abby she didn't really want to be there anyway. Not if the news was as good as it sounded.

"I'm moving here." Denny sounded as though he was about to burst. "Packing up my things and getting a new job quick as I can." Abby could hear Denny's smile, and a strange pang worked its way across her heart. It wasn't right. How come two people like Matt's parents could work things out and she and John—the couple everyone had always looked to as an example—couldn't find enough common ground to hold a conversation?

No answers ricocheted in Abby's heart.

"Dad, my gosh, are you serious?" Matt's voice rang with hope.

"Yep, and something else too . . ."

"Wait a minute," Jo interrupted. "Nicole, where's your mother? I want her to hear this firsthand." Jo's voice came closer, and Abby spun around expectantly as Jo and Denny entered the kitchen holding hands, with Nicole and Matt giggling close behind.

"Abby, I simply can't tell the kids what me and Denny decided without telling you at the same time." She glanced at the man beside her and shrugged her shoulders up and down like a high-school girl.

The towel in Abby's hand hung limp. "Okay . . ." She chided herself silently for not sounding more enthusiastic. The fact that Abby's life was a mess wasn't Jo's fault. The least she could do was be happy for the woman. She forced a smile.

Jo leaned forward, beyond excited. "We're getting married!" The words spilled out as though Jo couldn't hold them in a moment longer. A quick squeal escaped her lips. "Can you *believe* it? Me and Denny, after all these years?"

"My goodness, congratula—" Abby's voice was drowned in the celebratory shouts and exclamations from Matt and Nicole, both of whom now had their arms wrapped around the older couple.

Abby stood on the outside, awkwardly looking in, wait-

ing for the moment to pass. When it did, Jo drew a steadying breath, a smile taking up her entire face. To describe her
as beaming would have been a vast understatement.

"You know what it was, don't you, Abby?" Jo reached
out and placed her hand on Abby's shoulder.

Fate playing games with me? "Not really . . ." She smiled
again, hoping not to raise Nicole's suspicions by acting less
than enthusiastic.

Jo slapped Abby on the arm playfully. "Come on,
Abby. You're the one who told me about Him."

"Him?" The woman was loony. Abby had never seen
Denny until tonight.

Jo released an exaggerated sigh. "God. The Lord, God,
Abby. Remember?" Jo shook her head and let out a hearty
laugh. "I declare, you have the driest sense of humor this
side of Arizona." She poked Denny in the ribs and drew a
small laugh from him, as well. "This here's Abby who told
me about heaven and God and all the rest." Jo looked at
Matt and Nicole. "Then at your granddaddy's funeral . . .
well, that's when I first gave Jesus my heart. After that I
knew He was gonna give me something too. Not just eternity with Him, but my own sweet Denny back where he
belongs."

That said, Jo planted a lingering kiss square on
Denny's lips, causing a crimson glow to spread quickly
from the man's neckline right on up to his balding head.
"Uh, honey, let's say you and me take a walk outside
where it's quiet."

Abby hadn't thought it possible, but Jo's smile spread
even farther around her face at the suggestion. She bid the
others good-bye, and in an instant they were gone. Matt
and Nicole hugged in celebration of the moment, and

then Matt excused himself, leaving Nicole behind, her face glowing, eyes full of hope for the future.

"Can you believe it, Mom? Isn't God amazing?"

Abby's gaze fell to the dishrag still in her hand, and she began absently polishing the tiles on the counter. "Amazing."

Nicole hesitated for a beat, her smile suddenly faded. "You don't sound sure."

Recover, Abby. Don't give her a reason to doubt you . . . She looked up, feigning ignorance. "About what?"

Nicole crossed her arms and moved her weight to one hip. "About God. I said isn't He amazing and when you answered . . . you didn't sound sure."

Abby laughed as lightly as she could manage. "I'm sorry, honey. I guess I'm tired. It's been a long weekend. Watching Kade graduate, throwing the party, getting ready for your wedding."

A look of concern danced in Nicole's eyes. "You're not sick or anything, are you?"

Abby shook her head quickly. "Not at all, sweetheart. Just a little caught up in what's happening around here."

"But you're happy for Jo and Denny, right?" Nicole's voice still had an edge, and Abby was desperate to change the direction of the conversation.

Pour it on, Abby. "Oh, absolutely. They're just wonderful together. I mean, if that's not how God loves to work, I don't know what is."

Nicole's shoulders eased, and the lines on her forehead smoothed. "Exactly. That's what I was trying to say in the first place. I mean, those two back together is like . . . I don't know, it's like more than Matt and I ever imagined."

Abby felt herself relax as she folded the towel and set it

on the edge of the counter. She moved closer to Nicole and hugged her gently, pulling back enough to see Nicole's eyes. "You and Matt have been praying for them, haven't you?"

Nicole's eyes danced like they had earlier. "Every day."

This time Abby's smile was genuine. "Then that, my dear, is absolutely amazing."

They were still standing that way, face to face, Abby's wrists balanced on Nicole's shoulders when John walked in and stopped short. "Oh . . . I thought Nicole was with Matt."

Nicole twisted around and smiled at John. "Hi, Dad. Why, where's Matt?"

"Outside with his parents. I thought . . ." He looked preoccupied.

What is it now? Abby felt her insides tighten, and she released the hold she had on Nicole. "Go on out and join him, honey. You should be together at a moment like this."

Abby was grateful that this time Nicole didn't scrutinize their faces or look deeply into the reasons why John might want to talk to Abby alone. Instead she grinned and bounced off in the direction of the backyard. "They're probably down at the pier. Matt knows that's where we celebrate everything."

Abby felt her daughter's comment as strongly as if it were a physical blow to her gut. *"That's where we celebrate everything . . . that's where we celebrate everything . . ."* Abby turned and met John's gaze. "Is everyone gone?"

He swallowed and had trouble making eye contact with her. "Yeah. Everyone but Jo and Denny." He was quiet for a beat, but Abby refused to rescue him. *If you have something to say, say it. I can wait all night.*

John cleared his throat. "We need to talk."

Abby shrugged. "Yeah, for about five years now."

"Look—" John's tone was suddenly impatient, tired and impatient—"I don't need your sarcasm, Abby. I'm serious. The wedding will be here before you know it and we need to . . . there are a few things we have to discuss."

Abby stared hard at him. "I'm listening." Her voice gave away nothing.

He let his gaze drop for a moment and then pulled it back up again. "The papers are ready. I talked to the lawyer again yesterday." There was defeat in his voice—but something else too. Something more determined and set that hadn't been there before. "He wants you to stop in sometime this week and take a look before we sign."

The corners of her eyes began to sting. "You've seen them?"

John nodded. "It's just like we discussed. Everything's split. You get the house. I get the savings and the truck. Child support until Sean's eighteen. I keep adding to their college funds. It's all spelled out."

Listening to him was like hearing an autopsy report of their marriage. Abby tried to fight the sick feeling that welled up inside her, but it was a losing battle. She let her head drop some. "Fine. Whatever gets us out of this mess."

There was a distant sound of laughter, and Abby knew that Nicole and the others would be outside for a while. The evening was too nice to waste it inside.

Unless, of course, you had divorce details to work out.

John was staring hard at her. "The reason we're in this mess is because sometime . . . a long time ago . . . we stopped loving each other. It wasn't just me who stopped, Abby. It was both of us. You were busy with the kids, and I was—"

"Busy with Charlene."

He angled his head in frustration. "No. I was busy with work. And before we knew it we stopped talking to each other. Maybe we were too tired, or maybe we just ran out of things to say. But I can guarantee you one thing, Abby. This mess isn't because of me alone." He studied her, and for a moment she thought she saw a flicker of regret in his eyes. "I've made arrangements to stay with one of the PE teachers after the wedding. I'll have my things packed so I can leave when the reception's over."

The stinging was back. Abby blinked twice and struggled to make her voice sound normal. "When do we tell the kids?"

"After Matt and Nicole get back from their honeymoon."

Abby nodded slowly and walked over to the kitchen sink, staring out across the dark yard toward the lake and the pier and the happy voices that still rang out from that direction. "Okay."

For a moment neither of them said anything, and Abby wondered if John had left the room. Her breath caught in her throat when he came up behind her and let his hands settle on her shoulders. "I'm sorry, Abby. This isn't . . . I never thought . . ."

She was torn between jerking her body from his grasp and turning into his embrace. Instead she remained utterly still. "I know. I'm sorry too."

He withdrew his hands and cleared his throat. "I'll keep my promise about Charlene, though. Nothing until after the divorce is final. You have my word."

"You have my word . . . have my word . . . have my word." A silent, sad laugh started up Abby's throat and

died. She kept her back to him and blinked her tears away. "I'd like to be alone now, John, if you don't mind."

Without saying good-bye, without touching her again or asking if she was all right, John simply turned around and retreated. After a minute she heard the bedroom door close behind him, and she thought of the hundreds of times when that sound would have pulled her from a late-night task, beckoning her to the quiet intimacy of making love or whispering side by side under the covers or laying her head on his shoulder and merely listening to him breathe.

But tonight . . . tonight the sound marked the end of a business meeting between two coworkers who had gathered to discuss funeral arrangements for an associate. An associate whose imminent death was bound to be something of a relief.

Twenty-One

IN ALL HER LIFE NICOLE HAD NEVER FELT CLOSER TO God than she did during those weeks leading up to her wedding. Everything her parents had ever taught her about love, all that they had prayed for her and modeled in their own marriage, was finally about to culminate in the single, most glorious moment of her life.

It was Monday, an unforgettable summer morning, mere days from her wedding, and Nicole could barely wait another minute.

She opened a suitcase and set it on her bed. Maybe the camping trip would make the time pass more quickly. Nicole didn't know if it would, but she was glad she was going all the same. It was something she'd always dreamed of: a chance to spend a few days with the women closest to her and glean all she could from them and from God about what it really meant to love a man, to be partners for life in a bond that would last as long as life itself.

A gentle breeze sifted through the screened window, and Nicole gazed outside across the lake. She had always loved the fact that her room faced the back of the house. How many mornings had she sat in her window seat and written down the feelings in her heart while gazing outside? Something about the way the sun threw diamonds across the water always made her emotions rise to the surface, and today was no different.

Nicole stopped and stared, breathing in the summer air. There was nothing like summer in southern Illinois, and she and Matt had talked often about having a house much like her parents', a modest home with a lake view and plenty of room for . . . well, for children one day. Just last week they'd received news that Matt had passed his bar exam, and already he was receiving offers from two local firms and several in the Chicago area.

The thought of their future made Nicole feel all lit up inside.

She pictured her parents one day, not too many years off, having the chance to be grandparents, and she smiled . . . but just as the image took root, it changed, and Nicole remembered Matt's concerns about Charlene Denton.

There's nothing to be worried about. The woman's a floozy.

Her mood cooled considerably. Nicole crossed over to her dresser and pulled out two pairs of shorts she'd need for the campout. Charlene wasn't a threat to her parents' marriage. No way. Her father was deeply devoted to her mother and would be forever. They were in love. Busy maybe, but in love all the same.

Still, the more Nicole tried to shake the idea, the more threatened she felt by thoughts of the other woman.

Finally, she released a loud sigh and dropped to her knees near the foot of her bed.

"Fine." She hung her head and began praying out loud, in a whisper only she and the Lord could hear. "Okay, God, I don't like my thoughts, but maybe I'm having them for a reason. Maybe there's something about that woman that's causing my dad and mom some trouble." She struggled for a moment. "I mean, I don't think so, really. But still. Whatever this feeling is, I want You to take it, Lord. If Charlene's a problem, make her go away." She hesitated, allowing God's Spirit to lead the prayer. It was something she'd learned years ago when she first realized her habit of rushing ahead of Him. As she waited, she felt led in a specific direction. "What I'm really trying to say, God, is be with my parents. They've had a lot on their minds and . . . well . . . make their love new again. Use me and Matt if it'll help. Whatever it takes, just make sure they love each other forever. And help me not to waste any more time thinking about my dad and that . . . that woman. Love is from You, Father. And love is always what we've had in this family. Make it grow so that it's greater than ever before."

A peace came over her and calmed her anxious heart. Nicole smiled, relieved and grateful at the same time. "I can always count on You, God. Thank You ahead of time for what You're going to do on this camping trip." She was about to stand up when she thought of one last thing. "Oh, and make the hours fly, Lord. Please."

Abby lugged her suitcase into the hallway and leaned it against the others as she looked around for John. He had promised to load up the van, but as usual lately he had busied himself in the garage—his most common hiding place in the hours when he absolutely had to be home.

The others were already in the living room, talking in unison and swapping stories of earlier camping trips. Originally there were to be six of them, but Nicole's friends were both sick with the flu. That left Abby, Nicole, Jo, and Abby's sister, Beth, who had flown in for both the campout and the wedding and who was in an uncharacteristically upbeat mood.

Abby walked down the hallway and opened the door to the garage. "We're ready."

She didn't wait for John's reply, but let the door shut and turned to join the others in the living room. In seconds she could hear him moving luggage outside, and in no time he found them in the living room, slightly out of breath. "You're all loaded up."

He refused to make eye contact with her, but his tone was cheerful and she was sure the others hadn't picked up on it. Jo was on her feet first. "I declare, John Reynolds—" she walked up to him and patted his cheek much the way a favorite aunt might—"you haven't aged a bit since your playing days in Ann Arbor, Michigan." She winked at Abby and then turned back to John. "Oughta be against the law to look that good at your age."

The others laughed at Jo's directness. For the briefest moment, John caught Abby's gaze, and she looked away. *Get me out of here, God. What am I supposed to do, stand around and agree with her?* So what if he was good looking? She and John were counting down the days until the divorce.

Abby led the way out to the car with the other women trailing behind. The foursome piled into the van and bid good-bye to John. Abby was grateful that Nicole didn't comment on the fact that John hadn't kissed her as they left. In five minutes Abby merged onto the highway, and Jo seized an almost imperceptible break in the conversation.

"Well, girls, I think I need to tell you about the miracle of God." She was sitting next to Beth in the backseat, with Nicole in the passenger seat up front. Jo tapped Abby on the back. "You girls already know about this, but Beth here hasn't heard, and besides—" she giggled loudly—"I can't stop talking about it. I mean really and truly. It's worse than my fish stories. Everywhere I go it just sort of leaks out all over the place—"

Beth broke in. "What leaks out?"

"Well, my love for God and Denny and being together and marriage, and all the things I'd given up on long before I . . ."

This should be good. Abby leaned back in her seat and focused on the road. There couldn't possibly be anyone more cynical about the virtues of marriage than her sister. Beth had been married at twenty-one, had two baby girls at twenty-three, and been deserted at twenty-five. Beth liked to say joining someone for life was less marriage and more psychological warfare, and that if she were ever tempted to make a mistake like that again, she hoped someone would have her committed for insanity. Beth was one of those If-I-get-lonely-I'll-get-a-dog women, and so far she hadn't even done that. Every time the topic came up, she'd explain that being married three years cured her of loneliness for a lifetime.

Not until just now had Abby considered the sparks that might fly if Jo and Beth chose to get into the faith issue that weekend. *Well, God, whatever happens work it out for us . . . this is Nicole's campout.*

The prayer came easily, as though she'd been in conversation with the Father for months on end.

The appointed time is for you, daughter.

Abby's breath caught in her throat, and she tightened her grip on the wheel. It was one thing to let loose an incidental prayer, but to sense what seemed like an answer so quickly and surely in the depth of her heart . . . Abby blinked hard and pushed the words from her mind. She must be imagining things. The campout had nothing to do with her. Abby tuned out the Lord and honed back in on Jo's conversation.

"And so I just kinda leak all over about the Lord and His goodness and how He done worked a mighty miracle for me and Denny, and how He could do the same thing for anybody willing to take Him at His word."

Abby glanced in the rearview mirror and saw Jo grab a mouthful of air. Beth used the opportunity to clear her throat. "Well, I hate to be a kill-joy, especially when we're getting together for Nicole's wedding, but I for one found my miracle in being divorced. Something about making dinner night after night for a man who can't keep his pants zipped around other girls just doesn't smack with the feel of a miraculous God, if you get my drift."

Nicole shifted uneasily in the front seat and shot Abby a glance. Abby nodded. *Great.* She'd probably be playing referee all weekend at this rate. "Anyone want to stop for coffee before we head out toward the cabin?"

The drive to the cabin took two hours, but the last thirty miles were so remote Abby didn't think there was another person within fifty miles of them. The cabin belonged to a friend of her father's, and at least once a year the Reynolds family had use of it, even if only for a weekend of fishing. Abby knew the spot represented quiet and utter solitude to Nicole and the boys, and when Nicole requested it in lieu of a bridal shower, Abby hadn't been surprised. After all, they'd already had the couples' barbecue.

After they arrived, the four of them unpacked, after which Abby stood up and surveyed the group. "Okay, who wants to go for a walk?"

Beth was on her feet almost instantly. "Me."

Jo waved toward the door. "You go ahead." She patted the cover of her Bible. "Me and the Lord have some catchin' up to do."

Nicole looked at Abby as she spread out on the now-empty bottom bunk. "Mom, why don't you and Aunt Beth go this time. Jo had a few verses she wanted to share with me, okay?"

Abby felt a pit form in her stomach. If she and Beth were going to be alone, then maybe it was time to tell her the news. She nodded. "Sounds good, we'll take the path around the lake and be back in an hour."

They headed north on the gravelly trail that circled the water, walking in silence until the cabin was out of sight.

"Sure is beautiful." Beth was trim like Abby but more rugged, earthy almost. She spent her days as an advertising executive, but she'd worked her way to a position of seniority so that getting time off was not a problem. Although Beth could be cunning and brilliant in a business meeting, she was far more at home with hiking boots and walking shorts, taking in a few days on Silver Moon Lake.

"Hmmm. I love the trees. Especially this time of year." Abby fell in place easily beside Beth, and in no time the cabin was out of sight. "Like they're shouting the fact that summer is here."

Beth chuckled. "That's my sister. Always the writer."

They walked in silence for a moment, stopping to spy on a family of deer drinking at the lake's edge. The evening was cooling quickly, nightfall descending like a quiet blanket over the woods. Abby's heart beat so loud she was sure Beth could hear it. *Do I tell her now? Should I wait?*

"Beth, I—"

"So what's the—"

They laughed because it was something they'd done since they were children, rushed into conversation at the exact same moment. Abby nodded toward her sister. "You go."

Beth's smile faded. "What's the deal with you and John?"

An alarm sounded near the surface of Abby's heart. If Beth could sense a problem, what had the kids been feeling? Had she and John been that obvious? "What do you mean?"

Beth raised one eyebrow sardonically. "Look, big sister, I've been around the block a few times myself. Back at the house you and John were the only people still stuck in winter, like you were afraid you'd catch something if you exchanged so much as a passing glance."

Abby was silent, horrified that Beth had seen through what she and John thought was a perfect act. "We . . . we have a lot on our minds."

Beth said nothing, just cast Abby the look of a younger sister waiting for the whole story. She resumed walking, and Abby joined in beside her. They went on that way for another five minutes while Abby's stomach churned with the truth. When she could take it no more, she stopped and hung her head. The tears weren't something she thought about, just an overflow of emotion that had gotten too great to contain.

Beth saw the first teardrops splash against the gravel below, and she reached out, wrapping Abby in a hug that felt safe and warm and familiar. It made her miss the fact that she and Beth hadn't been closer over the years, and with a suddenly sure realization, she understood that the distance had been her fault. When Beth and her husband divorced, Abby had basically written her off. *What kind of Christian woman couldn't make things work with her husband?* Abby had wondered. And there had been nothing in the past decades to indicate Beth was drawing closer to God, so Abby had chosen to let the relationship wither.

The truth of her own judgmental spirit was almost more than she could bear, and in Beth's arms Abby's tears became heart-wrenching sobs that tore at her and uprooted all that remained of her belief that things worked out for the best.

"Tell me, Abby, it's okay . . . what's wrong?" Beth, normally tough and flippant, was now—in their own private world on the backside of the lake—as kind and caring as their mother would have been.

"You're . . . you're right about me and John." Abby kept her face hidden in Beth's shoulder. "Beth, we're getting a divorce."

As many times as she would have to say the words in the months and years to come, this was perhaps the only time when her statement needed no explanation whatsoever.

"Oh, Abby, I'm so sorry." Beth stroked Abby's hair and, thankfully, refrained from saying anything even remotely sarcastic. "Do the kids know?"

Abby shook her head. "We're waiting until after the wedding."

Beth exhaled through pursed lips. "Boy, Abby, I don't envy you." She paused and shook her head. "I mean, who'd have thought . . ."

After a few minutes Abby's tears subsided, and she pulled away, wiping at her wet cheeks, unwilling to make eye contact with Beth. Was this how she would always feel when someone asked her about her failed marriage? Like she had let the entire world down?

Love is patient and kind . . . love never ends.

The words from 1 Corinthians 13 ran through her head as they had so often these past months, and Abby shook them off. No matter how she had prayed about her marriage in years past, this time love was ending. Her husband wanted to be with someone else. It was over and there was no turning back, nothing to do but figure out a way to go on.

"Is there someone else?" Beth angled her head so she could make eye contact with Abby. "For either of you, I mean?"

Abby shrugged. "John's been seeing someone at work, but honestly our marriage died before she came into the picture."

Beth shuffled her feet absently in the gravel along the path. "You, too? Seeing someone, I mean?"

Abby thought about her editor. "No, nothing like John's situation."

They moved on in silence, more slowly than before. "Men can be such scum." Beth's statement wasn't meant to belittle Abby or the marriage that she and John had shared over the years. She was merely sharing her heart on the matter. "Still . . . you and John? I mean, I could sense something was wrong, but I had no idea . . ."A sigh eased from Beth's lips, and she stared up through the trees as she walked. "Makes you want to warn Nicole, doesn't it?"

Abby's defenses reared up at Beth's suggestion. No, she didn't want to warn Nicole! Marriage was still a good thing, the right thing for most people. What had happened to Beth and her husband, what was happening now with Abby and John, was still the exception. It had to be. Abby couldn't imagine a world where all hope for lasting love was nonexistent. "Nicole and Matt'll be fine." There was certainty in Abby's voice, and Beth raised an eyebrow.

"I thought you and John would be fine too."

"For a lot of years we were." Abby picked up her pace. She was suddenly anxious to be back with Nicole, to a place where new love still seemed full of promise and the reality of her divorce was weeks away.

"What happened, if you don't mind me asking?"

Abby sighed and stared out at the lake, her feet finding their own way as they rounded a bend. She'd had months, years to think about that question, but still the answer did not come easily. "I think it was the year Nicole made the Select soccer team. John was busy with football and the boys, and Nicole and I were gone almost every weekend."

Beth nodded but said nothing.

"We were so busy with the kids, so caught up in our separate lives, that when we were together . . . I don't know, it was like we were strangers or something. I'd get frustrated when he didn't ask about the kids' games or the articles I was writing; he'd feel the same way when I didn't ask him about practice or Friday night football games." She paused. "I don't know. He'd leave clothes lying around, and I'd forget to make dinner every night. We started getting on each other's nerves. Like too much had happened since the last time we were together, and there was no real way to catch up. Things I used to rush home and tell him seemed not so important anymore, and . . . our conversations became more functional small talk than anything else."

Abby felt the tears again and blinked so she could see clearly. "I can't really put my finger on it, Beth. It was like overnight all the things we used to laugh at weren't funny anymore. The details he used to share with me about football went unsaid. Our time together on the pier— where we used to talk, just the two of us—was forgotten. Things like that. I knew it at the time, and I guess that made it worse. I didn't want to hear about his players or the training routine; I was tired of caring about which sophomore might make varsity and which senior had the best shot at a blowout year. It just didn't matter. I wanted him to ask me about *my* day, act a little interested in what I was writing and which magazine was buying my work."

There was quiet for a moment as they kept walking. Finally Beth drew a deep breath. "You and John had some-thing most people never get in a lifetime."

A wave of overwhelming sadness washed over Abby, and she stopped in her tracks, wiping her eyes and trying to get a handle on her feelings. "When I think back to the man he was, the man I fell in love with . . . I can't believe we're going through with this."

"But the truth is you're not the same people you were back then, even I can see that." Beth made it sound so matter-of-fact, as though people like she and John simply changed, and marriages like theirs died every day of the week. It made Abby want to scream, made her want to stop the madness, race home, and shake John until both of them realized the mistake they were about to make.

But was it a mistake?

He was in love with Charlene now, and he hadn't so much as asked about Abby's day in more than a year. The truth that Beth was right made Abby even angrier. "Let's get back." Abby felt like she was carrying John and Nicole and Kade and Sean squarely on her shoulders, knowing that the burden would only get heavier, not lighter in the days to come. She wiped away the last of her tears and began moving forward once more. "Nicole'll be wondering where we are."

"I won't say anything. Obviously." Beth reached out and squeezed Abby's hand once. "I'm here for you."

Abby managed a smile. Beth meant well, and though Abby had spent a lifetime convincing herself she had little or nothing in common with her independent, cynical little sister, the days were quickly coming when they would share more similarities than Abby cared to think about. "Thanks."

They walked the remainder of the trail in silence and soon were back at the cabin. Abby opened the door, then stopped cold at what she saw. Jo and Nicole were sitting cross-legged on the same bottom bunk, facing each other and holding hands as they bowed in prayer. Beth caught a glimpse of them and moved back outside to a distant chair on the front porch.

But Abby couldn't bring herself to turn away. Here was her only daughter, the girl she herself had taught to pray, the one she had prayed over on countless nights year after year, now joined in prayer with a virtual stranger. A woman who until a few months ago was a divorcée who didn't know the first thing about having a relationship with the Lord. Yet here was Nicole praying with that very woman.

Probably the kind of prayer she might have prayed with Nicole back before . . . well, if things were different. Abby realized then that she had lost something of herself, the part that years earlier would have been sitting where Jo was. *Another casualty of our dying marriage.* Through her tears she wondered how—by what awful, miserable twist of fate—she had switched roles with the woman before her. And whether there was any way she could ever rise again from the pit she occupied to that graceful, peaceful place Jo Harter had somehow found.

The moment the van was out of sight, John set aside the bicycle gearshift he'd been working on, washed his hands, and wandered into the family room to his old easy chair. Sean had ridden his bike halfway around the lake to a friend's house, and Kade was working out at school, trying to gain another ten pounds before college.

The house was quieter than it had been in days.

How had none of them noticed? Wasn't it obvious that he and Abby hadn't so much as touched in front of the kids in months? John let the question hang in the rafters of his mind, and it occurred to him that he was thirsty. He made his way through the dining room into the kitchen and poured himself a glass of water. As he filled it, his eyes fell on the phone.

"I'll be home . . . call me if you want . . . call me if you want . . . call me if you want . . ."

Charlene's words played in his ears until he could feel

himself being pulled toward the receiver. *Help me out of this, God . . . Please. I promised Abby . . .*

Love bears all things, My son . . . love never ends.

The thought rattled around in his tinny heart and set his feet in motion, moving back through the dining room, away from the phone. Halfway to his chair he spotted a paper on the table and stopped to read the cover.

"Merits of the Eagle—A Senior Class Project by Kade Reynolds."

Kade had aced the paper, and for days now he'd been harping on John to read it. He reached down and picked it up, opening the first page and scanning the table of contents. "Traits of an eagle . . . What makes the eagle different . . . The eagle takes a mate . . ." The paper was ten pages long and looked tedious.

Read it, son . . . read it.

He was drawn to the report by something he couldn't see . . . couldn't explain. A silent voice almost like God's had once been, back when they had spent their days in conversation . . . but why would God want him to look at Kade's report?

Then another voice echoed through him.

Don't waste your time. Who cares about the eagle? You're a week away from moving out, and you have the house to yourself. Make the most of it.

As the thought slithered across his conscious, John pulled his eyes away from the paper in his hand and stared hard at the telephone.

"I'll be here . . . call me, John . . . I'll be here."

Without giving it another thought, he dropped the paper on the table once more. Refusing to think about promises to Abby or what kind of man he'd become, John lifted the receiver. But just as he was about to dial her number, the phone rang. John drew back as quickly as if Abby had walked into the room. He pushed a button and held the phone to his ear, his heart beating wildly. "Hello?"

"Dad?" It was Nicole, her voice dripping with tender nostalgia. "It's me. I'm on the cell phone at our old campsite. Can you believe it reaches from way out here?"

John's desire to call Charlene disappeared instantly. He forced his voice to sound normal, as though he'd been sitting around the living room watching ESPN. "Hi, honey. You having fun?"

"Yeah, we're gonna play Scrabble and stay up all night talking." She paused, and John could almost see the sparkle in her eyes. "Mom said I could call real quick and tell you good night."

A thin layer of sweat broke out across John's forehead and he gulped back his anxiety. "I'm glad you're having a good time, sweetheart." *Should I say it?* "And, uh, tell Mom I said hi."

Nicole sighed at the mention of her mother, and John had the feeling she was debating whether to speak. "Dad, I'm praying for you and Mom."

John's anxiety level doubled. "For . . . for us?" What had Abby told her? And why now, with her wedding days away?

Nicole giggled. "Parents need prayers, too, Dad. I figure as long as we're gone for a few days talking about love and stuff, I might as well pray for you guys. Maybe watching Matt and me get married on your anniversary will make you feel like newlyweds again. I figured it couldn't hurt."

There were a hundred things John wanted to say, but

he wasn't sure he should voice any of them. To defend their marriage was to lie to her, but to say nothing was to admit there was a problem. John drew a deep breath. "It never hurts to pray."

"Well, I gotta run. I just can't believe that a week from now I'll be on my honeymoon. It feels like my days of being a little girl are ending, you know?"

John's heart felt as if someone had ripped it from his chest and stomped on it. Dozens of snapshots of Nicole raced through his mind: toothless on her first day of kindergarten, decked out in blue and gray at one of his football games and cheering alongside the big girls, booting a soccer ball over the heads of three defenders in a tournament game her eighth grade year, playing the piano in her cap and gown hours before her high-school graduation. Where had the time gone? And what would happen to Nicole's smile in two weeks when the news was out?

There was a lump in John's throat, and again he had no idea what to say.

"Dad? You still there?" The connection was breaking up and Nicole sounded concerned.

"I'm here, honey. Try to remember it isn't so much an ending as . . . a new beginning."

"Right . . . that's what Mom said too." Thank goodness she was too excited about getting married to spend much time reminiscing. "Well, I'll see you in a few days, Dad. I love you."

John closed his eyes and dropped into the nearest dining room chair. "Love you, too, Nick."

He disconnected the call and left the receiver on the table, imagining the fallout that lay ahead. Before he could decide what to do next, the phone rang again. *What'd you forget this time, Nicole?* "Hello, honey, I'm all ears . . ."

There was a pause, then Charlene's voice sounded coolly on the other end. "That's nice . . . expecting me or someone else?"

John's head began to spin. He hated the crazy, confused web that his life had become. "I . . . I thought it was Nicole."

"Nicole." Charlene's voice was flat. "Not Abby, though, right?"

That was it. "Look, get off my back. I don't have to defend myself to you, Charlene."

He sighed and massaged his temples, his eyes closed. Nearly a minute passed in silence. "I'm sorry for snapping at you. I just don't want to talk to you right now . . . I need time."

There was a pause, and then he heard a sniffling sound. *Great, now I'm making two women cry.* Strangely, Charlene's tears only frustrated him more. "I've gotta go."

She cleared her throat. "Call me when you're ready . . . and not until then, okay?"

An odd sense of relief flooded John's soul. "Okay."

When he'd hung up, John planted his forearms on the kitchen table and stared out the window into the dark night. What had he almost done? Why was he going to call her in the first place? And how could he feel so strongly for her one minute and barely able to tolerate her the next?

It had never been that way with Abby, not in the beginning at least. Not after ten years, for that matter. With Abby he'd always looked forward to their time together. They'd shared a chemistry that had not let up with time.

So why'd you stop loving me, Abby? Why'd you lose interest in everything about me?

His eyes fell on Kade's report still lying on the table, and he could hear his son's voice. *"Take a look at it, Dad. I'm leaving it right here until you read it."*

Fine. Charlene wouldn't be calling again; he was alone for the night. Why not? He picked up the report and moved across the kitchen to his easy chair in the next room. When he was comfortable he turned to the first page. The report was well-written and informative, and despite every other emotion that warred inside him, John felt a surge of pride. Kade would do well at the University of Iowa, and not just on the playing field.

He read through the introduction and into the body of the report, remembering again how the Lord called His people to be like eagles. *Mount up on wings as eagles . . .* not crows or chickens or pheasants. Eagles. Key phrases from the report jumped out at him, information Kade had shared with him months ago. "The eagle eats only life-giving food. When it eats something that makes it sick, it flies to the highest rock it can find and lays spread eagle with its wings out against the surface of the rock. It stays there until the sun draws out the poison, freeing it to fly with the other eagles."

John let the image sink in again. The next section was about the eagle's mating habits.

"Female eagles like to test their male counterpart." *Counterpart?* Where did Kade come up with a word like that? John kept reading:

When the female knows a male is interested, she leads him on a chase through the skies, swooping and diving and soaring high above the hills. When the chase is nearly over, she flies as high as she can and flips onto her back, free-falling toward the ground. It is the male's job to place his body over hers and grasp her talons, flapping his wings with all his might to keep her from certain death. Moments before they hit the ground, the female pulls out of the dive and circles the male. Because he had been willing to stay even unto death, he will have proven himself as a mate. The eagles are joined for life from that point on.

John closed the report and set it down on the table beside him. He felt sick to his stomach, laboring under a mantle of guilt as heavy as any brick wall.

The comparisons were obvious. Of course he and Abby were destined for divorce—he had let go of her years ago, and now they were just two lonely eagles, free-falling hopelessly toward the ground. And as he pondered their plight he began to have a revelation unlike anything before in his entire life.

A revelation that could have come only from God Almighty Himself.

Twenty-Two

IMAGES OF EAGLES FALLING FROM THE SKY KEPT JOHN awake long into the night, so the next morning he was not only deeply troubled, but tired as well. He waited until nine o'clock to call Charlene.

"Hello?" Her voice was chipper and upbeat; she seemed unaffected by the phone call from the previous night. Didn't she know how upset he'd been? Wasn't she concerned by his reaction, his decision to avoid conversation with her? A brief thought occurred to John . . . maybe he was just a passing interest in Charlene's life. A conquest of some kind.

No . . . he and Charlene had known each other too long for that. "Hi. It's me."

"John! You called!" The excitement in her tone was instant. The last thing he'd done was agree to call her when he was ready, when he'd had enough time. His hand came up along the back of his neck and he massaged it idly. She had no idea what had happened since then.

"We need to talk. Can you . . . would you mind coming by this afternoon. Sometime after lunch?" He was trying to sound friendly but not suggestive. The last thing he wanted was Charlene showing up in a bathing suit ready to spend an afternoon along the lake.

"Our conversation last night didn't . . . well . . . it didn't work out so well. Are you sure you're ready to see me?"

John released a measured breath and flexed his jaw. "Yes. One o'clock."

"Perfect." She sounded upbeat and . . . triumphant. How well could she know him if she thought he could change his mind that easily?

As the morning passed, John read more of Kade's report. The eagle had two natural enemies: storms and serpents. He embraced the storm, waiting on the rock for the right thermal current and then using that to carry him higher. While other birds were taking cover, the eagle was soaring. An eagle would never fight against the storms of life.

He saved his fighting for the serpent. Especially when the snake threatened the eagle's young.

John put the report aside again. Did Kade know he'd been writing specifically for his own father? Could God have found any better example to show him how he'd fallen short?

He didn't think so. And though his marriage was over, though he'd messed up over the last few years, he felt the seeds of change taking root in his soul. If only he could get his life with God right again . . . maybe, just maybe he could remember what it was to be an eagle. The type of eagle he'd always wanted to be. The type that would embrace the storms of life.

And fight the serpent at all costs.

Charlene was right on time, wearing white shorts and a formfitting tank top. Her makeup was simple, and she looked twenty-five when John opened the door and invited her in. *Give me strength here, God. I don't have the words . . .*

I will tell you what to say and when to say it, My son. Wait on Me.

Wait on Me . . . wait on Me. The words rang in his heart, reminding him of another verse. The one in Isaiah that talked about waiting on the Lord . . . what was it? *"Those who hope in the Lord will renew their strength. They will soar on wings like eagles; they will run and not grow weary . . ."*

Eagles again. Okay, God, I'll wait on You.

He opened the door and motioned for her to follow him. "Thanks for coming."

John sat on the edge of his easy chair, and Charlene took the sofa seat closest to him. "I thought you needed more time." Her voice was confident—clearly she was expecting him to tell her it was time, maybe even take her in his arms and show her exactly how he felt about her.

Instead—in light of all God had showed John through Kade's report—he looked at her the way he might look at an old friend, one for whom he felt nothing but platonic concern. "Charlene, you have your whole life ahead of you. You're . . . you're young and beautiful and . . . I guess what I'm trying to say is I want you to take the job in Chicago."

She laughed nervously and adjusted her legs in a way that made them beyond attractive. John noticed, but was not in the least bit tempted. "You mean both of us, right? You've decided to apply for a coaching job there, is that it?"

John slid back in the chair and leaned over his knees. *Help me, God. Give me the words.* "No . . . I mean it could take months, years, Charlene. Abby and I might be through, but I can't just walk into another relationship with you. Not now anyway."

Momentary impatience flashed in Charlene's eyes. "I told you I'd wait. Why the big speech?"

John knew that on his own strength he'd lose a battle of words with Charlene. She had a way of finishing every conversation in complete control. He waited for God's wisdom. "You've allowed me to tie up your life long enough." He looked into her eyes and willed her to understand. "This'll sound funny to you, but next year when I'm living alone, I want to get things right with God. It's important to me."

Charlene raised a single eyebrow and seemed to stop just short of laughing out loud. "Right with *God?* You think you can divorce your wife and then spend the next year getting religious?" She dropped slowly to her knees and came to him, wrapping her arms around his bare legs and laying her head across his thighs. "It's not God you want; it's me."

A tingling sensation made its way through his body.

No! God, get me out of this. I've messed up one relationship; I won't do it again. Help me!

Gently, and with power that was not his own, he nudged Charlene off his legs so that she fell reluctantly into a cross-legged heap at his feet. "I can't. Understand?"

"Why?" Charlene's eyes filled with tears. "You've wanted to . . . we've both wanted to since the day we met. You're just scared, John. Let me love you. Please . . ."

He clenched his jaw. "Charlene, I'm telling you it's over between us."

Her face grew pale, and she retreated back a few feet. "What's that supposed to mean? I thought you just needed time."

"I need time alone with God." As difficult as this was, he was absolutely sure it was the right thing. And nothing Charlene could do would change his mind.

"With God? Come on, John. Like that mattered to you the other day in your classroom or that night on the football field."

He remembered the breakthrough from the night before and silenced her with an icy glare. How dare she throw that at him now? "I've made up my mind, Charlene. Do what you want about the job in Chicago. It's over between us."

Just as Charlene was about to say something, there was a knock at the door.

John's heart rate tripled. Were they home early? How would he explain Charlene being there? He stood on suddenly shaky legs and motioned for her to move up onto the sofa again. She did so, and he ordered himself to be calm as he opened the door.

The sight of Matt Conley was both a relief and a source of concern. "Uh, hey, Matt. What's up?"

Matt looked beyond him and saw Charlene in the next room. "Oh, I'm sorry, I didn't know you had company."

Charlene took the cue and stood up, grabbing her purse and making her way to the front door. She laughed lightly. "Don't mind me, gentlemen. I was just leaving."

She breezed up alongside them and, with Matt watching, she looked John squarely in the eyes. "About your suggestion, I think you're right. I can't pass up a job like that." She hesitated, and he could read in her face the things she wasn't saying: the pain and anger and resignation. "I'll probably find a place in Chicago before the end of the month."

John hadn't pictured ending it this way, talking in cryptic phrases while his future son-in-law hung on every word. He managed a smile, taking a step backward to keep the distance between them. "You'll do great." He patted her on the shoulder the way he might congratulate one of his players after a good performance. "Thanks for stopping by."

There were fresh tears in her eyes as she left, but John was fairly sure Matt hadn't noticed them. When she was gone, the two men moved into the living room. Matt fidgeted. "I didn't mean to run her off . . . I just thought . . ."

"Don't worry about it. She needed a little advice, and it was a good time to talk to her. She's taking a position in Chicago."

"I gathered." Matt wrung his hands and chuckled. "Nothing personal, but Nicole can't stand that woman."

"Charlene?" John's heart skipped a beat. He hadn't realized Nicole had an opinion on her, one way or the other.

"Yeah, Nicole thinks she has designs on you."

John's laugh sounded forced, but again Matt didn't seem to notice. "There's nothing to worry about where Charlene's concerned. We've been friends for a while, but she's moving on now."

John willed his heart to beat normally, stunned at the timing of Matt's visit and how his presence had caused Charlene to leave. He thought about Nicole's phone call the night before and the classroom announcement the other day. How close he'd come to . . .

God, You're so faithful! I've done nothing but live life on my own for so long, and yet here You are giving me all the help I need. Help me be an eagle, Lord . . . Help me learn to fly again.

"That's sort of why I'm here, I guess. I mean, you're amazing, Mr. Reynolds. Women like Charlene breathing down your back and still—after all these years—you and Mrs. Reynolds have this perfect marriage."

Okay, switch gears, John. Matt wasn't there to spy on him; he was there for advice. "Well, no marriage is perfect."

Matt stood up and walked from one end of the living room to the other and back again. "It's not that I'm getting cold feet." He stopped and stared earnestly at John. "I love Nicole more than I ever thought possible."

A flashback lit up in the corners of John's mind. He and Abby under the big oak tree on the University of Michigan campus: *"I'll never love anyone like I love you, Abby . . . like I love you . . . like I love you."* "I remember the feeling."

"But that's just it. You and Mrs. Reynolds never *lost* that feeling, you know? I mean how can I keep what's bottled up inside here—" he cupped his hand over his heart—"and make sure it never goes away?" His arm fell back to his side. "Like it did for my parents."

John started to open his mouth but the hissing voices were back. *Hypocrite, hypocrite, hypocrite! How dare you give this godly young man advice when you can't even keep a simple promise to Abby?* "I don't have the answers, Matt."

The young man before him was so serious, so intent on finding the secret to lasting love, that John wanted to crawl into a hole and never come out. How would Matt feel about him in two weeks?

Tell him about the eagle, My son.

The thought echoed through the place in his heart reserved for holy whispers.

Give me the words, God . . . one more time.

Matt moved back to the sofa and sat down, crossing his legs. "I know there's no set formula, but I want at least a clue." He ran his hand across his brow. "I should have asked you a long time ago. I just wasn't sure how to bring it up without you thinking I was having doubts. I mean, you're not just this great man I admire and look up to . . . you're Nicole's father. That made it tricky."

John was almost desperate to come clean with Matt, to stop the farce and let him know what a terrible husband he really was, how he and Abby had stopped trying years ago.

Remember My grace, son. Tell him about the eagle . . .

There it was again. He wasn't up to this, couldn't look Matt in the eyes and tell him anything that might—

"Maybe a scripture or something. I mean, I've studied all the verses about God hating divorce and how the two shall be one . . ."

John felt a knife of regret slice through his midsection. *I can't do this, God . . . make him leave.* "Have you ever studied the eagle?"

Matt grinned. "You mean like, Marion Eagles . . . the winningest football program in southern Illinois?"

John was suddenly bolstered by a strength he hadn't known in years. "In Isaiah, God says we'll soar on wings like eagles." He reached over and grabbed Kade's report from the nearby end table. "Kade did his senior project on the eagle, and I think there's a lot there."

Matt's expression twisted curiously. "About marriage?"

For the next ten minutes John talked about the eagle

and its ability to embrace the storms of life, how the eagle fought the serpent, keeping the snake from destroying its baby eaglets or the great eagle nest. He told Matt how, when it was sick, the eagle knew enough to get alone on the rock and let the sun soak the poison from its system. And most of all how the male eagle was born to cling to the female regardless of the fall, even unto death.

When he was finished, Matt no longer seemed concerned. From where he stood, on the doorstep of new love and commitment, the idea of clinging to Nicole for life seemed easy and exciting. John prayed it would always feel that way.

"That's perfect, just what I needed." They chatted awhile longer about the wedding and how quickly everything would take place that week. Finally, after nearly an hour, Matt stood to leave.

Though John still felt like a hypocrite, though he was certain the strength to talk to Matt had been supernatural, he walked Matt to the door and bid him good-bye.

"Four days, Mr. Reynolds. I can't wait." Matt was tall and handsome, and with his ability to reason, John was sure he would make a good attorney one day soon. But more than being an ample provider, John hoped his future son-in-law would be able to grasp the lesson of the eagle and the importance of never letting go.

A lesson John only wished he'd understood years earlier when he and Abby had first started to fall.

Abby stood alone in her driveway, tired and satisfied, as she waved good-bye to Beth and Jo. Nicole had already taken her suitcase inside the house, and if her outlook was any indication, the girls' campout had been a complete success. They'd laughed and talked and even prayed together. Now at home, Abby wandered around the side of the house toward the backyard and spotted John, adrift in their aluminum rowboat in the middle of the lake.

Probably feeling guilty. Didn't want to face us when we got in. She allowed her gaze to linger, and a dozen memories of happier times danced into view. The boat didn't seat more than three people, but there had been times when it seemed like a yacht, times when she and John could spend an afternoon in it, floating on the lake, soaking up the sun and sharing laughter and conversations. It was out in that very boat that they'd dreamed about Kade's football career and that she'd told him she was pregnant with Sean.

John wasn't rowing, and since his back was to her, she figured he didn't know they were home yet. And it occurred to Abby that this might be the last time she'd come home and find him out on the lake like this.

There was something peaceful and timeless about being on the lake, and John knew with the craziness of both the dress rehearsal and the wedding over the next few days there would be little time for anything resembling quiet. Besides, he needed to think, needed to imagine how different life might have been if he'd seen the split coming and done something, anything, to stop it.

Of course, it was too late now. Abby didn't love him, and no effort at holding on to her would make a difference at this point. In the free fall of life, they'd both crashed and burned. Now she was moving on to other territories.

He leaned into the boat, his back to their home and all

the joy and sorrow that would take place there over the next few weeks. As he stared into the sky, he watched a bird soar effortlessly into the air, crisscrossing over the water in search of evening fish. John stared at it more closely. It couldn't be. Not here and now, when so much was going through his mind, when Kade's report had been the trigger for the greatest change of heart he'd had in all his life.

But it was. It was an eagle. And as he watched it, he felt washed in God's grace and forgiveness, filled with a hope that had no reason for being.

John stared at the eagle as tears burned his eyes. Something about seeing the majestic bird in flight gave him strength. As though God wanted him to know it was possible to fly again, even after a lifetime of poison. And that was good because nothing was going to poison his system more than going before a judge and divorcing the woman he'd fallen in love with more than two decades earlier.

John watched the eagle until the sun set, and then, with a strange new sense of forgiveness and purpose, a sense of grace that had nothing to do with himself, he rowed back to shore where there were still no answers for the most important questions of all.

Tell me how, God . . . how do I find my way back to the Rock so the Son can rid me of all those years of poison? And how, with broken wings, will I ever learn to catch the thermal currents in life and fly again?

Twenty-Three

THE NEXT THREE DAYS PASSED IN A BLUR OF preparation. Party coordinators worked to make the back-yard perfect. Florists called to double-check the order for the church and the back porch. The DJ needed to set up a wooden platform and hadn't realized the yard was sloped. A carpenter was called in to make the platform level and to lay out a small dance floor, and by the time the rehearsal was underway, Abby was almost too tired to feel anything but drained.

Drained and cheated.

This should have been a time when all her energy was focused on Nicole. Instead Abby felt almost as though she was only going through the motions: the wedding, the divorce, Kade's move to the university—all of it. Like she was delaying her feelings in the here and now because to experience them might actually kill her.

For days she and John had passed like enemy ships in

the night, speaking only when necessary, yet still some-how avoiding the notice of the kids. Kade was getting ready to leave for Iowa, and Sean was busy with his friends, looking forward to a summer of fun. Everyone had his or her own life to worry about, including John—who no doubt already had plans with Charlene for the moment Nicole and Matt were gone from the wedding reception.

Well, she wasn't going to sit there and watch them. Abby had realized she needed to get away as soon after the wedding as she could. She made arrangements for Sean to stay with one of his friends and booked a flight to New York. She'd stay in a hotel downtown and catch a few shows with her editor. It was time they finally met, time to see if they would share anything lasting beyond their e-mail friendship. The days away would be good. Better than sitting around the house wondering what John and Charlene were doing.

Her flight was set to leave Monday morning and return Friday. The kids would be back from their honey-moon the following Sunday, and on Monday she and John had agreed to break the news. It still seemed unreal-istic, like the scary part of a horror movie. Only this time there would be no turning the channel, no getting up and walking away. The reality was upon them, and together—perhaps for the last time—she and John would have to help the kids understand.

The boys thought their dad was going fishing with some friends from work right after the wedding and that Abby had a business meeting in New York. The idea of their parents heading in different directions for the week didn't raise even a bit of concern among them. Nicole was too busy to think about it or she probably would have had questions.

That night, with the wedding set to take place in less than twenty-four hours, Abby delayed her office time and made her way across the house to Nicole's room. Her daughter was beaming, completely packed, and writing a letter. The moment Abby walked into the room, Nicole hid the paper under her pillow. "It's a surprise for Matt."

"Oh. That's nice." Abby wandered across Nicole's bedroom floor and kissed her. "I'm so happy for you, honey. I want you to know that."

The joy in Nicole's eyes was not something that could be contrived. It was the most real and satisfying thing Abby could have hoped to see the night before Nicole's wedding. "He's the one we prayed for, Mom. I love him so much."

Abby sat on the edge of Nicole's bed and smoothed a hand over her daughter's golden hair. "No matter what life brings, no matter what happens all around you, don't forget how you feel tonight. Keep that. Make your marriage first in your life."

Nicole nodded and some of the sparkle faded from her eyes. "God first, then my marriage. That's what you mean, right?"

Abby felt her face growing hot. Why hadn't she thought of that? Was she so far removed from God? So far away from—

"Are you okay, Mom? You've been kind of quiet these past few days."

Focus, Abby. She smiled, holding back tears. "I've had a lot on my mind." She put her arms around Nicole and pulled her close. "My baby girl is getting married tomorrow."

"Ah, Mom, but it's not like that with you and me. You

know that, right? This will always feel like home. I mean, Matt and I will come over for dinner and hang out playing cards with you and Dad, and one day we'll bring the grandkids here for you guys to baby-sit." Nicole's face was beaming again, caught up in the certainty of God's blessings and goodness.

Abby folded her hands in her lap and forced herself not to weep. Hadn't she felt the exact same way the night before her own wedding? Certain of their happy-ever-after? Yet the truth was none of Nicole's pictures of home would ever be the same after she and John were divorced.

The tears came of their own volition, and Abby leaned over, kissed Nicole once more, and bid her good night. "See you in the morning, sweetheart. You're going to be absolutely beautiful."

Nicole dabbed her finger under Abby's eyes. "Mom . . . you're crying."

Abby smiled, her vision blurred as another round of tears waited their turn. "Happy tears, sweetheart. That's all."

And when she left the room, sure that everyone else was asleep, Abby scurried toward the office where she could let loose and cry all night if she wanted to. She was almost there when she heard John's voice.

"Abby . . ."

She turned and saw him standing in the kitchen doorway. He still wore his dress slacks and white button-down from the rehearsal dinner, and Abby realized how little she'd looked at him that night. Though they'd sat next to each other all evening, they'd managed to carry on conversations with other people. Until now he hadn't said more than what was absolutely necessary to pull off their charade.

"What?" She was not up to a verbal battle. Not when it was all over but the walking away. Not when in twenty-four hours they would reside at different addresses.

"We haven't had a moment alone in a long time, and . . . I don't know, I thought we could talk."

Abby sighed. "It's too late, John. There's nothing to talk about."

There was a depth to John's eyes that hadn't been there in months. Years, maybe. *It's my imagination; nostalgia coming up against the finality of it all.* "Okay. Never mind." He hesitated. "Are you . . . will you be around this week?"

Abby sighed and felt her frustration level rising. How dare he ask about *her* plans when he'd be with Charlene? Of all the things he might want to talk about, why on earth would John want to know her plans for the coming week?

Don't say it, daughter—

"Let me guess, you and Charlene want to make dinner plans with me?"

John flinched as though he'd been slapped, and his eyes took on the hard look she was more familiar with. "Forget it, Abby." He studied her for a moment. "Someday I'd like to know what happened to the girl I fell in love with . . ."

"I—"

He put his hand up, cutting her off. "Never mind. I know it's my fault. It's all my fault, and I'm sorrier than you'll ever know. But years from now when this is behind us, take a minute and look in the mirror. And see if *you* even know who you've become." His tone wasn't hateful like she'd heard it before. It was more dumbfounded. And sad. And that only made Abby angrier.

She could live with the idea that he was finally taking credit for the train wreck of their marriage, but how *dare* he accuse her of changing. She hadn't changed; she'd survived. Back in the beginning, when their schedules had first taken precedence over their relationship, the woman he'd fallen in love with had been there just beneath the icy surface. She spread her hand across her chest and kept her voice low so the kids couldn't hear her. "That same girl is still in here somewhere, John. But a long time ago you stopped looking for her." New tears filled her eyes, and she blinked so she could see more clearly. "And now that you've fallen in love with someone else, maybe she'll stay hiding in there forever."

"I'm not in . . ." His voice trailed off, and his look of protest faded as he shrugged. "I'm going to bed."

With that he turned and trudged up the stairs toward the bedroom. When he was out of earshot, Abby stepped into her office and clenched her fist, leaning her back against the oak cabinet and sliding slowly down it until she was in a heap on the floor.

"I hate this, God . . . what's happened to me?"

John was right. The girl he'd married had become hard and angry and bitter. She smiled so rarely that when she did her face felt strange, like the muscles at the corners of her mouth had forgotten what it was like to work on their own. With no one around to hear her, she allowed her tears to come, crying for all that she would be losing the following day.

Her sides ached, but her heart hurt worse. It was really happening. John and Abby Reynolds were getting a divorce, breaking their greatest promise to each other, to her father, to Haley Ann, to the others. To God Almighty. Suddenly she longed to forget about the whole thing, follow John up the stairs, and crawl in bed beside him. She could feel the warmth of his skin against hers, hear herself telling him she was sorry, begging him for one more chance.

The idea fled as quickly as it came.

John had been seeing Charlene for years, no matter when the two of them had first become physical. Abby was a fool to have allowed the pretense of their marriage to last as long as it had. Rage built within her at the role he'd played in destroying their lives. *I hate you, John. I hate you for what you've done to us, to me.* "It isn't fair, God," she wailed out loud in a whispered voice. "Help me . . ."

Come to Me, daughter. The truth will set you free.

She shook her head and struggled to her feet to find a tissue. How could the truth set her free? If she knew the reality of how close John and Charlene were, it'd probably send her over the edge.

Another wave of quiet tears came and she was overwhelmed with the feeling of loss that welled up inside her. Loss of her marriage and her family. But mostly the loss of that young girl, the one John had fallen in love with.

The one Abby feared might not be hiding at all, but rather too far gone to ever find again.

The morning of Saturday, July 14, dawned more beautiful than any Nicole could remember. She had more than enough time to get ready, since the ceremony wasn't until three o'clock that afternoon. But she wanted to savor the day and that meant rising before anyone in the house and watching the morning come to life across the lake.

She'd been reading the Epistles lately, trying to understand the message Paul had for the church, especially his desire that they live in love and grace the way God would have them live. Nicole situated herself in her window seat and gazed across the lake. *Thank You, Father . . . the day is finally here.* Her heart felt as though it had been created for this time in her life, and she eased open the cover of her Bible, flipping to the thirteenth chapter in First Corinthians. She had read the verses a dozen times since getting engaged, and each time the Lord had showed her something new and revealing about true love, the kind she and Matt would share for a lifetime.

She read down to the fourth verse. *"Love is patient, love is kind. It does not envy, it does not boast, it is not proud . . . "* The words flowed from the pages straight into her heart, and she could feel them building her up, preparing her to love Matt the way God wanted her to. Nicole thought about the fact that sometime late that night, when the celebrating was finished, she and Matt would have their first opportunity to love each other with their bodies. She closed her eyes and felt a smile make its way across her face.

We actually managed to wait, Lord. We stayed within Your plan, and I know with all my heart that tonight will be only the beginning.

She thought about the times when they'd been tempted and knew that God's strength alone had brought them to this point, to a place where they could pledge their love to each other on their wedding day, knowing that they had kept themselves pure. Nicole could think of no greater gift to give Matt, no greater way to please the One who had brought them together.

God, You're so good. Just like Mom always told me, You've had a plan for me all my life, and today it's actually going to happen. She opened her eyes and found the place in

Scripture where she'd left off. *"Love always protects, always trusts, always hopes, always perseveres. Love never fails."*

Nicole let her gaze roam about the backyard of the house where she'd grown up. That was the trouble with too many couples. They didn't understand what it really meant to love. Oh, sure, it was the butterfly feeling that happened when two people first met, but it was so much more than that. She thought over the verses again. *"Love always hopes, always perseveres. Love never fails."*

It was an entire marriage manual in less than ten words.

She thought of her parents and how long they'd stayed together, and a strange cloud of concern blocked the sunshine of the morning. *What is it, Lord? How come I feel this way whenever I think of their marriage?*

Pray, daughter.

Her heart rate quickened, and Nicole felt the rumblings of fear deep in her gut. Pray? For her parents? Again? The insistent urging was the same one she'd felt before the camping trip, and it was beginning to make her wonder if her parents were hiding something. Today wasn't the right time, but when she and Matt returned from their honeymoon, she would take an afternoon and talk to Mom. Ask her straight out if she and Dad were having trouble.

Whatever it might be, it couldn't be serious enough to spend time dwelling on now, on her wedding day. Right?

Pray. Pray hard, dear one.

Okay, Lord, I hear You. The feeling was so urgent, Nicole's hesitation dissolved. Whatever the situation, her parents needed prayer. And for the next thirty minutes she lay aside all thoughts of her wedding and the things she needed to do to get ready and poured out her heart on behalf of the two people she admired most in all the world.

The excitement was so great in the minutes before the ceremony that for the first time in six months Abby wasn't consumed with thoughts of their divorce. Instead she was swept up in what felt like a dream scene, one she'd dreamed decades earlier when Nicole Michelle was still a newborn. Nicole was radiant, of course—the waist and bodice of her dress fit perfectly, the skirt and train billowed about her like a satin cloud trimmed in lace.

Abby and Jo had already lit the candles at the front of the church, and now Abby made her way through the tuxedoed men and stunning bridesmaids and sidled up next to Nicole. "You could've worn rags today and you'd have looked every bit as beautiful."

Nicole cocked her head and grinned, meeting Abby's gaze and holding it. "I'm so happy, Mom."

A light chuckle came from Abby. "It's obvious, sweetheart." She leaned forward and kissed Nicole, patting her gently on the cheek. "Kade's walking me down now. Next time I see you you'll be a married woman."

"Can you believe it, Mom? It's finally here!" Nicole squeezed Abby's hands. "You and Dad look so good. No one'll believe you're old enough to be my parents."

Yes, Abby had noticed. John looked more handsome than the groom in his black tux and baby-blue cummerbund. She smiled, hiding the way Nicole's comment pierced her heart. "I've got to go. Love you, honey."

"Love you too . . . and Mom?"

Abby waited. "Yes?"

"Happy anniversary!" The words poked daggers at Abby's heart, but she smiled at her daughter.

"Thanks, honey. Love you . . ." Tears welled up in Abby's eyes as she turned to find Kade. Happy anniversary? She'd almost forgotten that this day marked twenty-two years of marriage for her and John.

Maybe everyone else will forget . . . I can't get through it otherwise . . .

She spotted Kade a few feet off, chattering with one of Nicole's bridesmaids. As Abby walked up to him, she felt someone looking at her. She glanced over her shoulder. John was there, ten feet away, standing by himself near the church window. Was he smiling at her? Why? Why work so hard to pretend when the charade was only hours from being over? Abby turned away and linked arms with Kade as he promised the bridesmaid a dance at the reception.

"Flirting with the girls already, Kade?" Abby was desperate to preserve the lighthearted feeling she'd had moments earlier, before Nicole's happy anniversary wish . . . before she'd spotted John.

"Always, Mom. You know me." His grin faded and he studied Abby. "You're the best-looking mom a guy could have."

Abby bowed her head. "Thank you, kind sir."

"Oh, and happy anniversary." He grinned and the hurt in Abby's stomach was so great she wondered if she'd make it down the aisle. *I can't do this, God . . . help me . . .*

Kade was waiting for her. "You ready?"

She nodded, forcing herself to move ahead as the wedding coordinator opened the church doors. As Abby took in the church setting, her breath caught in her throat. It was like something from a movie, white satin ribbons adorned the ends of each pew, and huge sprays of pink roses fanned out across the altar. And so many familiar people, most of whom had known the Reynolds family since they moved to Marion. In fact, the church looked almost identical to the one she had entered twenty-two years earlier back when . . .

And the song. Was it the same one that had drifted down from the balcony all those years ago? Abby had to blink hard to remind herself where she was and who she was and that this was her daughter's wedding, not a flash-back of her own. They arrived at the front row where Kade kissed her cheek and winked at her. Abby took her seat and sat alone to watch the attendants make their entrance.

The bridesmaids wore light blue, the exact shade as the cummerbunds worn by the men. Sean was the youngest groomsman, and when the wedding party was lined up, Abby was struck by how beautiful they were. Suddenly the music changed, and every head turned toward the back of the church. As the crowd rose to its feet, Abby peered around them and was among the first to see Nicole and John as they made their way down the aisle. Halfway there, John leaned toward their daughter and whispered something that made them both smile. Abby felt the sting of tears in her eyes as she watched them.

Who are you, John Reynolds? I don't even know you any-more. The man who'd stood beside her mere months ago making promises to her dying father . . . the man who had kissed her so passionately that night, and who years ago had asked to her to listen to the music of their lives, who had begged her not to ever stop dancing with him . . . the man who shared with her the only memories of little Haley Ann . . . Was that the same man walking their little girl down the aisle? Or was he an impostor, going through the motions, biding his time until he could be free from them all?

Abby no longer knew.

She glanced at Matt. His eyes shone as he saw Nicole in her wedding gown for the first time. Surely any man who could look at his bride with that type of adoration would be faithful to her for a lifetime. But then, John's eyes had looked that way, hadn't they?

Abby wasn't sure anymore.

The minister cleared his throat. "Who gives this woman to be married?"

John smiled at Nicole in a moment shared between them alone, regardless of the nearly two hundred family and friends who watched. "Her mother and I do." Keeping his eyes trained on Nicole even after his words were said, John lifted her veil and kissed her on the cheek. A hundred images flashed in Abby's mind. John kissing Nicole's infant cheek and that same cheek again when she was hit by the car that awful afternoon. Always Daddy's little girl. Nicole had cherished the role, and as Abby watched them she was struck by a realization: the John Reynolds she remembered would have struggled greatly with this moment. In fact, it would have torn his heart wide open. For the past days and weeks and months, Abby had wondered if John was looking forward to the wedding. She figured he was, since it signaled the end of his attempt at staying clear of Charlene. But the truth— at least in part—had to be that John was dying inside. He'd dreaded the coming of this day since Nicole first made her way into his heart the morning of her birth.

Are you sad, John? Does it hurt the way you thought it

would, or have you already moved on, even from a moment like this?

Almost in response, she caught John's glance as he made his way next to her. His eyes were watery with tears, and the ceremony hadn't even begun. The fact reminded Abby that if things had been different, she and John would have had ample opportunity to grow close over the past six months. Sharing their thoughts on Nicole's wedding and reminiscing about their own love. Remarking at how fast her childhood had disappeared and wondering where the time had gone.

Abby sighed and stared at her hands, at the wedding band she still wore. John said nothing but positioned himself so that his shoulder was nearly touching hers. She could feel the heat from his body, and she tried to imagine what Beth must be thinking, sitting back a few rows. Probably the same thing they'd all think by the end of the next week.

That Abby and John Reynolds were world-class hypocrites.

John clenched his jaw as Pastor Joe commanded the attention of the crowd and began speaking about commitment and God's plan for marriage. The preacher was a man the Reynolds family knew well. He was the associate minister at the church, the man who had led the high-school youth group when Nicole was a teenager.

Had Nicole and Matt met with him to plan all this? And why hadn't John been more involved? He could have at least had a conversation with one of them about what scriptures they wanted read at the ceremony or what direction the message might take. Had he fallen that far from his daily walk with the Lord? John felt himself being suffocated in a blanket of shame, and he silently begged God to take it from him. *I'm so sorry, Father . . . never again will I let You go. I don't care what else happens; I can't make it without You.* He thought about Abby, how they had been unable to have even a pleasant conversation in weeks. *Lord, is there a way? Someday, down the road a year or two? Is it possible that she might forgive me and maybe even . . .*

"When two people marry, the commitment is life-long." Pastor Joe smiled at the congregation. "No matter what else happens along the way, they will be tied to that promise forever . . ."

John remembered a distant friend of his father's who had gotten divorced in his thirties and remarried his wife again twenty years later. And, of course, there were Matt's parents, Jo and Denny. If they could find a way back together after so many years then . . .

Maybe that'll be us one day, Lord. John considered the idea. *You're the only One who could make it happen, God.* He pictured the way Abby's eyes had grown hard, how she never smiled or laughed or allowed her feelings to show around him anymore.

Reconciliation seemed about as likely as snow in July.

With Me all things are possible . . .

John reveled in the return of the inner voice. God was beyond faithful, prodding him, encouraging him, bathing him in grace every moment since the night he'd read Kade's paper on the eagle. The deepest regret in all his life was that his restored relationship with the Lord was—for him and Abby—too late. He'd even started writing his feelings down in a journal, confessing his shortcomings, analyzing all that he'd done that had hurt their marriage. *Maybe someday when she's not so mad . . . maybe she'll read it, Lord. It's all my fault . . .*

Confess your sins to one another; talk to her; tell her.

For just a moment, he let his imagination take him down such a path—but he knew there was no way. *Abby's mind is made up, Lord. She has . . . other plans.* John's fingers tightened into a fist and relaxed again as a pang of jealousy gripped him. Kade had mentioned earlier that morning that the house was going to be quiet with Nicole and Mom gone. A few questions later, and John knew the truth. Abby was going to New York on business, which could mean only one thing. She was seeing her on-line friend, her editor.

Not that he could blame her. It was simply over.

Pastor Joe had moved from commitment to honor, and he seemed to be winding up. "I'd like to close by talking about the eagle for a moment." He grinned in John's direction, and John felt the blood draining from his face. Had someone told the pastor? His breathing seemed to slow to a stop as the man continued. "The bride's family has spent a lifetime calling themselves Eagles. Marion Eagles." A friendly chorus of chuckles sounded across the church. "But God also calls us to be eagles. Why? Well, lots of reasons, really."

Kade shot John a curious glance and raised an eyebrow. Obviously Kade hadn't told Pastor Joe about his report. He glanced at Abby and could tell from her unchanged expression that the message wasn't hitting a personal chord with her. *You're really trying to tell me something here, aren't You, God?*

Anyone who hears these words of mine and puts them into practice is like a wise man who built his house on the rock.

A hollow pit formed in John's gut. He was familiar with the scripture that wove its way through his mind, but it was too late to put anything into practice. At least where Abby was concerned.

The pastor smiled at Nicole and Matt. "But the main reason I want to talk about the eagle is because of something Matt shared with me. Something he learned from his future father-in-law, John Reynolds."

Abby looked skeptically at John, and he turned his attention back to the pastor. *That's okay. She doesn't know what's happened in my heart.*

"Before eagles choose a mate—" Pastor Joe paused, making sure he had the attention of everyone in the building—"the male eagle will lock talons with the female as she falls upside down toward the ground. At that point the male must pull her out of the tumble or die trying. In other words he grabs on to her and refuses to let go—even unto death." He smiled again at the couple. "And that's why—Nicole and Matt—God calls you to be like the eagle. Because the commitment that you make here today is one you make in the same way. Unto death. Let's pray."

John wasn't sure when the tears had filled his eyes, but sometime near the end of the message, he felt them on his cheeks. As he wiped them, he noticed Abby do the same thing. What was she thinking? Did she realize that they'd failed the eagle test? That they had done everything *but* stick together in the past years? That when life got busy and the kids' schedules even busier, they hadn't locked talons but simply set out on totally different flying patterns? And if she felt the sting of the message, what direction were her thoughts headed? Did she still hate him as she'd told him the night after Kade found Charlene in his classroom?

It was time for the vows. Pastor Joe asked Matt to repeat after him, and John realized how grateful he was that Nicole was marrying him. Matt was a good kid—a good man. He'd make a wonderful husband for Nicole. Matt finished his part, and it was Nicole's turn.

"I, Nicole Reynolds, take you, Matt Conley, to be my husband." John was struck by how calm Nicole seemed, and his mind diverted to the hazy memory of Abby saying similar words to him on a day not so different from this one. *Were we that way twenty-two years ago? Sure beyond any doubts that what we had would last forever?*

Pastor Joe was moving on to the ring part of the ceremony, and John shot a look at his gold band. How many times had he taken it off so he could work out in the morning with Charlene? Oh sure he'd told himself it was for safety reasons. Wouldn't want to crack the ring or hurt his finger on the free weights. But the truth—and he wasn't up to anything less at this point—was that he wanted to feel single. Even just for an hour.

It was something else he could write in the journal. *Lord, I have so much to be sorry for . . .*

And a promise to keep.

A promise? What promise?

"And now, by the power vested in me by the state of Illinois, I am honored to present to you, Mr. and Mrs. Matt Conley—" the pastor grinned at the couple and waved a hand toward the congregation—"whose promise before all of you today is the beginning of a lifetime of love." He looked back at Nicole and Matt. "You may kiss the bride."

It was during the kiss that John remembered the promise, and the realization cut like a dagger through his heart. It was the promise he'd made to Abby's father. A promise not too different from the one Nicole and Matt had just made.

That he would love Abby Reynolds as long as he lived.

As terrifying as the coming weeks seemed to Abby, nothing could have marred the joy in her heart as Nicole's wedding reception came to life. The house had been decked out in flowers and folding chairs, and the caterer had set up a series of white canopies for the buffet line. From the moment the wedding party arrived back at the house, the disc jockey seemed to have the perfect music playing in the background. The fading sun sent a glistening spray of light across the lake, and though the evening was warm, it was not humid. A faint breeze stirred the tops of the trees, and the sunset promised to be something out of a painting. Nicole and Matt sat closest to the house with the rest of the wedding party while their friends and family found places at tables situated about the yard on either side of the constructed dance floor.

Abby surveyed the gathering and noticed that many couples seemed happier than usual, as though they were touched, as people often are at weddings, by the reminder that they, too, had once shone as brightly as the bride and groom. And even though the memories were sad beyond words for Abby, she refused to let her sorrow win tonight.

Throughout dinner Abby sat next to John, talking mostly to Jo and Denny who were bursting with excitement over the next week's events.

"If it were up to me, I tell you, we'd stop the music, take our place up there on the dance floor, and say our vows right now." Jo pointed at the lake. "Then me and Denny would get out there and do what we always did best."

Jo jabbed her elbow gently at Denny's side, and he broke into a grin. When he noticed the odd looks from the others at the table, he cleared his throat. "Fishing. We'd go fishing; that's what we've always done best."

"Something the Lord Himself liked to do, I might add!" Jo nodded at Abby. "I've been doing what you said. Reading the book of John and learning all sorts of things about the Lord. When I got to that fishing part, I had to stop and clap my hands. I mean, I just knew I liked God from the get-go. Just wish I hadn't taken so long to figure it out. In fact, what was it I was reading the other day, Denny, you remember . . . about that—"

The conversation showed no signs of slowing. And while it might have been nice to talk to some of the other guests at the table, Jo and Denny's streaming dialogue took the spotlight off Abby and John so that no one at the table seemed to remember it was their anniversary or that they hadn't said a single word to each other since back at the church.

Dinner was winding down, and the DJ called the wedding party forward for a dance. Abby watched the young people laughing and swaying together, caught up in the joy of the moment. As the song ended, Abby heard the beginning notes to "Sunrise, Sunset," and she knew it was time for John to dance with Nicole.

"I'll be back." John made the general announcement to the table and eased onto the floor as the music began asking the same questions that rattled around in Abby's empty heart. What happened to the little girl Nicole had been? When did she get so old and grown-up? Wasn't it yesterday when she was just a child? Just skipping in from the lake, asking for a towel and a glass of juice?

Tears built up in Abby's eyes as she watched her football player husband dance the age-old number with their daughter.

And suddenly all Abby could hear was John's voice as he'd said it dozens of times before, as he'd never say it again. *Dance with me, Abby. Dance with me. Dance with me.*

As the reception wound down Abby found herself comparing this evening to the one six months earlier when John and Kade had won the state title football game. All the while she kept reminding herself that this was the last time she and John would entertain and socialize as a married couple. After all the years of frustration and pain and buildup over their divorce, they had finally arrived at this place, and now every minute brought them closer to the end. Abby knew that like the night of the big game, even the smallest memories made that evening would be savored in their minds forever. There was one difference, of course.

This time there were no winners.

"Beautiful wedding, Abby, tell Nicole she looked gorgeous . . ."

"Happy anniversary, you two . . . you look every bit in love as always . . ."

"Matt's going to make her happy; I can feel it my bones. Thanks for a great evening . . ."

"Wonderful party, Abby, give me a call sometime . . ."

One at a time friends and family left until it was Beth's

turn. She and her daughters would stay at a hotel in Chicago that night and catch a flight out tomorrow for the East Coast. Abby had already said good-bye to Beth's girls, and now Beth pulled Abby to a place on the back porch where no one could hear them. "Well, big sister, I don't envy you telling those great kids of yours the truth. But you've got to do it; there's no other way. I watched you and John today." Beth angled her head sadly and brushed a stray lock of hair off Abby's forehead. "It's gone between you, Abby. You're doing the right thing."

Abby wished she could feel some sense of victory in Beth's words, but there was none whatsoever. The fact that Beth was right brought little consolation to the reality of all that lay ahead for Abby, living life as the divorced mother of three grown children. The sound of it so chilled her heart that goose bumps appeared on her arms as she hugged Beth and wished her a safe flight home.

"I'll give you a call next week when I'm in New York." Other than the children, Beth was the only person Abby had told about her trip.

Beth nodded. "I know we haven't always been close, but I'm here if you need me." She squeezed Abby's hand and then found her daughters. "We'll be getting our things in the car. Tell Nicole and Matt I'll be ready to leave in five minutes."

Abby glanced at a clock on the wall inside. Quarter past ten and only the wedding party and Jo and Denny remained. Nicole and Matt disappeared into the house and came back dressed in sporty outfits.

"Okay, everyone," Nicole announced from the porch. "We're off to the airport." Abby had helped Matt and Nicole with the logistics of their honeymoon. Beth would drive them to a hotel near the Chicago airport where the bride and groom had reservations for the honeymoon suite. Like Beth, they would board a plane in the morning, but theirs would take them to an all-inclusive resort on the island of Jamaica.

John had been chatting with Denny down near the pier, but at Nicole's announcement both men made their way up to the porch.

"Bring home a tan for me." Kade pulled Nicole into a hug and kissed her on the cheek. "Love you."

Nicole's eyes glistened with tears. "Love you, too, Kade."

Abby's full-grown son turned to Matt and pushed him playfully in the arm. "Take care of my sister, okay, buddy?"

There was a smile on Matt's face, but his eyes were more serious than Abby had ever seen them. "Always."

One by one Matt and Nicole shared similar words with Sean and the others and eventually with Matt's parents.

"Don't know about you, sweetheart, but right next to that Bible of yours I'd pack myself a fine fishin' pole; wouldn't you, Denny?" Jo was completely serious, and despite the sadness at saying good-bye to Nicole and Matt and the impending doom of what was set to happen when everyone was gone, Abby had to stifle a giggle.

"Well, Jo, I thought about it and . . ." Nicole gazed into Matt's eyes, her entire face lit up with her feelings for him. "I decided we probably wouldn't have enough time to fish. Not on this trip anyway."

Abby watched a pretty blush fan across Nicole's cheeks and then noticed that Jo was astonished. "Not enough time to fish? When you'll be stuck out there in the middle of that warm Atlantic Ocean. Now listen, you two, if you change your mind you could always rent the—"

Denny gently placed his hand over Jo's mouth and nodded toward the bride and groom. "What she's trying to say is have a wonderful trip, and we'll see you when you get back."

Jo conceded and laughed lightly as Denny circled her waist with his arm and brought her close to him. "Okay, okay. Go. We'll fish later."

Watching them, seeing how Denny loved Jo, how Matt loved Nicole, Abby felt more alone than ever, drowning in an ocean of separateness and solitude. *Get me through this, God, please.*

Seek first My kingdom, and all these things will be added to you . . .

Abby sighed quietly. *Later, God. Let me get through this nightmare, and then I promise I'll come back around. After next week I'll need You more than ever. Okay, Lord?*

There was nothing in response, and Abby's lonely feeling worsened. Even God was against her these days.

John was next. He took the initiative and stepped up, placing one hand on Nicole's shoulder and the other on Matt's. That deep something or other was back in his eyes as he began to speak. "If it's okay, I'd like to pray before you leave."

Pray? An unnerving feeling worked its way down Abby's spine. Was this part of his act, his way of making sure Nicole and Matt would think things were fine back home while they celebrated their new marriage in Jamaica? Other than before football games, Abby couldn't remember how long it'd been since John had offered to pray.

"Lord, grant Matt and Nicole safe travel this week, but above all else, give them time to realize the beauty of the commitment they've made to each other. Help them be like eagles, Lord . . . now and forever, amen."

"The beauty of the commitment they've made?" Abby played John's words over and over in her mind and felt baffled by them. Was he so out of touch with the fact that he'd broken his own commitments to her? How could he pray for Nicole and Matt to be like eagles, to hold on forever, when he had determined years earlier to let go of Abby and all they had?

She pushed the thoughts from her mind. What difference did it make? Their fate had been sealed for months, years. They had been helpless to keep their marriage together. Even counseling hadn't helped. Why begrudge John the chance to pray for a different path for Nicole and Matt?

It was Abby's turn then, and she hugged first Nicole, then Matt, smiling through tears on the verge of spilling over. "It was a beautiful wedding, you two."

Nicole took Abby's hand and bent her head close, her eyes glowing with sincerity. "Thank you so much for everything, Mom. We couldn't have pulled it off without you and Dad."

Abby nodded. "You two go. Have a great time."

Nicole hugged Abby once more. "Love you, Mom. You're the best."

"Love you too."

Nicole leaned forward and whispered into Abby's ear. "Remind me to tell you what God's had on my heart lately. We'll talk about it when I get back, okay?"

When they got back . . . That would be when the meeting would take place, when she and John would finally tell the kids the truth about their marriage. Whatever Nicole wanted to talk about would probably be forgotten in the aftermath.

"Okay, sweetheart. We'll talk then."

In a flurry of motion, Nicole and Matt left the house and climbed into Beth's car, waving out the window as they drove away. Sean had already gone home with his best friend, Corey, since he'd be staying with his family that week. With the bride and groom gone, the others said their good-byes, and Kade set out with some friends. Jo and Denny were the last to leave.

"Abby, thanks for everything." Jo had tears in her eyes as she hugged Abby longer than usual. "Without you and John, your marriage and faith, I wouldn't have known what real love was."

The lump in Abby's throat was too thick for her to do more than nod her head. John reached for Denny's hand. "It's your turn next. When's the big day?"

"Two weeks. It'll be a small wedding, nothing like this, but we'd like you and Abby to be there."

Tension began gnawing at Abby's insides and she swallowed hard.

"And happy anniversary, guys." Jo reached out and pinched first her cheeks then John's.

Denny nudged his bride-to-be. "If we'd let 'em have a minute alone, they might actually get to celebrate. Come on, Jo, I'm taking you home."

"Bye! Thanks for everything . . ." Jo was still talking as Denny linked arms with her and headed for their car, leaving Abby and John standing in the doorway.

When they were gone, the house was silent, echoes of laughter and conversation from moments earlier still fading in the foyer. Abby took a step back and leaned against the wall for support. An overwhelming sense of dread settled over her, their home, the air between them.

John cleared his throat as he turned to face her. "I guess it's time."

The sadness in his eyes was too much for her, and she let her gaze fall to the floor. "Go, John. Don't make a long ordeal out of it. Just go."

His suitcase was already in the car, and Abby was sure his keys were in his pocket. But instead of leaving, John stepped a few feet closer. "Abby, I know you're mad at me, and I don't blame you." He came closer still and gently lifted her chin so that their eyes met. The tears that had been brimming spilled onto her cheeks, and she gulped back a torrent of sobs. "I'm sorry, Abby." His voice was tender, barely more than a whisper. "Sorrier than I've ever been in all my life."

Abby had no fight left in her. She looked down again and nodded her understanding as she managed to speak. "Me too."

"You don't have to believe me, but the other day—while you were on the campout with Nicole—I told Charlene to move on with her life." He hesitated. "The enemy of my soul wanted me to get sucked up in that mess, but God and I, well . . . we've been doing some talking. I ended it with Charlene, Abby. She's moving to Chicago in a few weeks."

Abby kept her eyes trained on the ground, not sure what to say. Not sure whether she believed him. When she found the strength to look at him again, she saw tears on his cheeks as well. "Abby, I made some awful mistakes and I'm sorry. I kissed Charlene twice when I never should have . . ."

Abby huffed under her breath. This wasn't true confession time. Abby didn't want to hear about Charlene now. *Go, John, get it over with.*

Instead he slid his fingers up the side of her face and continued. "There was never anything more between us, Abby. Never."

"John, this isn't the—"

"Wait . . . let me finish." His voice rang with sincerity, and again Abby was confused. *Why is he doing this? Breaking things off with Charlene—if he really had—and talking so tenderly to me? Why now when it's too late?*

He drew a deep breath and continued. "Look, Abby, I know you don't believe me, and that's something you have to work out, but it's important for me to tell you anyway. I made mistakes, but I was not having an affair with Charlene, and I was never in love with her." He sighed, his hand still framing her face. "For what it's worth, I think God wanted me to tell you."

Her soul felt like it was being strangled within her, and she remained motionless. *How much can I take here, God? What's he doing to me?*

He's lying to you, Abby. Taking you for a fool.

The answer came quickly, angrily, from some dark recess of Abby's being, and her back stiffened as she silently agreed with it. Of course he was lying. All those mornings and afternoons together and time alone when she was busy on the weekends? He must think she was incredibly gullible to believe there'd been nothing but a few kisses between him and Charlene.

"I'll always love you." He brought her chin up again and looked directly into her soul. "You know that, right?"

If he loved her, would he have taken up with Charlene in the first place? Her tears were falling onto the floor now, and her lack of response to his question caused fresh pain in John's eyes.

He captured a tear from her cheek and mingled it with one of his own. "We were supposed to be one; that's what we promised each other twenty-two years ago. And just because we stopped being one doesn't mean I stopped loving you."

A sob escaped from Abby's throat as she nodded again. "G-g-go, John. Please."

"Okay." He backed up toward the front door, his eyes still locked on hers. "I'll never forget the years we had together. No matter what the future brings."

See, there it was! The reference to Charlene and the future they'd have together. She hung her head and let the sobs come. They stood there, not speaking to each other for nearly a minute. When she finally found control again, she opened the screen door and held it that way. "Good-bye, John."

He nodded his understanding, his voice thick. "Good-bye."

With that he walked out of their home, out of the life they'd shared together. In years to come he would be little more than a stranger, someone she used to love a long, long time ago.

Feeling as though her arms were being ripped from her sides, Abby watched him go, watched him climb into his truck and drive away. She stayed there until his taillights disappeared and she could no longer hear his engine. Then she shut the door, locked it, and wandered back into the house like a child orphaned in battle, wounded and cut to the core. Her eyes fell on the back door, and she knew where she needed to be: on the pier. Even if she was all by herself, she needed to be there.

The air had cooled some, so she ran upstairs to find a sweater. Tears still streamed down her face as she made her way through their closet. It was emptier now, missing the items John had taken with him. It would all be gone soon, everything that might remind her of John's place in their home. His former place.

Her eyes fell on John's zip-up Marion Eagles sweatshirt. Gathering it to her, she buried her face in the soft fleece and felt another wave of sobs wash over her. It still smelled like him. She eased it off the hanger and slipped it on over her dress, relishing the way she felt small and protected inside it, as though John's arms covered her shoulders.

"Dear God . . ." She could barely speak for the force of her tears. "I can't believe he's gone . . ."

Again the pier beckoned her. Hugging herself tightly, she moved from the closet into their bedroom . . . then paused. A brown notebook sat on John's dresser. She blinked twice, clearing the tears so she could see more clearly. What was that? Abby had never seen it before.

Don't let it be from Charlene . . . please, God . . .

Abby almost walked past it, but something halted her, nudged her, and she went to take it gingerly in her fingers and open the cover.

It was John's writing. She turned a few pages and saw that there were several entries. Was it a journal? Could it be that her husband had kept notes she was completely unaware of? She flipped back to the first page and began reading:

July 9, 2001: I have made the most terrible mistake in all my life and I—

Abby closed her eyes. Was it a confession about what John had done with Charlene? If so she couldn't bear to read it, not now. She opened her eyes, terrified at what she was about to see. Unable to stop herself, she continued down the page.

> . . . *and I have no one to talk to, no place to share my feelings. That's why I'm writing now. Oh, God, what You've shown me in Kade's report. About the eagle and how he will hold onto his mate to the end. Even to death. My mistake is this: I let go of Abby. I loved her with all my being but someday, sometime, I let go. I'm sorry, God . . . if You're listening, let Abby know how sorry I am.*

Her heart fluttered strangely. What was this? What had he done that caused him to be so sorry? And why hadn't he told her in person? Suddenly her mind filled with the image of John trying to talk to her the night before, and she bit her lip. He *had* tried to talk to her, but she was too weary, too sure he was lying to listen. She swallowed a series of sobs and dried her face on the sleeve of John's sweatshirt. The next entry was on the same page.

> *July 10, 2001: There's nothing I can do to make Abby believe me. I've made mistakes, God. You know that. But I haven't lied to her about Charlene and me. The memory of every moment with Charlene makes me sick to my stomach . . .*

The room was spinning, and Abby had to sit on the foot of the bed to keep from falling on the floor. Was it possible? Had John been telling the truth all along?

A dozen times when she had ridiculed him, shouted at him, called him a liar played again in her head. What if she'd been wrong? What if he *had* been telling the truth?

She read the other entries, struck by John's humility, his transparency. Had he left the journal on his dresser intentionally, hoping she'd find it? The final entry answered her question:

July 13, 2001: Nicole is getting married tomorrow, the same day that I'll lose everything that ever mattered to me. One day . . . maybe ten years from now . . . I'll find the right moment to share these feelings with Abby. For now . . . there's nothing I can do. It's over between us, and it's all my fault.

Abby closed the book and set it down. A different kind of sorrow gripped her heart, suffocated her with the reality that she'd been wrong about John. Yes, he'd made mistakes. They both had. But clearly he wasn't in love with Charlene, and he hadn't lied about his relationship with her. Just the opposite. He'd tried to tell Abby every detail, to confide in her the feelings in his heart . . . but she had refused to listen.

Tears still pouring down her face, the sobs having their way with her, she followed the familiar path outside and down the damp, grassy hill, past the deserted tables and empty dance floor to the old wooden pier. There were two chairs there, and Abby took one of them, doing her best to get control of herself. No wonder he had left. She hadn't really listened to him in years, hadn't been the friend he needed to confide in.

Okay, Abby, let it go. He's gone. It's all over; you can open your eyes.

She was cold and alone, and the ache in her chest felt like it would kill her. John Reynolds, the man she had fallen in love with when she was barely more than a girl, was gone from her life. In part, at least, because she had refused to hear him, to believe him. *Lord, what have I done?*

Trust Me, daughter . . . look to Me. All things are possible with God.

But it's too late . . . I've pushed him away, and now we have nothing left.

The wind in the trees made it sound as though God Himself were holding a finger to His mouth. *"Shhhhhh,"* He seemed to say. *"It's okay. Trust Me, daughter . . . come home to Me . . ."*

I want to, God, I do . . . But I've made such a mess of things.

Abby had no idea how long she sat there, sobbing quietly, not sure she would survive the losses in her life. Finally, when she didn't think she had tears left to cry, her mind moved back to the wedding and the lovely bride Nicole had been.

Dear God, let her and Matt stay together forever; don't let her happiness be dimmed because of John and me.

Abby stared out at the water and imagined how Haley Ann might have looked if she'd been Nicole's maid of honor. Abby looked intently across the water. "Haley Ann, baby, we missed you today. I missed you."

There was a rustling of bushes and grass behind her, far up on the hillside, and Abby spun around. She had never felt nervous here, in this place where she had lived nearly all her married life. But now that she was alone, every sound seemed magnified. Nothing caught her eye, so Abby decided it must have been a deer making its way across the field.

She turned back to the water and stood up, her pale blue dress flowing in the breeze beneath John's sweatshirt. She moved to the edge of the pier, then reached down and moved her fingers across the water. *Mommy loves you, baby girl.* Haley Ann wasn't there, of course, but something about dipping her hand in the place where her baby's ashes lay gave Abby a sense of connection with her.

It was the closest she could come this side of heaven to holding Haley Ann, and right now it was the only thing that brought even a fraction of peace to Abby's heart. As she stayed there, the lake water moving between her fingers, her mind returned to John's final words in the hallway. So, he hadn't lied after all . . .

The reality left a sick feeling Abby knew would never quite go away. The death of their marriage was no longer something she could blame on John alone. It was her fault too. *Why didn't I see it sooner, Lord?*

Love covers a multitude of sins, My daughter.

If only it weren't too late . . .

Abby gazed into the starry summer sky and there, alone in the night, she was overwhelmed by the presence of God.

As I have loved you, so you must love one another . . . love deeply, Abby.

The unspoken words came at her again and again, and she ached for the chance to tell John about finding the journal. To think that everything he said had been the truth. That he hadn't wanted an affair, hadn't been sleeping with her. That Abby's mocking comments had probably driven him into Charlene's arms in the first place. That it had been both their faults . . . refusing to talk, watching love die . . .

Year after year after year.

The realization was suffocating, and she pulled her hand from the water, frozen in that stooped position at the end of the pier. *God, forgive me. What have I done? I could have believed him. Instead I convinced myself he was a cheater, a liar. And I treated him that way for years. Dear God . . . what kind of woman am I?*

Return to your first love, Abby. Love as I have loved you . . .

But how could she return to God now when she deserved nothing but condemnation? As if in response, Abby felt an overwhelming sense of grace wash over her. Grace: precious and undeserved. *I'm sorry, Lord. How much of what happened was my fault and I didn't see it until now? And why couldn't I have heard You this way before it was too late? Oh, God, please forgive me . . .*

A strong voice full of love and peace echoed in her being. *I died for you, child, and I have loved you with an everlasting love . . . All is forgotten, all is forgiven . . . Now, go . . . return to your first love.*

Return to my . . . ? Abby had thought the words in her heart referred to the Lord. But maybe . . . could it be? Could God want her to talk to John, to make peace with him somehow, to tell him she was sorry for doubting him?

Sadness and regret filled her to overflowing, but Abby recognized that in those sacred moments she'd been blessed with some sort of miracle, a private encounter with the Lord Almighty. Abby opened her eyes and gazed across the lake once more. Whatever God had done to her soul, her entire perspective was different now, changed in a divine instant.

"Haley Ann would have loved the wedding, don't you think?"

Abby gasped and spun around, rising to her feet at the sound of John's voice. He was on the pier, walking toward her, and Abby had to blink to convince herself she wasn't seeing things. "John? What are you . . . why . . . ?"

A million questions came at her, but she couldn't find the strength to voice any of them. He moved closer still until his feet were nearly touching hers. His eyes shone with tears, but there was a calm in his features now, a certainty that Abby couldn't explain, and it filled her with hope.

Could it be that the same holy realization that had dawned in her heart had dawned in his as well?

"Abby, give me your hands."

Her shock was so great she could think of no response but to do as he asked. Tentatively, she reached out, surprised at her body's reaction to his touch as he turned them palms up and linked his fingers over hers.

He blinked back tears as he started to speak. "I was two miles down the road when I realized that if I kept moving in that direction, away from all this, from my life here with you, then something inside me would die forever." He studied her eyes intently. "I couldn't have that, Abby. So I pulled over and started walking back."

Abby had to remind herself to breathe as she listened. "You . . . you walked back?"

He nodded, his gaze never leaving hers. "The whole way. I wasn't sure at first what I wanted to say, but I knew I had to say it."

Somewhere, in the newly illuminated alleys of Abby's bruised and broken heart, the seed of hope began to take root. "I don't understand . . ."

The lines in John's jaw hardened and then relaxed again. "I need to tell you about the eagle."

"The eagle?" Abby's heart rate doubled. What was he getting at? Was this a confession or another apology?

"Yes." He spoke slowly, every word steeped in sincerity. "A long time ago I made the mistake of letting go of you, Abby." He tightened his grip on her fingers. "I was crazy, and I don't blame you if you never forgive me. I started spending time with Charlene and . . . it was like everything fell apart between us. Like we were free-falling toward the death of our marriage and neither of us could do anything to stop it."

He massaged her fingers, never taking his eyes from hers. "It wasn't until you were gone on the campout with Nicole that I had a chance to read Kade's report."

Abby blinked and tried to make the connection. "Kade's report?"

"On the eagle, Abby. Remember?" He paused. "As I read it God spoke to me like I haven't heard Him speak in . . . well, in too long. And I knew then I could never be with a woman like Charlene. Or any other woman for that matter."

Fresh tears burned in Abby's eyes. "I found your journal."

John's eyebrows lifted. "What? I packed it . . . it's in the car with my clothes . . ."

Abby shook her head. "It's on your dresser. Right on top."

"That's impossible, Abby. I know I packed it . . ."

"It doesn't matter—" Her voice broke as still more tears filled her eyes. "I read it, John. How could I have thought you were lying . . . ?" She let her head fall against his chest. "I'm so sorry." Her eyes found him again. "Everything I accused you of . . . you were telling the truth, weren't you?"

"Yes." He studied her intently as a single tear slid down his cheek. "I did a lot of things I'm not proud of, I broke promises I should have kept." He looked at her again. "But I never lied to you, Abby."

"I'm sorry I didn't believe you. Sorry I . . ." Abby's throat was too thick to speak.

John shook his head. "It's okay, Abby. It was my fault, and that's why I'm here now. The truth is . . . I still love you." He came closer to her, their hands still linked. "I couldn't seem to find the right time or the right way to tell you these past few days, but . . ." He stroked Abby's palms with his fingertips. "I don't ever want to let go again, Abby. Never. I don't care if it kills me; I want to love you like an eagle loves his mate. Like the Lord *wants* me to love you. Holding on until death makes me finally let go."

Abby's head was spinning, her heart racing so fast she could barely breathe. "What're you saying, John?"

"I'm saying I can't divorce you, Abby. I love you too much. I love the history I have with you and the way you are with our children, the way you brighten a room just by walking into it. I love that you share every important memory of my entire life and that you loved my father and I loved yours . . ." Two more tears made their way down his cheeks, but he ignored them. When he spoke again his voice was only a broken whisper. "And I love . . . the way only you understand how I feel about Haley Ann."

He cocked his head, pleading with her. "Please, Abby, stay with me. Love me forever the way I want to love you. Take time away with me and talk to me. Laugh with me and grow old with me. Please."

John's words unlocked something in Abby that sent what remained of the walls around her heart tumbling down. She came to him slowly, fitting her body against his and laying her head on his chest as she sobbed tears of unabashed joy. "You're . . . you're serious?"

He pulled back and stared at her once more. "I've never been more serious about anything in my life. God's worked on my heart, Abby. I want to go to church with you again and read the Bible with you and pray with you. Forever." He looked deeper into her eyes. "I love you, Abby. Please don't hide from me anymore. You're the most beautiful woman I know, inside and out." He hesitated. "Do you think . . . could you forgive me, start over with me here and now and never let go again?"

A sound that was part-laugh, part-sob came from Abby as she clung to John. "Yes, I can do that. I love you too. I realized tonight that I never stopped loving you, even when I . . . even when I said I hated you."

"I'm so sorry, Abby." John whispered the words into her hair, clinging to her the way a dying person clings to life. "Why did we do this to each other?"

Abby was suddenly confused as well. Why hadn't they had this talk months ago, years ago, back when they'd first grown apart?

A shiver of terror ran through Abby's body as she nestled deeper into John's chest. What if she hadn't found his journal? What if he'd kept driving and never looked back? What if they hadn't embraced the grace of God, swallowed their pride, and admitted that divorce was the most wrong thing they could ever do?

Thank You, God . . . thank You. Abby's tears were those of gratitude now, and she felt humbly awed at the power of Christ's love, the power to turn them from certain destruction and send them back into each other's arms.

She would cancel her trip, he would bring home his suitcase, and the kids wouldn't know how close they'd come. Not now, anyway. Someday, when the time was right, they would share some of what they'd gone through. So the kids would know that no marriage is perfect, and only by God's grace did two people—no matter how right they seemed for each other—ever stay together.

Abby and John talked about that and other aspects of what had happened for nearly an hour, acknowledging their mistakes and pronouncing their love for each other as they never thought they'd do again.

Finally they were quiet, and slowly, gradually, his arms still around her, John began to sway.

"Do you hear it, Abby?" His voice was low, filled with a love that would bear all things, forgive all things. A love that would never end.

She closed her eyes and listened to the subtle creak of the pier in the water, savored the sound of crickets around them, and the steady thud of John's heartbeat against her chest. In the trees a gentle wind carried with it echoes of long-ago memories. The announcer saying, *"Ladies and gentlemen, your 2000 state champions, the Marion Eagles!* The precious jingle of Haley Ann's cry . . . Nicole's sweet, clear voice promising a lifetime of love to her young man . . . her father using the last of his breath to pass the baton to John. *Love her . . . love her . . . love her.*

It was music. The same music John had asked her to listen to all those years ago. "I hear it."

John eased back and kissed her then, tenderly, sweetly, with a longing that was undeniable. The same way he had kissed her twenty-two years earlier, and Abby was filled with certainty that somehow, miraculously, they had again gone through the fire and come out stronger on the other side.

They were caught in the moment, and as John led her across the pier in time with the music of their lives, he whispered to her soul the words she had never expected to hear again.

"Dance with me, Abby." He brought his lips to hers once more and their tears met and mingled somewhere in between. "Please, Abby . . . for the rest of my life, dance with me."

Nicole and Matt were at the hotel counter checking in as Mr. and Mrs. Conley for the first time when Nicole's breath caught in her throat. "Did you hear that?"

They were waiting for the attendant to get their room key, and Matt glanced at her, his expression blank. "Hear what?"

"Wow." Nicole grinned. "I guess it was God, maybe. It was so loud I thought everyone heard it. Like a voice told me my prayers had been answered."

Matt slipped an arm around her. "Of course they have, honey," he teased. "Look who you married."

She laughed, but shook her head. "No, I think it was my prayers for my parents."

"Your parents? You weren't really worried about them, were you?"

Nicole remembered the burden she'd felt, the heavenly insistence that had preceded her prayers for her mom and dad those past months. "Yeah, I guess I was. God kept putting them on my heart, and I kept praying."

"Then you did the right thing." Matt smiled. "Better safe than sorry."

"You think it was God then, telling me my prayers were answered?"

"Probably." He shrugged. "But it couldn't have been anything serious. Not with your parents."

Nicole grinned, her heart and soul bathed in peace. "You're probably right. Whatever it was, God's got it under control."

A man approached them from the other side of the hotel check-in counter. "Here you go, sir. Room 852, the honeymoon suite." He handed Matt a set of key cards. "Enjoy your stay."

Matt took her hand and led her toward their room— and into the beginning of a marriage that Nicole knew had been destined by God Himself. A marriage she prayed would always feel this wonderful and amazing, one that with the Lord's help would survive whatever life gave them and somehow wind up stronger, more beautiful on the other side.

A marriage just like her parents'.

Author's Note

When I think of the divorce situation in society today, I am and always will be deeply grieved. In the dance of life, the casualties of our instant, self-serving, self-indulgent society abound among us. Brokenhearted men and women who struggle through life alone; toddlers whose lives are built around two houses, two bedrooms, and two sets of parents; teenage boys and girls who have no idea how to honor one another or keep commitments.

None of this is how God intended love to be.

If nothing else, I pray that *A Time to Dance* made you compassionate. Compassionate for people suffering through divorce, for children whose parents have separated. Compassionate toward the spouse you might—even now—be walking away from.

There are obvious exceptions—abuse or infidelity or abandonment, for instance—and for those of you hurting in such a situation, I pray miraculous intervention and healing. But even still divorce is deeply displeasing to our Lord. Scripture tells us God hates it, that what He brings together no one should separate. Strong words, really. Strong enough to make us consider how greatly the enemy of our souls wants to destroy our relationships.

But for every marriage that dies a painful death, there are others like Abby's and John's. Marriages that we are too quick to throw away, marriages where a joyous, boundless, restored, and renewed love might be discovered if only we would be willing to dig deep enough to find it. Willing to humble ourselves and hear our God on this issue that is so close to His heart.

If you or someone you love is in the throes of divorce, please do not hear condemnation in this letter. Hear compassion and hope and, above all else, love. Because where there is God, there is faith, there is hope, and there is always love.

Love that perseveres. Love that never ends.

Fight for your marriages, friends. Pray for wisdom and godly counsel; seek God and find a way back to the place where love began, a place where love can begin again.

For some of you that might mean renewing a relationship with the Creator and Savior. For others it might mean starting such a relationship where one never existed. The process is fairly simple. In the most definitive example of love ever, Christ died to pay the price for your sins, for mine. In doing so, He gave us the choice of abundant eternal life now and forever as an alternative to hell. Perhaps it's time that you admit your need for a Savior and commit your life to Him. Find a Bible-believing church, and study what the Scriptures say about having a relationship with Jesus Christ.

Once you understand that kind of love and grace, it'll be easier to love others around you. Easier to let them love you.

Finally, know that I have prayed for each of you, begging the Lord to meet you where you are, dry your tears, and bring beauty from ashes. That He might help you and your spouse find a place of love greater than anything you've known before. Let us all love deeply, friends. No matter how impossible it feels, God is pulling for you, waiting, watching. Ready to help if only together you will let Him.

If you or someone you love is divorced or separated from a spouse who has been unwilling to try, then know God is there for you, also. Keep praying. As God was faithful to answer Nicole's prayers for her parents, so He will be faithful to answer yours. His grace and mercy know no bounds, and with your hand in His, He will one day lead you to that place you long for.

A place of magnificent, boundless, unimaginable love.

Thanks for journeying with me through the pages of *A Time to Dance.* May God bless you and yours until our next time together.

Humbly in Christ,
Karen Kingsbury

P.S. As always, I would love to hear from you. Please write me at my e-mail address: rtnbykk@aol.com.

Discussion Questions

The following questions may be used as part of a book club, bible study, or group discussion.

Relationships do not change overnight. What were some of the signs that Abby and John were having trouble? Why is it easy to miss such signs?

Name three things that caused a strain in the Reynoldses' relationship. What can people do to safeguard against the common problems of busyness, distractions, and judgmental attitudes?

Many of the Reynoldses' problems stemmed from a lack of trust. What could John have done differently so that Abby might have believed him from the beginning? What could Abby have done differently to keep the lines of communication open between the two of them?

Share what you feel about your spouse's friendships with members of the opposite sex? What guidelines should a married person follow when it comes to such friendships?

When was it clear that John and Abby were crossing into dangerous territory with their outside friends? How can married people avoid reaching out to strangers to have their needs met?

What did you learn about the eagle in *A Time to Dance*? In what ways can we learn from the eagle's example?

How was it apparent that Nicole's prayers for her parents were being answered?

What were the individual breakthroughs John and Abby needed to experience? What lessons did they have in common?

What role do our memories play when we're faced with the temptation to walk away from our spouse? How does attending a conference like "Women of Faith" help us remember what's important?

Marriages—like all relationships—are tapestries woven with an assortment of colors and fabrics. The dark colors and brilliant hues make up the beauty of our lives together. Think of three moments of sorrow and three moments of celebration in your own marriage. Recall a time when you knew you would love your spouse forever. If you don't feel that way still, what has changed? What can you do, with God's help, to take the first step toward healing?

AN EXCERPT FROM *A Time to Embrace*

THE KID MADE COACH JOHN REYNOLDS NERVOUS.

He was tall and gangly, and he'd been doodling on his notebook since sixth period health class began. Now the hour was almost up, and John could see what the boy was drawing.

A skull and crossbones.

The design was similar to the one stenciled on the kid's black T-shirt. Similar, also, to the patch sewn on his baggy dark jeans. His hair was dyed jet black and he wore spiked black leather collars around his neck and wrists.

There was no question Nathan Pike was fascinated with darkness. He was a gothic, one of a handful of kids at Marion High School who followed a cultic adherence to the things of doom.

That wasn't what bothered John.

What bothered him was a little something the boy had scribbled *beneath* the dark symbolism. One of the words looked like it read *death*. John couldn't quite make it out from the front of the classroom, so he paced.

Like he did every Friday night along the stadium sidelines as the school's varsity football coach, John wandered up and down the rows of students checking their work, handing out bits of instruction or critique where it was needed.

As he made his way toward Nathan's desk, he glanced at the boy's notebook again. The words scribbled there made John's blood run cold. Was Nathan serious? These days John could do nothing but assume the student meant what he'd written. John squinted, just to make sure he'd read the words correctly.

He had.

Beneath the skull and crossbones, Nathan had written this sentiment: *Death to jocks.*

John was still staring when Nathan looked up and their eyes met. The boy's were icy and dead, unblinking. Intended to intimidate. Nathan was probably used to people taking one glance and looking away, but John had spent his career around kids like Nathan. Instead of turning, he hesitated, using his eyes to tell Nathan what he could not possibly say at that moment. That the boy was lost, that he was a follower, that the things he'd drawn and the words he'd written were not appropriate and would not be tolerated.

But most important, John hoped his eyes conveyed that he was there for Nathan Pike. The same way he had been there for others like him, the way he would always be there for his students.

Nathan looked away first, shifting his eyes back to his notebook.

John tried to still his racing heart. Doing his best to look unaffected, he returned to the front of the classroom. His students had another ten minutes of seatwork before he would resume his lecture.

He sat down at his desk, picked up a pen, and grabbed the closest notepad.

Death to jocks?

Obviously he would have to report what he'd seen to the administration, but as a teacher, what was he supposed to do with that? What if Nathan was serious?

Ever since the shooting tragedies at a handful of schools around the country, most districts had instituted a "red-flag" plan of some sort. Marion High School was no exception. The plan had every teacher and employee keeping an eye on the classrooms in their care. If any student or situation seemed troublesome or unusual, the teacher or employee was supposed to make a report immediately. Meetings were held once a month to discuss which students might be slipping through the cracks. The telltale signs were obvious: a student bullied by others, despondent, dejected, outcast, angry, or fascinated with death. And particularly students who made threats of violence.

Nathan Pike qualified in every category.

But then, so did 5 percent of the school's enrollment. Without a specific bit of evidence, there wasn't much a teacher or administrator could do. The handbook on troubled kids advised teachers to ease the teasing or involve students in school life.

"Talk to them, find out more about them, ask about their hobbies and pastimes," the principal had told John and the other faculty when they discussed the handbook. "Perhaps even recommend them for counseling."

That was all fine and good. The problem was, boys like Nathan Pike didn't always advertise their plans. Nathan was a senior. John remembered when Nathan first came to Marion High. His freshman and sophomore years Nathan had worn conservative clothes and kept to himself.

The change in his image didn't happen until last year.

The same year the Marion High Eagles won their second state football championship.

John cast a quick glance at Nathan. The boy was doodling again. *He doesn't know I saw the notebook.* Otherwise wouldn't he have sat back in his chair, covered the skull and crossbones, and hidden the horrible words? This wasn't the first time John had suspected Nathan might be a problem. Given the boy's changed image, John had kept a close eye on him since the school year began. He strolled by Nathan's desk at least once each day and made a point of calling on him, talking to him, or locking eyes with him throughout the hour. John suspected a deep anger burned in the boy's heart, but today was the first time there'd ever been proof.

John remained still but allowed his gaze to rove around the room. What was different about today? Why would Nathan choose now to write something so hateful?

Then it hit him.

Jake Daniels wasn't in class.

Suddenly the entire scenario made sense. When Jake was there—no matter where he sat—he found a way to turn his classmates against Nathan.

Freak . . . queer . . . death doctor . . . nerd . . . loser.

All names whispered and loosely tossed in Nathan's direction. When the whispers carried to the front of the classroom, John would raise his eyebrows toward Jake and a handful of other football players in the class.

"That's enough." The warning was usually all John had to say. And for a little while, the teasing would stop. But always the careless taunting and cruel words hit their mark. John was sure of it.

Not that Nathan ever let Jake and the others see his pain. The boy ignored all jocks, treated them as though they didn't exist. Which was probably the best way to get back at the student athletes who picked on him. Nothing bothered John's current football players more than being looked over.

That was especially true for Jake Daniels.

No matter that this year's team hadn't *earned* the accolades that came their way. The fact that the team's record was worse than any season in recent history mattered little to Jake and his teammates. They believed they were special and they intended to make everyone at school treat them accordingly.

John thought about this year's team. It was strange, really. They were talented, maybe more so than any other group of kids to come through Marion High. Talk around school was that they had even more going for them than last year's team when John's own son Kade led the Eagles to a state championship. But they were arrogant and cocky, with no care for protocol or character. In all his years of coaching, John had never had a more difficult group.

No wonder they weren't winning. Their talent was useless in light of their attitudes.

And many of the boys' parents were worse. Especially since Marion had lost two of its first four games.

Parents constantly complained about playing time, practice routines, and, of course, the losses. They were often rude and condescending, threatening to get John fired if his record didn't improve.

"What happened to Marion High's undefeated record?" they would ask him. "A good coach would've kept the streak going."

"Maybe Coach Reynolds doesn't know what he's doing," they would say. "Anyone could coach the talent at Marion High and come up with an undefeated season. But losses?"

They wondered out loud what type of colossal failure John Reynolds was to take a team of Eagles football players onto the field and actually lose. It was unthinkable to the Marion High parents. Unconscionable. How dare Coach Reynolds drop two games so early in the season!

And sometimes the wins were worse.

"That was a cream puff opponent last week, Reynolds," the parents would say. If they had a two-touchdown win, the parents would harp that it should have been four at least. And then John's favorite line of all: "Why, if *my* son had gotten more playing time . . ."

Parents gossiped behind his back and undermined the authority he had on the field. Never mind the fact that the Eagles were coming off a championship season. Never mind that John was one of the winningest coaches in the state. Never mind that more than half of last year's championship squad had graduated, placing John in what was obviously a rebuilding year.

The thing that mattered was whether the sons of John's detractors were being used at what they believed were the proper positions and for enough minutes each game. Whether their numbers were being called at the appropriate times for the big plays, and how strong their individual statistics appeared in the paper.

It was just a rotten break that the biggest controversy on the team had, in a roundabout way, made Nathan's life miserable. Two quarterbacks had come into summer practices, each ready for the starting position: Casey Parker and Jake Daniels.

Casey was the shoo-in, the senior, the one who had ridden the bench behind Kade up until last year. All his high-school football career had come down to this, his final season with the Eagles. He reported in August expecting to own the starting position.

What the boy hadn't expected was that Jake Daniels would show up with the same mind-set.

Jake was a junior, a usually good kid from a family who once lived down the street from John and his wife, Abby. But two years ago, the Danielses split up. Jake's mother took Jake and moved into an apartment. His father took a job in New Jersey hosting a sports radio program. The divorce was nasty.

Jake was one of the casualties.

John shuddered. How close had he and Abby come to doing the same thing? Those days were behind them, thank God. But they were still very real for Jake Daniels.

At first Jake had turned to John, a father figure who wasn't half a country away. John would never forget something Jake asked him.

"You think my dad still loves me?"

The kid was well over six feet tall, nearly a man. But in that instant he was seven years old again, desperate for some proof that the father he'd counted on all his life, the man who had moved away and left him, still cared.

John did everything he could to assure Jake, but as time passed, the boy grew quiet and sullen. He spent more hours alone in the weightroom and out on the field, honing his throwing skills.

When summer practices came around, there was no question who would be the starting quarterback. Jake won the contest easily. The moment that happened, Casey Parker's father, Chuck, called a meeting with John.

"Listen, Coach—" the veins on his temple popped out as he spoke—"I heard my son lost the starting position."

John had to stifle a sigh. "That's true."

The man spouted several expletives and demanded an explanation. John's answer was simple. Casey was a good quarterback with a bad attitude. Jake was younger, but more talented and coachable, and therefore the better choice.

"My son cannot be second string." Casey's father was loud, his face flushed. "We've been planning for this all his life! He's a senior and he will not be sitting the bench. If he has a bad attitude, that's only because of his intensity. Live with it."

Fortunately, John had brought one of his assistants to the meeting. The way accusations and hearsay were flying about, he'd figured he couldn't be too careful. So he and his assistant had sat there, waiting for Parker to continue.

"What I'm saying is—" Chuck Parker leaned forward, his eyes intent—"I've got three coaches breathing down my neck. We're thinking of transferring. Going where my kid'll get a fair shake."

John resisted the urge to roll his eyes. "Your son has an attitude problem, Chuck. A big one. If other high-school coaches in the area are recruiting him, it's because they haven't worked with him." John leveled his gaze at the man. "What exactly are your concerns?"

"I'll *tell* you my concern, Coach." Chuck pointed a rigid finger at John. "You're not loyal to your players. That's what. Loyalty is everything in sports."

This from a man whose son wanted to toss his letterman's jacket and transfer schools. As it turned out, Casey Parker stayed. He took snaps at running back and tight end and spelled Jake at quarterback. But the criticism from Casey's father had continued each week, embarrassing Casey and causing the boy to work harder to get along with Jake, his on-field rival. Jake seemed grateful to be accepted by a senior like Casey, and the two of them began spending most of their free time together. It didn't take long to see the changes in Jake. Gone was the shy, earnest kid who popped into John's classroom twice a week just to connect. Gone was the boy who had once been kind to Nathan Pike. Now Jake was no different from the majority of players who strutted across Marion High's campus.

And in that way, the quarterback controversy had only made Nathan's life more miserable. Whereas once Nathan was respected by at least one of the football players, now he didn't have a single ally on the team.

John had overheard two teachers talking recently.

"How many Marion football players does it take to screw in a light bulb?"

"I give up."

"One—he holds it while the world revolves around him."

There were nights when John wondered why he was wasting his time. Especially when his athletes' elitist attitudes divided the school campus and alienated students like Nathan Pike. Students who sometimes snapped and made an entire school pay for their low place in the social pecking order.

So what if John's athletes could throw a ball or run the length of a field? If they left the football program at

Marion High without a breath of compassion or character, what was the point?

John drew a salary of $3,100 a season for coaching football. One year he'd figured it came out to less than two bucks an hour. Obviously he didn't do the job for the money.

He glanced at the clock. Three minutes of seatwork left.

Images from a dozen different seasons flashed in his mind. Why was he in it, then? It wasn't for his ego. He'd had more strokes in his days as a quarterback for University of Michigan than most men received in a lifetime. No, he didn't coach for pride's sake.

It was, very simply, because there were two things he seemed born to do: play football . . . and teach teens.

Coaching was the purest way he'd known to bring those two together. Season after season after season, it had worked. Until now. Now it didn't feel pure at all. It felt ridiculous. Like the whole sports world had gone haywire.

John drew a deep breath and stood, working the tendons in his bum knee—the one with the old football injury. He walked to the chalkboard where, for the next ten minutes, he diagramed a series of nutritional food values and meticulously explained them. Then he assigned homework.

But the whole time there was only one thing on his mind: Nathan Pike.

How had a clean-cut student like Nathan once was become so angry and hateful? Was it all because of Jake Daniels? Were Jake's and the other players' egos so inflated that they couldn't coexist with anyone different from them? And what about the words Nathan had scribbled on his notebook? *Death to jocks.* Did he mean it?

If so, what could be done?

Schools like Marion High grew from the safe soil of Middle America. Most did not have metal detectors or mesh backpacks or video cameras that might catch a disturbed student before he took action. Yes, they had the red-flag program. Nathan had already been red-flagged. Everyone who knew him was watching.

But what if that wasn't enough?

John's stomach tightened, and he swallowed hard. He had no answers. Only that today, in addition to grading papers, inputting student test results in the computer, holding afternoon practice, and meeting with a handful of irritated parents along the sidelines, he would also have to talk to the principal about Nathan Pike's scribbled declaration.

It was eight o'clock by the time he climbed into his car and opened an envelope he'd found in his school mailbox just before practice.

"To whom it may concern," the letter began. "We are calling for the resignation of Coach Reynolds . . ."

John sucked in a sharp breath. *What in the world?* His gut ached as he kept reading.

"Coach Reynolds is not the moral example we need for our young men. He is aware that several of his players are drinking and taking part in illegal road races. Coach Reynolds knows about this but does nothing. Therefore we are demanding he resign or be let go. If nothing is done about this, we will inform the media of our request."

John remembered to exhale. The letter wasn't signed, but it was copied to his athletic director, his principal, and three school district officials.

Who could have written such a thing? And what were they referring to? John gripped the steering wheel with both hands and sat back hard. Then he remembered. There had been rumors in August when practice first started up . . . rumors that a few players had drunk and raced their cars. But that's all they'd been: rumors. John couldn't do anything about them . . .

He leaned his head against the car window. He'd been furious when he'd heard the report. He'd asked the players straight out, but each of them had denied any wrongdoing. Beyond that there wasn't a thing John could do. Protocol was that rumors not be given credence unless there was proof of a rule violation.

Not a moral example for the players?

John's hands began to tremble and he stared over his right shoulder at the doors of the school. Surely his athletic director wouldn't acknowledge a cowardly, unsigned letter like this one. But then . . .

The athletic director was new. An angry man with a chip on his shoulder and what seemed like a vendetta against Christians. He'd been hired a year ago to replace Ray Lemming, a formidable man whose heart and soul had been given over to coaches and athletes.

Ray was so involved in school athletics he was a fixture at the school, but last year, at the ripe age of sixty-three, he retired to spend more time with his family. The way most coaches saw it, much of the true heart of Marion sports retired right alongside him. That was especially true after the school hired Herman Lutz as athletic director.

John drew a weary breath. He'd done everything possible to support the man, but he'd already fired the boys' swim coach after a parent complaint. What if he took this absurd letter seriously? The other coaches saw Lutz as a person drowning in the complexities of the job.

"It just takes one parent," one of the coaches had said at a meeting that summer. "One parent threatens to go to Lutz's boss, and he'll give them what they want."

Even if it meant firing a coach.

John let his head fall slowly against the steering wheel. Nathan Pike . . . the death threat against jocks . . . the change in Jake Daniels . . . the attitude of his players . . . the complaining parents . . . the inexplicable losses this season . . .

And now this.

John felt eighty years old. How had Abby's father survived a lifetime of coaching? The question shifted his thoughts and he let everything about the day fade for a moment. Thirteen hours ago he'd arrived at school, and only now could he do what he wanted more than anything else. The thing he looked forward to more with each passing day.

He would drive home, open the door of the house he'd almost lost, and take the woman he loved more than life itself into his arms. The woman whose blue eyes danced more these days, and whose every warm embrace erased a bit more of their painful past. The woman who cheered him on each morning, and filled his heart when he couldn't take another minute of coaching and teaching.

The woman he had almost walked away from.

His precious Abby.